HOW AUSTRALIA DECIDES
Election Reporting and the Media

In recent years, the Australian media have come under fire for their reporting of politics and election campaigns. Political reporting is said to be too influenced by commercial concerns, too obsessed with gossip and scandal, and too focused on trivia and 'sound bites' at the expense of serious issues. There are accusations of bias, sensationalism, 'lazy' journalism and 'horse-race' reporting that is obsessed with opinion polls.

How Australia Decides is the first book to put these allegations to the test. Based on a four-year empirical study, Sally Young reports the results of the only systematic, historical and in-depth analysis of Australian election reporting and weighs up the evidence to assess how well Australians are served by those who report and comment on politics. This groundbreaking book shows how election reporting has changed over time, and how political news audiences, news production and shifts in political campaigning are influencing media content – with profound implications for Australian democracy.

Sally Young is Senior Lecturer in the School of Social and Political Sciences at the University of Melbourne and Senior Research Fellow at the Centre for Advanced Journalism.

Australian Government
_____
Australian Research Council

This research was supported under Australian Research Council's Discovery funding scheme (project number DP0663208).

This publication is supported by a grant from the Research and Research Training Committee, Faculty of Arts, The University of Melbourne.

HOW AUSTRALIA DECIDES

Election Reporting and the Media

SALLY YOUNG

CAMBRIDGE
UNIVERSITY PRESS

CAMBRIDGE UNIVERSITY PRESS
Cambridge, New York, Melbourne, Madrid, Cape Town, Singapore,
São Paulo, Delhi, Dubai, Tokyo, Mexico City

Cambridge University Press
477 Williamstown Road, Port Melbourne, VIC 3207, Australia

Published in the United States of America by Cambridge University Press, New York

www.cambridge.org
Information on this title: www.cambridge.org/9780521147071

First published 2011

Cover design by Tanya De Silva
Typeset by Aptara Corp.
Printed in Australia by Ligare

A catalogue record for this publication is available from the British Library

National Library of Australia Cataloguing in Publication data
   Young, Sally.
   How Australia decides : election reporting and the media / Sally Young.
   9780521147071 (pbk.)
   Includes bibliographical references and index.
   Elections – Press coverage – Australia.
   Political campaigns – Press coverage – Australia.
   Press and politics – Australia.
070.449324

ISBN 978-0-521-14707-1 Paperback

Promoting sustainable forest management - For more info: www.pefc.org

PEFC/21-31-17

To Jay and Abigail

CONTENTS

Part III: Elections in mediated times

TABLES, FIGURES AND BOXES

Tables

Figures

Boxes

ACKNOWLEDGEMENTS

The research for this book was made possible by a three-year Discovery Project grant from the Australian Research Council (DP0663208) and, before that, an Early Career Researcher Grant from the Arts Faculty at the University of Melbourne. The Arts Faculty also provided a publication subsidy grant and the University of Melbourne provided a semester of sabbatical leave to complete the project, gratefully acknowledged here. I tested my findings in a few different forums along the way, including *Inside Story*, *Journalism Studies*, *Media International Australia*, a workshop at the University of Sydney organised by John Keane and Rod Tiffen, the *Future of Journalism* conference at Cardiff University in 2009 and when I delivered the *Senate Occasional Lecture* at Parliament House, Canberra in 2008. I thank all those involved for the invitations, support and feedback.

I had a wonderful team of research assistants and coders who helped me collect and analyse election and media material for this book. I especially thank Stephanie Younane-Brookes, who was head of the coding team and provided expert research assistance throughout the project. A special thanks also to Leah Kaufmann, who did all of the quantitative data entry and most of the statistical results. The coding was a laborious task that took eight months and I was fortunate to have such a conscientious and engaged team. My thanks to Saskia Bourne, Brie Callahan, Mary Helen McIlroy, Violeta Politoff, Hannah Quigley and, for the 2001 and 2004 elections, William Bowe and Jennifer Pfeiffer.

I also owe a special debt of gratitude to Rodney Tiffen, who read a draft of this book, sent me resources, made valuable suggestions and gave me encouragement at crucial times. I am also indebted to William Burlace and Andrew Kennedy of Roy Morgan Research who were extremely generous in providing me with information from Roy Morgan surveys. Andrew also patiently answered my many questions about the data. Murray Goot read a draft of Chapter 2 and generously gave me feedback and access to his unpublished work.

There were many other friends, colleagues and interview subjects who provided information, answered my questions and pointed out things I'd missed. For assistance of one kind or another, I gratefully thank: Batoul Alamein, Steve Allen, Mark Bahnisch, Eric Beecher, William Bowe, Peter Brent, Peter Browne, Paul Chadwick, Peter Chen, Simon Cottle, Paul Cutler, David Denemark, Glenn Dyer, Angelos Frangopoulous, Michael Gawenda, Jock Given, Christian Guerra, Therese Iverach, Paul Jones, Christian Kerr, Randal Mathieson, Rod McGuinness, Brian McNair, Peter Meakin, Emelia Millward, Dennis Muller, Margaret Simons, David Speers, Graeme Turner, Lisa Walsh, Ian Ward, John Westacott, Jason Wilson and Graham Young. And, at Cambridge University Press, a special thanks to Susan Hanley and Debbie Lee.

In Chapters 8–12 of this book, I quote several media texts – especially newspaper articles – that I was unable to cite in full in the reference list due to space limitations. An online search using the sentences quoted will, in most cases, bring up the reference, but for any reader who requires more details, please contact me at s.young@unimelb.edu.au.

Finally, to my family – especially Jay, Kathy, Frances, Joe and Maree – 'thank you' is not enough for all the support, childcare and encouragement that made this book possible.

PREFACE

The 2010 election was the first in Australia to feature a female prime minister. It came only 24 days after Julia Gillard replaced Kevin Rudd in an unprecedented, overnight deposition of a sitting prime minister. It also produced an unusual result – a hung parliament and two weeks of machinations and deliberations before a minority Labor government was formed. Understandably, the more unusual elements of the campaign attracted most attention but there were still familiar patterns including an important paradox, which is explored in this book.

For those interested in following the campaign, more detailed and constantly updated information was available from multiple news sources. Yet there was also a sense that the election was playing out before an unusually disengaged electorate. On this latter point, the signs were mixed. The percentage of people casting an informal (invalid or blank) vote in 2010 went up, but not all of these were deliberate protest votes. Voter turnout only went down slightly, but this masked a bigger problem – declining voter enrolment. Over a million eligible Australians were missing from the electoral roll.

Of those who did vote, over 80 per cent gave their first preference to one of the major parties. However, a 4 per cent swing to the Greens, their success in winning a lower house seat for the first time, and the role four independents played in determining government encouraged claims that a 'new politics' was being forged out of a growing disillusionment with the major parties and 'business-as-usual' politics. Whether the 2010 election was really the beginning of an enduring sea-change in Australian politics remains to be seen but, certainly in the connections between politics and the media, there was much that *was* business-as-usual.

Although there was now a different government from the one that had been in power during the 2001, 2004 and 2007 elections, many of the same techniques were still evident. Government media advisers continued to outnumber journalists under the Rudd and Gillard governments. Like the Howard government before it, the Rudd government was accused of misusing government advertising to promote a partisan message (in this case, about its ill-fated mining tax) in an election year. Reportedly, the major parties then spent over $60 million on political advertising during the campaign and even the Greens spent around $2.5 million – more than double their 2004 spending.

Just as had happened under the Howard government, there were interventions by media owners and allegations of election-year policies designed to win their support. In February 2010, the Rudd government had given a $250 million hand-out to commercial TV networks in the form of a reduction to their licence fees after the Minister for Communications had been skiing in Colorado with Seven Network chief Kerry Stokes. After a personal meeting with Rupert Murdoch – who had competing interests in pay TV – Liberal leader Tony Abbott blasted the hand-out as 'dodgy' and an election-year bribe to buy favourable coverage.

Conservative critics continued to accuse the ABC of left-wing bias in its news and current affairs broadcasting as well as on its websites. But the most vehement allegations of bias in 2010 were directed at the Murdoch press. Critics described a News Limited 'war on Labor' and even the News Limited-owned *Australian* acknowledged 'talk of [a] News [Limited] bid to get Rudd'. Although there had been similar talk in 2007, the allegations were far more public in 2010 and were made not just by Labor supporters or left-wing bloggers but also by a range of respected journalists in mainstream media outlets.

Allegations of bias were part of a broader perception that the media were unusually active in politics in 2010. Media reporting of opinion polls had played a major part in Rudd's demise – as it had in the downfall of Kim Beazley, Simon Crean, Brendan Nelson and Malcolm Turnbull. However, it was also being reported as credible that a single newspaper article in the *Sydney Morning Herald* (which had reported that Rudd's chief of staff had been sounding out caucus members to see if they were going to defect to Gillard) had been the trigger for the 23 June leadership challenge.

Journalist Laurie Oakes, a veteran of four decades of political reporting, played an important role during the campaign. Two days before the election was announced, Oakes dramatically confronted Gillard at her Press Club address and recounted a leaked insiders' account of the night she deposed Rudd. Oakes then had another scoop in the second week of the campaign when he reported damaging Cabinet leaks against Gillard. The extraordinary leaks – designed to undermine Gillard and hurt Labor's re-election chances – animated the media with frenzied speculation about the identity of the leaker.

This temporarily punctuated a general narrative about the uninspiring nature of the campaign. Australian journalists have been decrying the boring, stage-managed nature of modern election campaigns in earnest since 1996. But, in 2010 there was a level of intensity about this, a chorus of complaints that the election was dull and vacuous. Perhaps there is nothing quite so boring as the media constantly describing how boring an election is, though, because disillusionment about the campaign in general also extended to media reporting of the campaign.

Many of the anti-media complaints were also familiar: that the media were too focused on the machinations of politics and on horse-race calling instead of policy. That they didn't explain complex issues well or investigate matters. That there was too much 'he said, she said' journalism, commentary-on-commentary and journalists talking to journalists. However, there was also a backlash against the hypocrisy of journalists who reported the stage-managed events but then lamented that the campaign was so staged. Like the complaints against politicians, the criticisms were amplified by an online environment characterised by ongoing chatter and feedback.

Critics called for journalists to 'get off the bus', away from the routine of, as one journalist described it, reporters asking 'polite questions in polite settings, followed by coffee and a buffet . . . supplied by the political parties' (Purcell 2010). The bus rolled on with politicians still manufacturing campaign events for the accompanying media, including visits to schools and factories, but there was a new emphasis on the media manufacturing events of their own.

One obvious pseudo-event was Channel Nine's hiring of former Labor leader Mark Latham to file a report for *60 Minutes* (which also raised questions about who or what was a journalist). Latham confronted Gillard on the campaign trail and then, during a live TV report about the incident, Oakes criticised his own employer for hiring Latham. All of the drama fitted nicely with the way Channel Nine promoted its election coverage, especially its polling night broadcast. In ads similar to those Nine had used to promote its crime drama series *Underbelly*, the election was described as 'the drama event of the year'.

News Limited engineered an unprecedented degree of control in staging campaign events when it organised two 'People's Forums' through its New South Wales/Victorian tabloids and Sky News at Rooty Hill RSL and Brisbane Broncos League Club. Part of a growing emphasis in political reporting on 'ordinary people', these were billed as a chance for voters in crucial seats to put their questions directly to Gillard and Abbott. News Limited paid Galaxy (one of its favoured pollsters) to conduct the selection process for choosing the audience.

Viewers were told that the audience consisted largely of undecided voters but, after the Rooty Hill event, some commentators argued that the audience and questioners seemed more hostile to Gillard than to Abbott. One man who had asked Abbott a question was later identified as the son of a former Liberal MP and former *Big Brother* contestant who had said he was a Young Liberal. In an era marked by both scepticism and a desire for 'authenticity', like reality TV itself, the 'People's Forums' raised questions about whether the media were really showing 'authentic' glimpses of 'ordinary people' in unscripted situations or were manipulating events for effect. The ABC created two special episodes of its *Q&A* program using a similar format of 'ordinary' people asking the leaders questions and it too was accused of having an unrepresentative audience.

Politics was most newsworthy in 2010 when adapted to fit the 'event' TV model of sporting and reality TV finals. Media organisations were willing to organise and pay for the 'big' events. Nine reportedly paid $10 000 to Latham and Seven reportedly paid $1.5 million for Labor strategist Graham Richardson to join its polling night panel. Polling night was an extravaganza that even Channel Ten – which had eschewed an election night broadcast in 2007 for a repeat of *The Empire Strikes Back* – could not ignore, broadcasting a special edition of its news-focused *7pm Project* and moving between regular programs and updates. Yet even 'big' politics could not compete if it was put up against the 'real' thing. The leaders' debate had to be rescheduled to avoid clashing with Ten's *MasterChef*.

The 2010 election was the first to be reported by two local 24-hour TV news channels after the ABC launched its 24-hour news digital TV channel during the campaign. Reflecting economic models for news production modelled in the 2000s, the channel was delivered with no new resources. Journalists were being asked to do more, package up existing material, work faster and file for multiple platforms. Politicians also had to feed a more voracious news cycle. The ultimate manifestation of this was Tony Abbott campaigning non-stop and without sleep for 36 hours in a reality TV style *Amazing Race* in the final days of the campaign.

The new ABC news channel was criticised when Sky News beat it to an Abbott policy announcement by half an hour. This showed increased expectations about speed, but the criticism was also part of a larger campaign by commercial media organisations against competition and the increasing strength of public broadcasting. That strength has been especially evident in online media and in the ABC's ability to attract politically interested audiences. For example, in 2010, almost twice as many viewers watched the ABC on polling night as watched Seven.

In 2010, there was a continuation of the blurring between politics and entertainment and between serious and soft news. Politicians appeared on FM radio and TV comedy shows, including Tony Abbott on Nine's *Hey, Hey it's Saturday* and Liberal Julie Bishop's staring contest with a garden gnome on the ABC's Chaser satire *Yes We Canberra!* This was filmed on the *Lateline* set with *Lateline* host Tony Jones switching from good-natured target of satire to serious newsreader when the *Lateline* music started. The ABC's *Gruen Nation* – a panel-style program exposing political advertising tactics – also achieved high ratings.

In news reports, there was a continued focus on major party leaders, on reporting the meta-campaign – the campaign staged for media – and on opinion polls although, this time, predictions of a close race were right! Female candidates – usually marginalised and under-reported in election coverage – received far more attention because of the presence of a female prime minister, but that attention was sometimes accompanied by an intense focus on Gillard's physical appearance and marital status.

There were proclamations in 2010 – as there have been since the 1998 election – that this campaign would be 'the one' to demonstrate the power of the internet, tinged with disappointment that political parties and the media were missing interactive opportunities. There were signs of growth, including a jump in traffic to news websites on polling night, especially to the ABC, Ninemsn and online newspapers. Twitter was to 2010 what YouTube had been to 2007. Viewers' tweets were broadcast during *Q&A*

and journalists – especially Annabel Crabb – built up a popular Twitter following.

However, there were also examples of the fragility of the online business model for smaller, alternative outlets, including the closure of *New Matilda*. Some alternative voices were lured across to mainstream media outlets, such as the psephology blogger *Mumble* (Peter Brent), who was hosted on the *Australian*'s website in 2010 despite being part of an anti-blogger tirade that the *Australian* had run in 2007 (Chapter 10).

Overall, the big media companies were still dominant and continued to show signs of both struggling with, and adapting to, a different media environment. TV was still where most citizens got their news and where the parties focused their attention. The increases in specialist fare accessed by political junkies and the big event-style TV extravaganzas therefore did not negate the need for regular politics coverage in general outlets such as primetime news.

In 2010, the media generally despaired about the stage-managed, pseudo-event style of campaigning but also served it. After the election, reporters were accused of being part of the 'old' system of politics that voters were rejecting, and of being unable to adapt or view politics as anything more than conflict or a two-horse race. There was intense criticism of media-centred politics during and after the election. This book looks at how we got to that point and whether the criticism is fair.

Chapter 1

ELECTION REPORTING IN THE 2000s

When the 2001 election was held, the *Bulletin* was still published. *Nightline*, *Sunday* and John Laws were still on air. The ABC website consisted of a string of text articles – no interactive maps, no video and no live vote-counting. The Packer family – with Kerry Packer in charge – still owned Channel Nine and the station was the undisputed ratings winner of the previous year. Only about 20 per cent of homes had pay TV (AFC 2005:62). Sky News existed but had not broadcast a dedicated election channel yet. Stephen Mayne's email newsletter *Crikey* had only begun the previous year. The *Age* and *Sydney Morning Herald* websites were updated irregularly. Wikipedia had only been in operation for a year. There was no YouTube and no Twitter. (They began in 2005 and 2006 respectively.) Blogging had begun in 1994 but 'was not a recognised force in the political world' and there was no social networking site 'until Friendster in 2002, MySpace in 2003, and FaceBook in 2004' (Schudson 2009:368).

It is not only media and technology that have been transformed. Reporting styles, journalism practice, audiences and the way politics is conducted have also changed. It will be a very different political reporting environment in another ten years' time. While we cannot anticipate all that will occur in the future, we can learn much by examining the recent past and thinking about how political reporting works, how it has changed and what we have both lost and gained in recent times. This book focuses on election reporting in the first decade of the 21st century – a decade marked by great expectations for journalism as well as grave concerns.

The concerns stemmed from fears about the repercussions of massive change that was occurring in news production and news access, including technological change and the search for an economic model that could sustain journalism in an era of declining mass audiences, the rise of free content and shifting concepts of what was 'news'. In the period between the elections of 2001 and 2007, every traditional news medium lost market share, including newspapers and television (the most dominant and accessed news sources over the past 30 years), but at the same time there was much more 'news' floating around, including through pay TV, websites, social networking, blogs, instant messaging, free commuter newspapers, radio news bulletins and comedy shows with a topical bent.

Even the traditional media increased their news output, if not their audience size. Newspapers went online but also produced more supplements, sections and newspaper-inserted magazines. On television there were more news bulletins; longer morning programs focused around news as well as panel-style commentary shows; and live breaking news broadcasts and news specials on a variety of topics. Richard A. Posner (2005) noted: 'The public's consumption of news used to be like sucking a straw; now it's like being sprayed by a fire hose.'

Audiences became more fluid, 'nomadic' and mobile in the 2000s. They were no longer the '"sitting ducks" of mass media communication', but were now 'splintering across ever more platforms', both harder to reach and to measure, simultaneously 'everywhere and nowhere' (Dahlgren 2009:45). This made an interesting paradox: there were fewer fixed news audiences, but there was far more news around. These factors were challenging many of the fundamentals of traditional journalism, especially its audience base and business models. So dramatic were the changes that commentators feared that a 'crisis' in journalism was at hand (see MEAA 2008; Young 2010).

However, if there were new concerns about journalism, there were also still old ideals and high expectations. The Media Alliance (formerly the Australian Journalists' Association) code of ethics encapsulated these in describing what journalists do:

> Journalists describe society to itself. They convey information, ideas and opinions... They search, disclose, record, question, entertain, suggest and remember. They inform citizens and animate democracy. They give a practical form to freedom of expression... scrutinise power, but also exercise it (Alliance Online 2009).

News outlets continued to promise a great deal. They promised to provide 'agenda-setting journalism that is accurate, independent, compelling, trustworthy, and of the highest quality' (*The Age* Online), 'in-depth coverage and analysis' (*The 7:30 Report*) and 'a provocative, challenging and intelligent window on today's world' (*Lateline*); to tell 'the big stories of the world' (*60 Minutes*), to cover 'the issues that affect you and your family' (*Today Tonight*), to have 'the nation's leaders discussing the big news stories of the day' (*Meet the Press*), to 'improve the lives of our readers with campaigns, exclusive stories and in-depth investigations' (*Daily Telegraph*) and reveal 'the inside word on what's really going on in politics, government, media' (*Crikey*).

Yet despite – or perhaps because of – these promises, the litany of complaints about political reporting was very long. And because election campaigns are seen as the ultimate test of traditional journalism and of how the media fulfil their role in a democracy, for many critics, election reporting in the 2000s was strong evidence of how the media fail to provide either what they promise or what is needed for a well-functioning democracy. Others strongly defended journalism, but even they didn't deny that the media are powerful and that whether they are working well or not matters.

Elections

Elections in Australia are highly mediated events. Most Australians don't have any direct contact with election candidates. Instead they rely on information from television, newspapers, radio and, increasingly, from the internet. These media have been described as 'the major sites, the privileged scenes, of politics' today (Dahlgren 2009:35). During elections, this takes on special significance because media reports provide information on which people might ultimately base their vote. This assumption is so powerful and so widely held that, for decades, politicians have been centring their election campaigns around obtaining favourable media coverage – especially television coverage (Denemark, Ward and Bean 2007:90; Tiffen 1989:138; Ward 1995:202).

Less convinced, academics have been testing the thesis of media effects on voting behaviour in earnest since the 1940s. There have been many conflicting findings because media effects are notoriously difficult to isolate, but the weight of evidence suggests that election campaigns *do* matter to the behaviour of citizens at elections, even if their impact varies for different voters in different circumstances and even if they are but one influence among many on voting decisions (Farrell and Schmitt-Beck 2002; Iyengar and Simon 2000; Weaver and Drew 2006). Media content seems to play an especially important role in encouraging or discouraging awareness of particular issues and in 'priming' people's evaluations of parties, leaders and candidates (see Chapter 5). Media content seems to have the greatest influence on undecided voters. This means that, in the past three decades, there has been a renewed interest in its effects because a diminishing number of Australians identify themselves with a particular party and more are entering election campaigns unsure about their vote (Denemark, Ward and Bean 2007; McAllister 2002).

There are estimates that between 35 and 40 per cent of Australian voters now decide their vote *during* the election campaign (McAllister 2002:24–5; McCarthy 1993:206; Young 2004:45). In 2007 pollsters were reporting that, with only four days to go until polling day, one in five voters had still not made up their minds and were only likely to decide who to vote for on election day ('Pollsters point to many undecided voters' 2007). Given that Australian elections 'are regularly won by [only] 2–3% of votes', this makes media content potentially very powerful in shaping election outcomes (Denemark, Ward and Bean 2007:107). The impact is likely to be particularly sharp in Australia because compulsory voting ensures that a high proportion of voters, including the less interested, participate on polling day and make some form of voting decision. Between the 1990 and 2007 elections, an average of 95 per cent of registered voters cast a vote (AEC 2009). Most relied on media content for information and impressions of national politics.

Media power and responsibilities

A capacity to influence election results is not something that media outlets usually promote overtly. There are exceptions, though. Most famously, in 1992 the British tabloid the *Sun* claimed 'It's the *Sun* wot won it' on its front page after it had run an anti-Labour Party campaign and the Conservative Party unexpectedly won the general election. In Australia, the *Daily Telegraph* (also owned by Rupert Murdoch) claims that its readers 'are the people who decide federal elections'. However, it states this on its website aimed at advertisers – including political parties and governments, which are big advertisers – rather than in its general content, which is aimed at readers (Newsspace 2009b).

It is more traditional for media outlets to draw upon the journalistic ideals of a 'fourth estate' and an impartial 'watchdog' role, and to claim a mandate to represent 'the people' and uphold democracy. In this view, based on classic democratic theory, reporting an election campaign is considered one of the most significant activities the media can ever perform in a democracy. Through effective reporting, media outlets are thought to increase transparency and accountability; deter fraud, illegal activities and corruption; make citizens more knowledgeable and better informed about elections, candidates and current issues; analyse candidate platforms; and provide voters with the information they need to make an informed choice on election day. At the most elementary level, they inform voters about the basic mechanisms of formal politics including the date of the election, voting hours and polling site locations.

Box 1.1

The role of the media in elections: 'classic' democratic theory

The traditional, and still widely held, view of the role of the media in elections is that the media 'play an indispensable role in the proper functioning of a democracy' including:

- a 'watchdog' role, providing 'unfettered scrutiny and discussion of the successes and failures of governments, [to] inform the public of how effectively its representatives have performed and help to hold them to account';
- 'enabling full public participation in elections by:
  - educating the voters on how to exercise their democratic rights.
  - reporting on the development of the election campaign.
  - providing a platform for the political parties to communicate their message to the electorate.
  - allowing the parties to debate with each other.
  - reporting results and monitoring vote counting.
  - scrutinising the electoral process itself in order to evaluate its fairness, efficiency, and probity' (ACE 2009).

Whether media reports affect the way people vote is therefore only one measure of influence (although it has tended to be the central preoccupation of those who study election media effects). There are broader impacts. These include influencing how people feel about politics and their society, including whether they are interested in the election and its outcome and whether they think their own participation matters. Significantly, the international literature suggests that many voters can 'be either engaged or "turned off"' elections by 'the quality of the campaign communications they receive' (Blumler 1987). Although an average of 95 per cent of registered voters voted between 1990 and 2007, there were an estimated 1.2 million who were eligible to vote but were not on the electoral roll (JSCEM 2009:23, 81). How many of these Australians were not registered because they did not believe their vote mattered or because they were 'turned off' politics?

Political reporters themselves acknowledge the great responsibility of the many democratic roles that are assumed. Veteran political reporter Laurie Oakes has said that political reporters must have:

> a commitment to accuracy, a determination to get the facts right . . . an obligation to inform the public to the best of their ability about issues, policies and actions of government, the political parties and people involved in the political process. And because we are in a sense, proxies for the voters, we have a duty to hold politicians accountable, and we also have a credo of objectivity. We're supposed to present things fairly. (ABC Radio National, *Background Briefing*, 15 August 1999).

However, politics is not only communicated by political reporters with a specific journalistic creed. There are also a multitude of other sources that report 'news' and contribute to political communication, including comedy shows, talkback radio hosts and callers, websites, blogs, YouTube clips, social networking comments, emails and electronic newsletters. Not all of these forms ascribe to journalistic principles but, in conjunction with news media, they contribute to making 'the media' the central arena through which politics are conducted and communicated.

Election reporting: the debate

Despite all of the important functions expected of (and claimed by) the media, many critics have expressed serious concerns about how politics and elections are reported. It is not surprising that politicians have been among the most vocal critics. Politicians are in close contact with media reporters, care passionately about politics and have a personal stake in it and first-hand experience. They are frequently on the receiving end of unflattering representations and unwanted intrusions. Politicians have argued that Australian political reporting is too influenced by commercial concerns and political vendettas (Keating 2000), too obsessed with gossip and scandal (Evans 1998) and too focused on trivia and 'sound bites' at the expense of reporting serious issues. Former Prime Minister Paul Keating (2000) stated more broadly that the Australian media were 'an industry that operates behind a cloak of secrecy and insider knowledge. It is riddled with nepotism, back-scratching and interlocking interests.'

In 2002, federal Liberal Party president Shane Stone said political reporting in Australia was biased and out of touch. He accused reporters of relying on gossip and rumours, and of using each other as sources of news rather than conducting interviews with people involved in news events. He argued that political reporters existed 'in isolation from the mainstream of their fellow Australians' and wrote and spoke 'in a language that most Australians don't relate to' (Grubel and Cole 2002). Former Labor leader Mark Latham (2005:58) claimed in his notorious 2005 diaries: 'There is no quality journalism in Australia, only the pretence of it.'

Concerns are not of course new, nor are they confined to Australia. Famously, Tony Blair outlined his views in an important speech in which he said that a fragmenting media system was causing media outlets to lose audiences and to seek 'impact' above understanding. In Blair's view, this had changed the nature of political reporting so that:

> ... scandal or controversy beats ordinary reporting hands down. News is rarely news unless it generates heat ... today's media, more than ever before, hunts in a pack. In these modes it is like a feral beast, just tearing people and reputations to bits ... rather than just report news, even if sensational or controversial, the new technique is commentary on the news being as, if not more important than the news itself. So – for example – there will often be as much interpretation of what a politician is saying as there is coverage of them actually saying it ... Things, people, issues, stories, are all black and white. Life's usual grey is almost entirely absent ... It's a triumph or a disaster. A problem is 'a crisis'. A setback is a policy 'in tatters'. A criticism, 'a savage attack' (Blair 2007).

Concerns were also voiced by experienced political reporters. Laurie Oakes argued that 'political reporting has become too negative, and based too much on personalities' (ABC Radio National, *Background Briefing*, 15 August 1999) and Paul Kelly (2001) said that political reporting in the early 2000s was 'obsessed with tactics and there's not enough focus on issues . . .'. Both Margo Kingston (2001) and Michelle Grattan (1998; 2005) expressed concern about how relationships between journalists, politicians and their advisers were influencing political reporting. Grattan (2005) also claimed that 'political investigative journalism [was] not strong' in Australia.

There was also some evidence to suggest that the Australian public was dissatisfied. Journalists were frequently ranked among the least admired of the professions. In 2007, they ranked below politicians (and only just above estate agents, advertisers and car salespeople) in a survey of the most trusted occupations (RMR 2008). In a 2000 AC Nielsen AgePoll, 37 per cent of respondents said they were dissatisfied with the media and an amazing 96 per cent said they thought journalists 'distort[ed] their reports in order to sell newspapers or boost ratings' (Colebatch 2000). Public complaints to the Australian Press Council increased every year between 2005–06 and 2008–09 (APC 2009b). Newspaper circulation and television news and current affairs ratings all declined between 2001 and 2007 (see Chapters 3 and 4).

The horse-race

Academics are also frequently critical about the news values and frames that shape coverage of politics. One of the most common criticisms is that the media report elections as if they are a horse-race with a focus on who's winning, who's losing and the competitive stakes, including an obsessive focus on opinion polls (see Chapter 9). Elections are also reported using the metaphors of games or sporting contests (Lichter and Smith 1996) or as 'battles', complete with military terms such as 'ad blitz', 'poll fight', 'battle', 'campaign headquarters' or 'war-room'. These narrative frames position conflict between the party leaders as the central focus, and attract criticisms that political reporting has become too adversarial and too cynical (see Tiffen 1999:2). A former politician argued: 'Conflict is the basis for news coverage. It is exaggerated where it exists and created or simulated when it does not' (Greiner 1992 quoted in Latham 2005:99). Laurie Oakes (2008:iv) observed that a 'sneering tone creeps into much... political commentary.' According to some studies, this negativity can lead the public to disengage from politics (Cappella and Hall Jamieson 1996).

A focus upon leaders was also widely held to have personalised politics. Television in particular was said to focus upon the 'star qualities' of individuals and party leaders (Ward 1995:188), leading to a 'presidentialisation' of politics and a tendency to ignore broader factors such as parties, policies, ideas and institutions. This frame is especially misleading in Australia, where prime ministers are not directly elected. When politics is seen through a prism of individual self-interest, the reporting of tactics tends to dominate and critics fear that personalisation reduces elections to a form of 'beauty contest' in which superficial matters – such as gaffes and personal appearance – play an inordinate role.

Dumbing down, entertainment and interpretation

Almost as common as the claim of 'horse-race' journalism is the lament by critics that a more entertainment-focused approach to reporting politics has led to a 'dumbing down' of content. These claims have been made of public broadcasters as well as commercial broadcasters and newspapers, but are more often associated with commercial media organisations that, it is argued, focus on politicians as celebrities and politics as entertainment in order to simplify politics and attract a mass audience that is profitable. 'Infotainment' and 'soft news' are now said to be the dominant modes of reporting (Thussu 2007). For many critics, these modes are disappointing because they are not about journalism, research or detailed reports on 'serious' topics, but about 'human interest' stories, lifestyle, consumerism and celebrity marketed in a way that fits with advertising and commercial imperatives (Barnhurst 1998:202).

For some critics, the entertainment values are not just about commercial media, but are more medium-specific and associated with television. Neil Postman (1985) famously stated that television was leading us to 'amuse ourselves to death' and that it promoted 'incoherence and triviality' (see also Kellner 1990). Journalist Paul Kelly also blamed television for making 'entertainment the dominant format for the representation of life' including political life (ABC *Media Report* 27 December 2001). Others, by contrast, have defended television. Oakes, who is well known for his televised political interviews, argued that: 'Quality is not necessarily equated with boredom' and that television is very valuable as it 'gives an extended look at a politician . . . [their] character . . . what [the politician] stands for, and what his [sic] intentions are' (ABC *Media Report* 7 September 2006; Wilson 2000).

Similar allegations centred around claims that a 'straight' reporting style focused upon 'the facts' had declined and that instead there had arisen an 'interpretive', commentary style. Newspapers certainly gave more space and prominence to op-eds – opinion pieces written by staff writers, regular columnists or external contributors. The rise of chat-style news and political commentary programs on television also reflected this changed style. For some, this 'interpretive turn' represented 'an excess of interpretation' and 'empty pontification' (McNair 2000:5). Yet defenders claimed that the changes had made journalism far more accessible, interesting and honest than older styles of reporting (Lumby 1999; McNair 2000, 2006; Chapter 13).

The media: too strong or too weak?

For some critics, the media were no longer acting as a watchdog before the powerful but had instead become too weak and too complicit (e.g. Hewson 2006). British political reporters following the 1996 election remarked that their Australian counterparts were noticeably timid and complicit in acquiescing to political candidates' conditions (*Media Rules* 1996). For those inside journalism, this trend is often seen as the result of declining access to politicians and information and the greater degree to which election campaigns are today controlled, choreographed and stage-managed by politicians.

In the 1990s, politicians began to favour talkback radio interviews, political advertising and direct mail and the press conferences of bygone years declined. Politicians argued that they wanted more direct ways of communicating with voters. However, the changes were seen by journalists as manoeuvres by politicians to evade scrutiny and the 'Gallery heavyweights' knowledge of history, context and policy, and their propensity to upset the leaders with brusque, unfawning questions' (Suich 2004a). Journalists increasingly claimed that they had been reduced to being theatre critics and spectators by the controlled nature of politicians' campaigning (Grattan 1998).

This was seen to be a consequence of politicians' heavy-handed political PR techniques, whereby an army of political professionals 'hijacked' news content so that it was now heavily influenced by – or in some cases came straight from – press releases and other information provided by politicians (e.g. Butler 1999:113; Chapter 8). The internet aided the ability of politicians to self-promote and self-publish and journalists reported that they were 'drowning in paper – the transcripts of the radio and television interviews the leaders and frontbenchers... [perform]. Correspondents now are textual analysts as much as reporters' (Suich 2004a).

By contrast, politicians and other media critics argued that such claims of declining media influence were disingenuous and that the media had inordinate power. Reporters were said to be players who could make or break political careers and influence electoral fortunes (Ellis 2002; Evans 1998; Latham 2005:270) and the active role played by some reporters and media owners led to ongoing accusations of bias in political reporting (see Chapter 11).

Information subsidies

The extent to which politicians' political PR is unwanted interference in the process of journalism is an issue of debate. Contrary to the view of an indignant media being harangued by politicians and their spin doctors, others suggest that journalists benefit significantly from their reliance on political PR because politicians' media management efforts subsidise the mass media and provide material for which news outlets would otherwise have to pay. According to this view, press releases, media advisers, staged picture opportunities and other set events were all very useful 'information subsidies' for the media (Herman and Chomsky 1988). Street (2001:149) argued, for example, that it was the desire of the media for news that was 'attractive and accessible' that led journalists to be very receptive to politicians' 'neatly crafted sound bites and photo-opportunities'.

Lazy journalism is a related complaint. Critics say that journalists all too frequently cut-and-paste from press releases or Wikipedia and don't leave their desks, cultivate new sources or chase difficult investigative stories any more. Economic pressures within media companies as well as reductions in journalism staff and the newsroom model of multiskilling are all seen to have contributed to this. However, there is also the compounding factor of the much faster news flows seen today, with 24-hour news cycles and a focus on 'breaking news' encouraged by the advent of 24-hour news channels and online news. This, it is argued, has led to less time for checking facts, gathering diverse viewpoints and conducting detailed reporting, as well as less time for reflection or follow-up; the focus instead is on being first, being live and being up to date at the expense of accuracy, depth and reflection (see Lewis, Cushion and Thomas 2005).

The Press Gallery

Reporters from the Press Gallery have been 'collectively responsible for the great majority of stories about federal politics that appear in Australian print and broadcast media' (Ward 2006:370; see also Lloyd 1988). The Gallery is a body of approximately 250 journalists plus their editors, producers and technical staff (Fitzgerald 2008:14). Unusually, by international standards, the Australian Press Gallery is formally accorded space within Parliament House. This has led to accusations that reporters work too closely with politicians and their advisers and are therefore too subject to their influence. In 2008, an editorial in the *Australian* ('Detachment matters', 15 March 2008) called this 'the bubble-like world of the parliamentary triangle', but claimed that the problem worked both ways and that politicians were also unduly influenced by journalists and needed to be wary of this because the 'interests and opinions of [Gallery] journalists . . . rarely reflect those of the majority of voters.'

This statement reflects another common criticism: that the Gallery is 'out of touch' with citizens because journalists in Canberra are so removed, geographically (but also socially and economically), from the interests and concerns of far-flung viewers and readers. The Press Gallery is said to operate like a 'club' in which reporters share similar backgrounds and mindsets and engage in a type of 'group thinking' (McGuinness 2002; see also Simons 1999). Jack Waterford, editor of the *Canberra Times*, has questioned whether 'political journalists write more for each other than for their public' (APC

1999). This, it has been argued, leads reporters to adhere to a type of 'editorial orthodoxy' that makes them provide 'a safe interpretation of events, aware that these would be shared by most other senior political reporters' (Suich 1988). As a result, according to Waterford, reporters' 'circle of contacts is too narrow' and 'their output is depressingly similar' (ABC *The Media Report* 11 August 2005).

Paul Kelly (2001) has also commented that there is a sameness and uniformity in editorial output. This is not only related to the working conditions of Gallery reporters – including their propensity to work and socialise together, for example – nor the media-management techniques of politicians and their staff (which tend to see journalists provided with the same stock information), but also to a commercial media need for content that appeals to the broadest possible audience. Yet other Gallery journalists deny these allegations of 'pack' reporting and point to differences in journalistic styles and opinions, as well as the competition that occurs for scoops and exclusives.

There is a hierarchy within political journalism in Australia. Margaret Simons (1999:23–5) has described how several journalists were called the 'God correspondents' because they were viewed as so influential among their peers. Who was in and out of this group varied over time, but the two names that were most consistently mentioned as influential in the 2000s were Laurie Oakes and Michelle Grattan. Both Oakes and Grattan had been reporting on federal politics for over three decades. Oakes covered every federal election since 1966 and Michelle Grattan began in the Press Gallery in 1971. An indication of their gravitas was the comments made by journalist Margo Kingston that 'There's two names in the Gallery. If they make a serious assessment about news they're automatically believed. They are Oakes and Grattan' (quoted in Henderson 2002).

Outside the Press Gallery, there are also a raft of political commentators and columnists such as Andrew Bolt, Miranda Devine, Janet Albrechtsen and Phillip Adams (see Chapter 13). Although not necessarily based in Canberra, these commentators are often viewed as political 'insiders' and, sometimes, as having too-close connections to particular politicians or even overt political agendas of their own (e.g. see Lucy and Mickler 2006). Commentators work across print, radio and television (and are especially prominent on programs such as *Insiders* and *Meet the Press*), but they also exist outside the mainstream media in blogging communities, social networking sites and alternative media outlets (see Chapter 10).

Editorialising and meta-coverage

For some critics, reporters today have become more overt 'players' in politics because there is so much editorialising in modern journalism. Journalists increasingly 'write themselves into the story'. According to Esser, Reinemann and Fan, this is because the media have entered a third stage of political journalism. Stage one was 'issue coverage', which ran from 1900 to about 1972; stage two was 'strategic coverage' (1972 until 1988) and the third stage of 'meta-coverage' began in the late 1980s. Meta-coverage is 'the news media's self-referential reflections on the nature of the interplay between political public relations and political journalism'. This includes a heightened focus in media reporting on the tactics of campaigning, including a 'behind-the-scenes schema', a reliance on 'spin doctors as news sources' and a 'focus on media manipulation' (Esser, Reinemann and Fan 2001:16–17).

Pippa Norris has argued that self-referential framing by the media is a way journalists 'fight back' to maintain control over their product as a wave of political professionals try to exert more control over media reporting (Norris 2001b). Journalists are especially reporting on how politicians try to manipulate the media. Commentators such as Stebenee have said that these changes in reporting style are 'a logical outgrowth' of the increased awareness in the media of their central role in political events such as election campaigns (Stebenee 1993:88 quoted in Esser, Reinemann and Fan 2001:18). Kerbel has also described self-referential coverage as 'part of "a natural progression"' (Kerbel 1999:87).

In some accounts, meta-coverage is viewed as a way for the media to acknowledge their own power as part of a political institution and to 'deal more constructively with their own involvement and power in . . . politics' (Cook 1998:175 quoted in Esser, Reinemann and Fan 2001:22). Esser, Reinemann and Fan comment:

> From a democratic-normative standpoint . . . [this is] to be welcomed as a new style of reporting that is potentially self-critical, self-analytical, contextualizing, and revealing about the hidden promotional powers in modern politics. (2001:39; see also McNair 2006).

Others remain unsure about whether the new emphasis on self-reflection is a vain distraction that lessens accountability and fails to honestly reflect on media power and how news is produced (see Chapter 9).

Difference and diversity

The way in which media content marginalises differences, including those of ethnicity, sexuality, class and gender, has been a source of much concern. As in media content more broadly, these concerns have all been said to apply to political reporting; however, the reporting of female politicians has been singled out for particular attention (e.g. Norris 1997b; Baird 2004). Studies have suggested that female politicians are represented differently from men in media reports and that unfair 'double standards' of behaviour are applied, particularly regarding physical appearance, sexuality, morality, private lives and domestic roles. Former Democrats leader and Labor MP Cheryl Kernot, who was the target of a series of media stories focusing on her private life, remarked that this was particularly true in Australia:

> I think that's something about the Australian media... about women in politics and in public life where you're either a madonna or a whore. There seems to be something about punishing women... it doesn't happen in the UK. (AAP 2005).

If media reporting of female politicians contributes to women's marginalisation in public life, it presents a significant barrier to women seeking and obtaining positions of political power (see Chapters 8 and 9).

Analysing election reporting

The list of complaints against media reporting of politics and elections is long, but it is also highly contradictory. For every accusation there is a counter-claim or counter-accusation. The focus of this book is to test the main complaints to find out how well we are served by those who report and comment on elections and how political news changed in the 2000s when many of the most virulent accusations of poor reporting surfaced.

This book therefore focuses on the three federal elections of that decade – 2001, 2004 and 2007.

Given the mass of content produced during those campaigns, it would be easy enough to find examples of sensationalist, inaccurate or seemingly biased election reports but, although this sometimes suffices for some critics, isolated examples are not enough. In order to understand election reporting, we need to view it in a broader context. Five aspects are crucial: (1) audiences; (2) news organisations, reporters and how they create election news; (3) politicians and how they campaign and interact with the media; (4) the content of election reports; and (5) the impact of this reporting on Australian democracy. This book is arranged to broadly follow this structure. (See also Appendix A for more details on the methodology.)

All pieces of writing involve choices of inclusion and exclusion as well as choices about how to contextualise and frame different ideas and concepts. This applies not only to election reports but also to this book, and so the approach I have taken needs to be explained. To begin with, I need to outline how I defined 'politics' and 'political' news.

'Politics' and 'political' news

Four months before the 2007 election, the American heiress Paris Hilton was sentenced to a 45-day prison sentence for driving offences. Was this a 'political' issue? Perhaps, but only in a very broad sense and defining something as 'political' tells us nothing about its relative value or impact. This book focuses on 'formal politics' – parliaments, parties, policies, politicians, governments, governing, elections, the media and their political role. Admittedly this is a much narrower definition of politics but it is a stable one, whereas the boundaries of informal politics are fluid, indistinct and, in some cases, stretched so far that the term becomes meaningless.

My emphasis on formal politics and the ballot box is out of step with some theorists, who have been arguing that conventional electoral politics are becoming less significant. For these theorists, the concept of 'representative democracy' is outdated and is being replaced by a new model. In some accounts this is seen as an 'audience democracy' (Manin 1997:218–35), or as a democracy involving 'monitorial' citizens (Schudson 1998), or as a 'monitory democracy' (Keane 2009) (see Chapter 12).

Most recently, John Keane (2009:14–15) has argued that 'a "post-Westminster" form of democracy' has emerged characterised by 'extra-parliamentary power-scrutinising mechanisms' and 'different types of power-monitoring devices that never before existed within the world of democracy'. These include courts, workplace tribunals, citizens' juries, think-tanks, blogs and other forms of media scrutiny. In such a system, parliaments and elections become less significant. Peter Mair (2008:130) describes a situation where:

> As citizens are offered more opportunities for direct participation, and as non-political agencies and 'guardian institutions' take on a more decisive role, it makes less sense to speak of power being acquired through a competitive struggle for the people's vote.

This view certainly has some theoretical appeal, but even its proponents do not suggest that the mechanisms of formal politics and representative democracy are in immediate danger of oblivion. In Australia, now and into the foreseeable future, we rely on representative democracy to convert individual needs into action, and ideas and principles into law. Competitive elections and freedom of speech, freedom of political expression and freedom of the press (media) are still fundamental and have a very real influence on the lives of those who are governed. As Richard S. Katz (2008:294) notes:

> there is occasionally talk that . . . social movements and governance networks will supplant [political] parties as the leading institutions channelling political participation and structuring government [but] experience to date offers little reason to suspect . . . that this will happen any time soon.

As flawed and imperfect as it is, our democracy and the formal political mechanisms that underpin it still remain vital. This is not to deny that democracy is an ongoing project and that political processes – including citizenship and concepts of representation – are in flux. Indeed, part of the brief of this book is to try to understand the changes that are occurring – not only in media reporting of politics, but also in its conduct and reception. All of these aspects are linked and, in the 'post-parliamentary democracy' that some theorists foresee, the media are identified as a key institution that exercises and scrutinises power. Understanding the role of the media, both in terms of their relationship with formal politics and independently from this, is therefore more crucial than ever.

Old media, new media: the past, the future

If this book focuses more on 'old' representative, conventional politics than some theorists will think appropriate, it also focuses more on 'old' media than some new media enthusiasts will think is warranted. The internet is influencing news production and consumption in highly significant ways that are discussed throughout this book (especially in Chapter 10). Mobile technology is also of growing significance to the future of news journalism. But I pay most attention to older media – particularly television and newspapers and, to a lesser extent, radio. There are a number of reasons for this.

While the internet had important effects on political participation and reporting in the 2000s, we were not yet at a point where it was the major source of political news for the majority of Australians. That distinction still applied to television, as it had for several decades. While media use is changing rapidly, even in the second decade of the 21st century, television remains the news medium that is used most often by the largest number of Australians. It is sometimes too easy to forget this, especially if one is a heavy internet user.

My focus also stems from an observation that 'old' media – television, radio and newspapers – have not yet been adequately covered in empirical research in Australia. This is partly because studying television and radio in particular is expensive and time-consuming and poses a raft of practical difficulties. However, many of the expectations that are now held for the internet – including that it will revolutionise political practice and reporting – were also held for television in the 1950s, and there has been insufficient attention paid to whether television ever actually *did* fulfil those expectations. Focusing on the 2001, 2004 and 2007 elections provides important evidence about this, which is not only valuable for its own sake – given the significant role television played in politics during these years – but also helpful in clarifying expectations about the internet and working out practical ways to measure its impact.

Like any book, this one captures a particular moment in time. It is an occupational hazard for anyone who writes about the media that, by the time their book is printed (let alone read in later years), the outlets and programs they mention may be embarrassingly out of date. This is especially true in a rapidly changing media environment. It was also a sobering experience when, in my research for this book, I consulted media/politics books by scholars from the 1960s to the 1980s and found that they included predictions that have since proved thoroughly incorrect, assumptions that have been roundly quashed or trends that have since reversed. One of my favourites from the 1980s argued that Rupert Murdoch had little business sense and was unlikely to last in the media industry! Predicting what will happen in media consumption and organisation is even more fraught than predicting election results.

Even when we are dealing with the safer task of analysing the past rather than trying to predict the future, making sense of news content to draw conclusions about the role of the media leads to a wide range of interpretations and views. The scope and ferocity of debate about election reporting demonstrates this well. As a political scientist, my own standards for assessing how 'well' the media report politics are admittedly high, shaped as they are by theories of political engagement, deliberative democracy and an animated public sphere. However, to return to the beginning of this introduction, they are often no higher than the purposes and responsibilities that journalists ascribe to themselves.

Conclusion

This book is about election news – how it was produced and how it changed in the 2000s. To begin an analysis of this kind requires us to take a step backwards and to start with audiences, because all media content is created for an audience. To know about audiences is to know who journalists think they are talking to when they produce election news. To know whether those audiences grew or shrunk in the 2000s also brings us much closer to understanding changes in production and content.

Democratic theory assumes that all citizens should be informed; but just who is in the political news audience and who is missing? Those who are interested in politics – including those interested enough to read a book on the topic (or to write one, for that matter) – have a tendency to assume that everyone else is just as interested or, from a normative viewpoint, *should* be just as interested in politics. This assumption is put to the test in the first part of the book as I map the actual existing political news audience in Australia to reveal how many people cared about political news and followed it through the media in the 2000s (Chapter 2); what the differences were between audiences for different types of media (Chapters 3 and 4) and how audiences influenced election news and vice versa (Chapter 5).

Part I

POLITICAL NEWS AUDIENCES AND OUTLETS

THE POLITICAL NEWS AUDIENCE

How many people watch, read or listen to political news? This is an important question because it influences everything about the way elections are reported. If no-one wants to follow political news, then media organisations (especially commercial ones) have little incentive to devote resources and time to it. Even if the media generate the best political journalism in the world – however this is defined – what is its value if no-one is paying attention?

Most theories about the media and politics assume that media audiences need information and opportunities to participate politically. The media are seen as crucial for delivering this and for facilitating the formation of public opinion, ideally through universal access and an unfettered flow of information and ideas (Habermas 1989). Yet this view may not necessarily fit with how media audiences see themselves and their media use, or with how news producers conceive of their audiences.

Media organisations place great significance on market research and audience profiling. However, while they seem to know a good deal about their audiences, they cannot always predict their desires or satisfy them; some of the key allegations of poor political reporting stem from claims that news producers do not understand their audiences as well as they think they do. According to some critics, news producers underestimate their audiences' information-processing abilities and overlook their democratic needs. Yet others imply the opposite: that news producers know their audiences only too well and pander to their 'worst' instincts. Tabloid newspapers and commercial television are criticised for indulging their audiences' desire for triviality, sensationalism and scandal, while broadsheets and public broadcasting media are accused of providing content that is boring, elitist and of interest only to political insiders.

One thing we need to get to the heart of such allegations is an understanding of the audience for political news. This chapter starts the process by focusing on the size of that audience. I begin with the classic fare of social science research – surveys – and what these tell us about levels of political interest in Australia; then I propose a different measure, using media audience data to gain a sense of how many people want political news and what sorts of news and media they prefer.

Who cares about politics?

How many Australians care about politics and pursue that interest? This is not an easy question to answer, because interest can wax and wane over a person's lifetime and can be expressed through a range of activities from discussing politics with others to watching political news on television, voting, joining a political party, attending political meetings or writing a politics blog. In other countries, voter turnout is often used as the standard gauge to measure political interest but in Australia, because of compulsory voting, it is not. A better way is to examine public opinion surveys of a representative sample of voters. In Australia, the Australian Election Study (AES) surveys, which have polled thousands of Australians and been conducted after each federal election since 1987, are the most comprehensive on attitudes to elections.

We need to keep in mind a few things about interpreting survey results. People who complete written surveys like those produced by the AES tend to have higher education qualifications than most citizens (Goot 2000:47–8). In general, when people report on their behaviour in surveys, there is also a tendency to overestimate 'good' qualities such as political participation and civic involvement. Then again, anyone who is willing to fill in a 28-page election survey form and post it back probably *is* unusually politically interested and civically minded. Also, the nature of politics at the time a survey is conducted has an influence on people's interest in politics. Factors such as the degree of competition (or lack thereof) between the major parties, the rise of a minor party and related media attention (One Nation in 1998), a new leader (Latham in 2004), a particularly controversial policy (the Goods and Services Tax in 1993) or an impending change of government (2007) can all make a particular election more exciting, competitive or otherwise 'interesting'.

Bearing these factors in mind, a high proportion of respondents to AES surveys in the 2000s reported they were interested in elections. The data in Table 2.1 suggests that, if anything, Australians became more, not less, interested in politics over the 2000s if you include those who expressed 'some' interest as opposed to 'none' or 'not much'. In 2007, 81 per cent said they had 'a good deal' of, or 'some', interest. This figure was higher than for both 2004 and 2001, when the equivalent proportions were 74 per cent and 70 per cent respectively.

Table 2.1 Interest in election campaigns, Australian Election Studies, 1969–2007 (percentages)

Election	A good deal	Some	Not much	None at all	No. of respondents
1969 election	33	37	30	n/a	(1873)
1993 election	49	35	14	2	(3023)
1996 election	34	41	21	4	(1795)
1998 election	36	41	17	4	(1897)
2001 election	31	40	23	6	(1975)
2004 election	30	44	21	5	(1735)
2007 election	40	41	15	4	(1830)

Note: 'n/a' means that respondents were not asked this question at the time.

Sources: For 1969, 1993–98 figures, Goot 2002:17. For 2001–07 figures, Bean, Gow and McAllister 2002; Bean et al 2005; Bean, McAllister and Gow 2008.

Yet while it is one thing to profess an interest in politics, it is another to act on it in ways that are demanding because this requires a degree of time, effort or money, and the same studies show that indicators of extensive (or deep) participation in formal politics are low. According to surveys, during an election campaign less than 5 per cent of Australians usually attend political meetings and only about 4 per cent are members of a political party (Passey and Lyons 2005:68; McAllister and Clark 2007). Tiffen and Gittins (2009:44) report that only 1.5 per cent of the Australian electorate were members of a political party in the 1990s.

Although a large proportion of Australians said they were interested in politics, a significant number also said they were not satisfied with the way it was conducted or communicated. Even in 2007, a year that saw unusually high interest in politics, one in four Australians said that politics had 'little connection with my life' and 34 per cent felt that 'sometimes politics seems so complicated that I can't really understand what's going on' (Phillips et al 2008). Seventeen per cent acknowledged that they had 'not much' or 'no' interest in politics and 12 per cent said they might not vote at all if it were voluntary (Bean, McAllister and Gow 2008).

The survey evidence builds up a picture of two extremes of a spectrum of political interest – about 5 per cent of Australians are highly interested and engaged in formal politics, while 12 per cent are so uninterested that they might not vote at all if voting were not compulsory; the other indicators suggest that up to 20 per cent are indifferent. In other words, for every Australian who is highly engaged with politics, there are at least two who aren't very interested at all. The majority of Australians are in between these extremes. To understand how this relates to media audiences and the reporting of elections, I now propose to use a different way of measuring political interest that reflects on actual behaviour by analysing audiences for political news.

Before outlining what the audience data shows, we should note that there have been long-standing controversies about audience measures such as television ratings and newspaper circulation figures. Media companies use this data to attract advertisers and the figures can sometimes seem suspiciously high (e.g. Simons 2008a; 2009). A different critique relates not to the accuracy of audience data but to what it purports to measure. Todd Gitlin (1983:54) has noted that television ratings 'only sample sets tuned in, not necessarily shows watched, let alone grasped, remembered, loved, learned from, deeply anticipated or mildly tolerated'. Audience measures are increasingly inadequate, especially in relation to use of the internet – which is still frustratingly difficult to measure – but also as a result of the marked trend towards multiple media use at the one time. (Think here of someone watching television with a laptop on their lap and a mobile phone in hand.) However, despite these difficulties, the data can still give us a good (albeit broad) sense of how many people follow traditional political news.

Political news audiences

Most Australians are interested in news. In 2007, over 80 per cent interviewed for the Australian Survey of Social Attitudes said that catching up with the news was a regular part of their day (Phillips et al 2008). But there are many different types of news including sport, finance, world news, entertainment and celebrity gossip. Overseas research has found that, while many people are interested in news (and there is even quite a large proportion who can be characterised as 'news junkies'), only a small portion are 'political news junkies – the rest prefer other types of news' (PRC 2006). Overseas studies have found that people who are very interested in politics and political news (colloquially called 'political junkies') tend to have very specific media preferences. They prefer a broadsheet newspaper to all other media; indeed, broadsheet reading has been found to be *the* defining feature of a political junkie. When they watch television or listen to the radio, they have a strong preference for public over commercial broadcasting (Kingdon 1970; Newton 1999; Norris 1996, 2000; Weaver and Drew 2006).

These media preferences are not surprising, given that content analyses have found that broadsheets and public television and radio tend to be the most politics-heavy of traditional news media (Henningham 1988; see also Denemark, Ward and Bean 2007; McNair 2000:16; PEJ 2007). For example, John Henningham (1996: 30) found that broadsheets such as the *Canberra Times* and the *Australian* devoted more than twice the amount of space to politics as did tabloids such as the *Herald Sun* and the *Daily Telegraph*. The findings tend to confirm what we might intuitively expect – that people who are highly interested in politics choose the media that devote the most space to it. However, there has been little research done on this in Australia and older studies of political junkies do not always take into account the growing range of specialised political news sources that have become available including 24-hour news channels, internet websites and blogs.

Figure 2.1 seeks to identify Australian political junkies based on what we know about media preferences and which media devoted the most time or space to political news in Australia in 2007.[1] It shows that political junkies could only have been a very small proportion of the population. Less than 1 per cent of Australians subscribed to the email newsletter *Crikey* (which

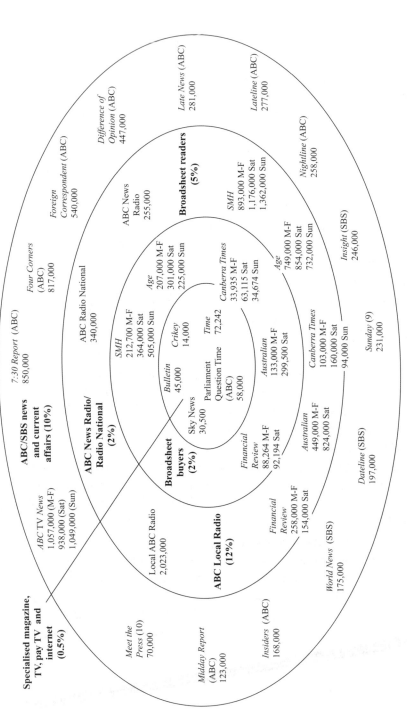

Figure 2.1 The audience for political news (2007) (raw figures and as an approximate percentage of the Australian adult population – 15 years+)

Sources: for sources and notes see Chapter 2 endnotes.

focuses on politics, business and media news); watched Sky News (then Australia's only locally produced 24-hour pay TV news channel), watched *Parliament Question Time* when it was broadcast on the ABC, or read news magazines such as the *Bulletin* (which closed in 2008) or the Australian version of *Time*. During the 2007 election, the ABC broadcast a series of debates between ministers and shadow ministers (on topics such as health and treasury) organised by the Press Club. These debates had only 85 000– 118 000 viewers. It is interesting that this is the same proportion as the 0.5–1 per cent of the population shown in Figure 2.1 who were the most dedicated political junkies.

There was a larger group of about 2 per cent of Australians who bought a broadsheet newspaper,[2] and listened to the only local 24-hour news radio station (ABC News Radio) or the ABC's Radio National, which focuses on journalism, politics and the arts. Beyond this, there were 5 per cent of Australians who read a broadsheet newspaper (but didn't buy it themselves) and 10–12 per cent who watched ABC or SBS television news and current affairs programs and listened to their local ABC radio. Taken as a whole, this sort of broadsheet/public broadcasting audience is sometimes called the 'attentive elite', because people in this group tend to be more politically interested but also wealthier and more educated than the general population (see Chapter 3). The media they favour are also often designated as 'elite' media. The use of this term is not meant to imply some inherent superiority in these products, but rather that the audience for them 'mainly comprises those whom social statisticians would place above the societal average in terms of income, educational level, or profession' (McNair 2000:14).

We cannot assume that all of the audience members shown in Figure 2.1 were politically interested. We cannot know, for example, whether someone bought a broadsheet for the political news or for the lifestyle magazine or IT supplement. Likewise, someone might have switched on ABC News for the weather report rather than the politics stories. However, those who seem to best fit the profile of a political junkie were in the inner circles of Figure 2.1 and the size of that group has significant implications for the reporting of politics and elections. Those media outlets that devote more time or space than others to the detailed coverage of politics tend to attract smaller audiences. Public broadcasting aside, this is clearly no incentive to commercial organisations seeking to make large profits unless, as in the case of broadsheet newspapers, they are able to do so, not on the basis of audience size (on readers paying for the newspaper), but rather from selling advertisers access to this small but lucrative audience and from the classified advertising contained in the newspaper. These economic models are now under threat (see Chapter 10).

Figure 2.1 reinforces the idea that there is only a limited audience for what is usually called 'quality journalism'. This has practical consequences not only for media economics but also for any theory that assumes a ready-made public of 'active citizens' who want engagement with politics via detailed news presented in the media. Most Australians are not particularly interested in politics and only a small minority are highly engaged. What role, if any, news organisations and media companies have played in this outcome is a key issue to be explored in coming chapters.

There are many limitations in a mapping process as broad as the one I have undertaken in Figure 2.1. My map only gives an average and a broad sense of the audience for particular media products at a particular point in time. It cannot pinpoint those who tune in and out to political news – who 'dip in and out' as their attention is sparked by a particular issue but then recedes. It only covers the main media products and neglects alternative and regional and rural media. Aside from *Crikey* – which is subscription based, so subscriber figures are available – accurate, comparative indicators of website audiences are difficult to obtain. These audiences are instead discussed separately in the next two chapters as well as in Chapter 10.

The most difficult part of the mapping exercise is that it cannot identify the cross-overs between audiences. Most news consumers 'use a combination of three or four media formats' and news junkies typically use six or more (PEJ 2008). This means many of the audience members for the different elite media products were the same people. Someone who subscribed to *Crikey* might also have bought a state-based broadsheet newspaper and a national one, watched *The 7:30 Report* and SBS News and listened to ABC radio. It would be useful to know how media consumption overlaps, but this is beyond the scope of what raw audience figures can tell us.

Despite the limitations and however broad the figures calculated in Figure 2.1 are, it is significant that they do seem to match up with other evidence. The 5 per cent figure is similar to the proportion of people who expressed 'deep' interest in politics in surveys (who attended meetings, for example). We know from international research that when the 'attentive elite' watch television they overwhelmingly favour public broadcasting, so a simple test is to add up primetime television news viewing on the public channels assuming – given working hours and programming schedules – that it is unlikely that even the very keen would watch all. Combined, the three main evening news bulletins on public television garnered an audience that equated to 9 per cent of the population, very close to the 10 per cent outer edge of elite political news interest in Figure 2.1.

In the 1960s, pioneering media academic Henry Mayer (1964:259) estimated that the audience for 'serious' news in Australia was around 10–15 per cent, which suggests that the proportions have not have changed much despite the increasing proportion of Australians with tertiary education (a variable strongly correlated with broadsheet reading). A final corroborating piece of evidence is that international comparisons have found remarkably similar proportions. In the US, the Pew Research Center estimates that 11 per cent of Americans are 'politics junkies' (PEJ 2008:44).

Figure 2.2 is not meant to imply that other media consumers, such as readers of tabloid newspapers or talkback radio listeners, are not interested in politics. Transport, hospital waiting lists, schools, the behaviour of politicians and other political issues frequently grace the pages of state-based tabloids or are at the centre of talkback discussion. In 2009, News Limited CEO John Hartigan argued that many important political stories in Australia – including Liberal leader John Howard's broken leadership promise to Peter Costello – had broken in tabloids.

It is also important to note that broadsheets are not all about political news or 'serious' journalism. They have large sections devoted to sport, movies, entertainment, human interest, lifestyle, supplements, magazines and advertising. Overall, they contain a mix of 'serious and less serious material' (Sparks 2000:32). However, even if there is an interest in politics that is shared by some audience members across popular and elite media and both types of media include a mix of formal politics and entertainment, the presentation of political issues still tends to be quantitatively and qualitatively different. Their audiences are also very different in demographic terms as well as in terms of their political attitudes and opinions (see Chapters 3, 4 and 5). This is why I think it is important to consider them separately rather than conflate them.

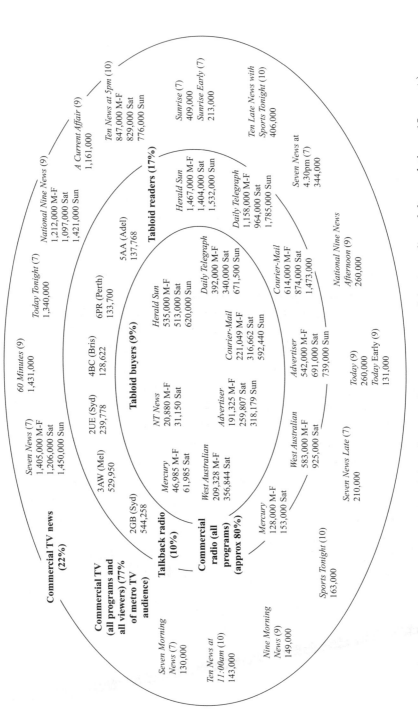

Figure 2.2 The general news audience (2007) (raw figures and as a percentage of the Australian adult population – 15 years+)

Sources: for sources and notes see Chapter 2 endnotes.

The popular news audience

Figure 2.2 maps those who followed news on commercial television and radio as well as those who listened to commercial talkback and read tabloid newspapers.[3] These audiences were much larger than for elite media and, while television's dominance as a news medium declined in the 2000s, Figure 2.2 reminds us that it was still a pervasive force. Every day, over 9 million Australians watched commercial television and 4 million specifically watched commercial news at primetime (FTA 2008). Others watched current affairs, breakfast and midday programs and even those who turned on television only to watch movies or sitcoms were still likely to see occasional news breaks.

Radio was also a major medium. Almost eight in ten Australians listened to commercial radio every week (CRA 2008). Talkback was particularly identified with political content due to its mix of talk, music, news and interviews with politicians (Ward 2002a). On commercial FM 'top 40' stations, political discussion was not as prevalent but listeners were still likely to have heard news bulletins between music and other programming (even if many were 'rip and reads' from newswires) and would also have heard presenters, comedians and callers talk about the 'news' of the day, which included election news during campaigns.

Increasing numbers of Australians were also seeking out, or coming across, news content on the internet including headlines and articles from Google, Ninemsn, news websites and search engines (see Chapters 4 and 10). So up to 90 per cent of Australians either actively sought out political news or saw and heard it anyway as part of their daily use of media.

Following elections through the media

Even if most people are not normally interested in politics, for 'the average citizen', an election campaign provides 'the single most compelling incentive to think about [politics and] government' (Riker quoted in Banducci and Karp 2003:444). But does this mean that more people switch on to political news during elections? The best way to assess this is by looking at television audiences. More than three-quarters of Australians said they followed the 2007 campaign via television (Bean, McAllister and Gow 2008). This does not mean that there was a sudden stampede for election news on television, though. The ratings for television news programs do not tend to dramatically rise just because an election is on. In fact, in 2007, there was a slight dip in the ratings of the two most-watched news programs in the first and last weeks of the campaign (CMH 2004; FTA 2007, 2008). However, there are two specific televised election events that have become a ritualised part of election reporting in Australia – the leaders' debate and the polling night vote count – and these are better indicators of audiences that are tuning in specifically for election content.

A leader's debate (often called the '*Great Debate*') has been held between the Labor and Liberal party leaders during every federal election since 1984 (with the exception of 1987) (Senior 2007). In 2007, it was shown on Sky News as well as on Channel Nine and the ABC. Combined, these three programs had an audience of over 2.8 million (OzTAM author data and Tadros 2007). However, many people were not watching television at all that night and, of those who *were* watching free-to-air, 57 per cent chose to watch something else. The top-rating individual program of the night was *National Bingo Night* on Channel Seven, followed by comedy show *Kath and Kim* and *Seven News*. For a political event, the debate certainly received high ratings and an impressive 43 per cent of the free-to-air television viewing audience but, in 2007, this was still only 21 per cent of registered voters.

In the 2007 AES survey, 47 per cent of respondents claimed to have watched the debate held between John Howard and Kevin Rudd on 21 October 2007. If this were true, the ratings would have been about 6.4 million instead of only 2.8 million across Australia. One likely explanation for the difference between the two figures is the way the AES is skewed towards the more interested and/or better educated. It may also demonstrate the differences that can occur between self-reported and actual behaviour, or it could be that respondents interpreted the question to include later seeing news breaks or news program stories on the debate rather than watching the whole event live.

The other major televised election ritual in Australia is the election night count of votes. In 2007, three out of the five free-to-air news channels broadcast live from the National Tally Room in Canberra and competed to be the first to call the result (the ABC, Channel Nine and Channel Seven). The other two channels broadcast shorter verdict programs later in the night – SBS at 9:30 pm and Channel Ten at 10 pm – meaning that, at some points in the evening, free-to-air viewers had little choice but to watch the vote count. In total, these five programs had a cumulative audience of over 3.2 million. However, the overall polling night audience still represented only 23 per cent of registered voters.

If we match up the figures with information from Figures 2.1 and 2.2, they suggest that the major rituals of television election viewing tend to attract those people who are already broadly interested in politics. And impressive as the viewing figures seem, the number of people who watched the debate and polling night broadcasts was not even equivalent to the number of people who would watch a nightly news bulletin. There were still around 80 per cent of Australians who avoided even these relatively popular mediated election events.

Table 2.2 Polling night cumulative audiences (mainland capital cities), 2001–07

	2001	**2004**	**2007**
ABC	664 570	890 700	1 075 000
Channel Nine	1 160 000	1 014 000	763 000
Channel Seven	–	–	967 000
SBS	n/a	n/a	120 000

Sources: OzTAM data supplied to the author; Carbonne 2001; Smith 2004.

Because these election rituals attract the politically interested, they do reveal important details about the elite–popular media split, though. Table 2.2 shows the audiences of polling night programs from 2001 to 2007. As we have noted, the 2007 election garnered more interest than usual. Those who watched on *commercial* broadcasters increased to 1.7 million. This is equivalent to 10 per cent of the population and broadly matches the tabloid newspaper buyers (9 per cent) and talkback radio listeners (10 per cent) mapped in Figure 2.2. This is the politically interested segment of the population who prefer commercial media. On the ABC, polling night attracted about 6 per cent of the population which is, broadly, the proportion of political junkies mapped in Figure 2.1, although it's also likely that some political junkies watched polling night on Sky News and/or on websites instead, including the ABC website.

What this broadly suggests to me is that, in 2007, an interesting and competitive election led the approximately 20 per cent of the population who were politically interested to switch on to their preferred outlets – about 10 per cent turned to elite media while the other 10 per cent chose popular media. There was not, however, a massive influx of attention from what might be called the 'politically shy' and the majority of the Australian electorate still failed to switch on for those events.

Election audiences

We can now start to tease out some characteristics of the elite news audience and the popular news audience, a process that is continued in the next two chapters. The available data allows us to examine characteristics relating to age, gender and class in particular. Unfortunately, there is no data available on ethnicity, race, sexuality or religious preference, which could give us an even better sense of how news use relates to social advantage or disadvantage.

Table 2.3 Characteristics of audiences for televised election events, mainland capital cities, 2007 (percentages)

| | | Leaders' | Polling night | | |
	Population	Debate	ABC	Channel 7	Channel 9
Men	49	52	50	48	51
Women	51	48	50	51	49
0–17 years	23	3	6	9	9
18–24 years	10	6	7	6	7
25–39 years	22	15	17	24	23
40–54 years	21	20	25	25	24
55 years+	24	56	46	37	38
Managers, administrators and professionals (ABs)	18	16	20	13	14
Para-professionals (including clerks, teachers, salespeople)	17	18	16	23	22
Tradespeople, plant and machine operators and labourers	12	7	5	12	11

Note: Occupation groups as defined by OzTAM. Tradespeople, plant and machine operators includes drivers and police. No figures were available for the Channel Nine version of the debate (which was a *60 Minutes* special).

Source: OzTAM data supplied to the author.

Table 2.3 shows the television audiences for the 2007 leaders' debate on the ABC and the election night specials broadcast at primetime by the ABC and by Channels Seven and Nine. It compares these audiences to the general population. What stands out immediately is how old the election news audience is – especially the ABC's: over half the audience for the ABC broadcast of the debate was over 55. With their more entertainment-focused approach, Seven and Nine's polling night broadcasts attracted a younger audience, more para-professionals and more than double the number of tradespeople and labourers than were attracted by the ABC – but their audiences, too, were disproportionately old.

The older audience is partly because television itself is increasingly an older person's medium. As more media options have become available, the free-to-air television audience has declined and remaining viewers tend to be older, with people over 55 watching the most television (Young 2009b:154). However, the data also reflects how interest in politics is strongly correlated with age (Norris et al 1999; Ofcom 2005). Ian McAllister (1992:35–6) has argued that voters tend to become more interested in politics as they age because they have had more time to observe it, have greater experience and knowledge with which to evaluate it, and have a larger economic stake in society. Young people tend to be less interested in formal politics (JSCEM 2007; Vromen 2008; Ward 1992). Australians aged 18–21 are significantly less likely to be enrolled to vote and less than half say they are interested in politics or consider it important to vote (EMC 2009:118–19). Aside from age, gender, class and ethnicity also play a role in political interest and use of news media for political news (see Chapter 3).

Declining interest in politics or media representations of politics?

Although a high proportion of survey respondents say they are interested in politics, voter turnout levels in established democracies with voluntary voting actually saw a 'a near universal decline' between the 1960s and 2000s (Hay 2007:42–3). A number of studies argued that citizens in advanced democracies had been withdrawing from formal politics and, overall, were less active and less interested in it than in the past (e.g. Dalton 1996; Hay 2007; Lijphart 1997; Putnam 2000). Research found that citizens increasingly avoided activities such as voting, joining political parties, attending political meetings, signing petitions and contacting MPs or government agencies and had less confidence in politicians and governments (Norris 1999; Putnam 2000).

There did seem to be a rise in the proportions participating in 'informal' politics including consumer boycotts, citizens contacting the media (as opposed to MPs) and various forms of protest, but this does not negate concern about declining participation in formal politics. As Hay (2007:27) points out, declines in formal political participation still matter because 'alternative modes of political participation' are not 'a substitute for... formal political participation.'

A range of theories have been proposed to explain declining interest in formal politics. The most commonly known is Robert Putnam's (2000) thesis of declining social capital, which suggests that low levels of electoral participation are part of a broader decline in community and civic/public duty on the part of citizens. Putnam especially nominates the influence of television as a factor. By contrast, Pippa Norris (1999) has interpreted the empirical evidence very differently and argued that high levels of political dissatisfaction and disengagement should be welcomed, as they reflect the rise of the 'critical citizen' who is less naive, more critical and more willing to express dissatisfaction than previous generations.

Not everyone agrees with the decline thesis or that the situation is as dire as it might seem (e.g. Goot 2002). Interpreting the evidence on political disengagement provokes much debate (see for example Holtz-Bacha and Norris 2001). Some theorists interpret lack of interest as a sign that most citizens are largely content with the status quo and willing to leave politics to others. Others take a very different view and see political indifference – especially because it tends to be concentrated among those who are marginalised in society – as symptomatic of an unhealthy, unequal political system that breeds political alienation.

When researchers ask citizens about their lack of interest, some cite feelings of powerlessness, apathy and cynicism about how politics works, and many report that they feel 'the mechanisms of democracy do not allow for their view to have much impact' (Dahlgren 2009:16). Feeling excluded is not just a psychological state but is grounded in reality when very real structural inequalities still exist. In Australia, the wealthiest 10 per cent of the population owns 'about 45 per cent of the total wealth' and the 'top 50 per cent owns over 90 per cent of the wealth', leaving half of all Australians to live on just 10 per cent (Stillwell and Jordan 2007:5). In 2007, less than 30 per cent of Commonwealth parliamentarians were women, only six of the top 200 Australian companies had a female CEO and women's average weekly earnings were still only 84 per cent of men's (OFW 2007). Aboriginal and Torres Strait Islander people were the single most disadvantaged group in Australia (SCRGSP 2007).

The spread of resources necessary to participate in politics – including education, time and money – is uneven. Everyday economic realities and social exclusion are barriers to political participation and civic engagement, but so too are the 'profoundly stressful circumstances under which large segments of the population live' (Dahlgren 2009:17). Work, raising children, fostering personal relationships and enjoying leisure time are far more pressing and relevant concerns for many people in their daily lives than a political process that often seems remote and inconsequential.

What most of the theories about declining political participation have in common – even if they disagree about whether lack of interest is increasing or whether we should worry about it – is a focus upon citizens and their attitudes to politics. Hay asks whether citizen discontent might not instead reflect the changed 'character of the appeals and invitations to participate that [citizens] receive' from politicians and political elites (Hay 2007:44) The context of politics – not just in terms of candidates and policies but also of avenues for participation – clearly matters and this refers not only to politicians but also to the media. As we saw in the previous chapter, there are many critics who claim that the way in which politics has been communicated to citizens has led them to lose interest and withdraw. Part of the evidence often cited for this view is that citizens are turning away not only from formal politics but also from traditional journalism and news media.

Although television was still the most used medium for election news in the 2000s, fewer Australians were using it to follow election campaigns than had in the past. This raises the possibility that people were dissatisfied with the political news in traditional media and were turning to other sources of campaign information instead. However, there was no concurrent rise in the use of other media (such as the internet) for political information.

The number of AES respondents who keenly followed elections on television (that is, 'a good deal' or 'often') halved between 1987 and 2001 (Table 2.4). The keen use of newspapers for election news also halved between 1987 and 2004; in 1998 and 2004 there was a very slight renewal of interest and in 2007 a more significant degree of enthusiasm. In 2007, more respondents than in 2004 used television, radio and newspapers to

Table 2.4 High use of the media to follow election campaigns, Australian Election Studies, 1987–2007 (percentages)

	1987	1990	1993	1996	1998	2001	2004	2007
Followed the election on TV 'a good deal' or 'often'	51	42	41	31	32	26	28	37
Followed the election on radio 'a good deal' or 'often'	27	21	21	15	18	16	14	19
Followed the election in newspapers 'a good deal' or 'often'	30	26	29	18	21	16	15	21
Used the internet 'many times' for election news	–	–	–	–	1	2	3	5

Note: Question response was 'often' in 1987 and 1990. From 1993, it was 'a good deal'.

Sources: Bean et al 2005; Bean, Gow and McAllister 1998, 2002; Bean, McAllister and Gow 2008; Jones et al 1993; Jones, McAllister and Gow 1996; McAllister and Mughan 1987; McAllister et al 1990.

follow the campaign. Even so, this increase, which coincided with the first change of government since 1996, still amounted to fewer Australians than had keenly followed elections in the late 1980s and early 1990s. In 2007, high use of the internet was confined to only 5 per cent of respondents and these are most likely to be the political junkies identified in Figure 2.1.

On the evidence of the AES, the number of people who keenly follow elections through the media declined. It is difficult to know whether this represented diminished interest in politics or diminished interest in representations of politics by the media. There was a general retreat from traditional news media in the 1990s and 2000s. Australians were watching fewer news and current affairs programs on television, buying fewer newspapers and generally spending less of their free time following traditional forms of news (Young 2009b). This was despite the proliferation of sources available. The drift dated to pre-internet times. So, although changing technology was having an impact, there seemed to be deeper factors involved.

Conclusion

Mapping political interest and political news audiences is a very inexact science but the evidence presented in this chapter, although it comes from a range of sources, is surprisingly consistent. When it comes to following political news through the mass media, only about 20 per cent of Australians did so actively and only half of these chose the more detailed, elite 'quality' media. The proportion of people who were only casually interested in following elections through the media grew, while those who identified themselves as very keen were a shrinking group. Although a particular election may spark more interest than usual, the vast majority of Australians still do not switch on.

In other words, there was an odd paradox at work in the 2000s: respondents said they were more interested in politics, but fewer were following it closely through the media. Is this because people *were* interested in traditional politics but found its actual conduct disappointing? Or was it because people were dissatisfied with the way the media reported politics? (Haswell 2001:144). The remaining sections of this book are dedicated to exploring this. The first step is to examine in more detail the two major audiences outlined in this chapter – the elite and popular – because these audiences are the key to how news is produced and received.

Chapter 3

THE ELITE PUBLIC SPHERE

Those who avidly follow politics are sometimes called 'the politically active', 'the political participatory class' or 'the attentive elite' in academic literature but, informally, are often known as 'political tragics', 'politicos' or 'political junkies'. Overseas studies have found that people in this group are disproportionately 'older, white, more affluent, well-educated, and male' (Norris 1996:477; Norris et al 1999). They are also active media consumers who use multiple news sources (Saad 2005). In other words, political junkies tend to be news junkies and, as we saw in the previous chapter, they favour media such as broadsheets and public broadcasting. These elite media are consumed by 'key policy and decision-makers, opinion-formers and issue-definers: elites in the political, business and cultural spheres, as well as university-educated professionals' (McNair 2000:23). In many theories, this audience and its favourite media are the key to explaining media content and its power.

Whether their style of news is called 'hard', 'serious' or 'quality', elite media are usually viewed as the most information-rich and the 'best' examples of journalistic excellence. Studies have found people who access the 'serious' media tend to know more about politics, to participate more and to believe that their participation matters (Curran et al 2009; Newton 1999; Norris 2000; PRC 2007). For some political theorists, the politically active and well-informed citizens play such a crucial role that democracy can safely be left in their hands. Economist and political scientist Joseph Schumpeter (1943) argued that it was unrealistic and undesirable to expect other citizens to so actively participate in democratic politics. Michael Schudson (1998) has also questioned the assumption that democracy requires an active, fully informed citizenry (see Chapter 12).

However, in critical theories about the elite media, it is seen as no coincidence that those who have the most power – politically, economically and socially – are those who also access the 'best' news sources, are better informed and are better able to participate in and shape political life. Conversely, women, the poor and the less educated, who largely miss out on the 'quality' sources, have been found to know less about politics, be less interested in participating and less confident that their participation would make a difference (Curran et al 2009; Jones and Pusey 2008). They therefore miss out on key ways to influence decision-making and to improve their own circumstances.

The most strident version of this critique argues that the dominant group in society – Marxists would call it 'the ruling class' while feminists would call it the 'patriarchy' – uses the media to strengthen and maintain its control, to 'manufacture consent' among the governed (Herman and Chomsky 1988). In this view, while the most information-rich media are accessed by the elite, the general population is led instead to 'tabloid' news, 'soft news' and 'infotainment'. These popular media are viewed not only as commercial strategies that put profit-making ahead of informing citizens, but also as political strategies because, when marginalised citizens receive a diet of celebrity gossip and pop culture, their attention is diverted from more important matters, including recognising their own disadvantages and demanding remedies.

A very different way of thinking about elite media is proposed by other theorists who agree that there *is* something of a 'knowledge-class conspiracy . . . by "opinion leaders" against the led' but argue that 'serious' journalism is the problem rather than the solution (Hartley 1999:125). For theorists in this camp, often from cultural studies, the virtues of elite media are illusory because the 'serious', 'objective', 'rational' approach to news that those media promote is a fallacy. John Fiske, in particular, has argued that the news reported in 'quality' sources such as broadsheets reinforces the domination of the elite because it is 'official news' and its 'tone is serious, official, impersonal and is aimed at producing understanding and belief. *It is generally the news which the power-bloc wants the people to have*' (italics added). According to Fiske, news of this kind produces a social reality that is

Table 3.1 Characteristics of elite news source audiences, 2007–08 (percentages)

	Population (14 years+)	Newspapers					Radio				Television	Pay TV	Internet websites and online newspapers				
		AFR	Australian	SMH	Age	Canberra Times	ABC Radio National	ABC News Radio	ABC 702 (Syd)	ABC 774 (Melb)	ABC/SBS news or current affairs	Sky News	Abc. net. au/news	Crikey website	Australian online	SMH online	Age online
Men	49	76	63	56	52	50	54	66	56	56	54	59	63	63	69	62	64
Women	51	24	37	44	48	50	46	35	44	44	46	41	38	37	31	38	36
Have university education	41	86	75	73	75	62	71	68	71	61	51	40	75	78	74	76	77
Personal income under $15k	33	7	15	21	23	21	22	24	22	20	29	37	19	18	23	20	20
Personal income $70k+	14	59	36	29	22	30	26	25	30	21	18	17	28	34	31	32	29
Professional/ manager	18	70	42	35	33	35	31	33	35	28	22	23	40	45	42	43	45
White-collar worker	19	14	20	22	28	19	20	19	21	21	18	18	25	22	20	23	25
14–17 years	7	0	1	3	4	7	1	1	1	2	2	2	2	2	3	3	2
18–24 years	12	8	9	10	10	8	2	4	2	2	6	4	9	9	18	15	15
25–34 years	17	18	15	16	16	15	9	11	9	7	12	12	22	24	21	26	29
35–49 years	27	42	28	27	27	22	25	29	30	28	26	34	30	38	31	30	31
Over 50 years	38	32	47	45	43	49	56	56	58	61	54	48	37	27	27	26	23

Note: Broadsheet newspaper readers: characteristics of M-F readers and figures relate to readers (not buyers). Figures are rounded. The *Australian Financial Review* is included as a broadsheet based on the characteristics of the paper and its readers rather than paper size of the newspaper. Radio audiences are an average of the Melbourne and Sydney audiences. The 'Have university education' category includes those 'now' at university and those who 'have diploma or degree'. Website audiences refer to news sites visited in the last four weeks by survey respondents.

Source: data supplied to the author by Roy Morgan Research (Single Source Australia, July 2007–June 2008).

'the habitat of the masculine, educated middle class', so when marginalised groups reject it they are not missing out on a vital avenue of participation (as the critical view would suggest) but are instead performing a subversive and empowering act (Fiske 1992:47, 49).

In order to make sense of these different theories and their implications for election reporting, which are explored in Chapter 5, this chapter builds a profile of the elite audience in Australia, including which media forms and outlets they access and how those preferences changed in the 2000s. Table 3.1 contains a summary of the elite media outlets that will be examined in this chapter. It contrasts a socioeconomic profile of the average Australian adult population with the audiences for 16 specific elite media products. This table is designed as a comparative overview, so it is lengthy and contains a great deal of information. I will now elaborate on its contents by focusing on specific media forms.

Printed broadsheets

Studies have found that people in the elite audience have a preference for newspapers and 'the printed word' (Kingdon 1970:259–60; PEJ 2008; Western and Hughes 1983:30). Even in the age of the internet, as the American Project for Excellence in Journalism noted in 2007: 'People who love to follow the news, and especially those who love politics, prefer newspapers over every other medium' (PEJ 2007). But this was changing in the 2000s. While older political junkies (and the group is generally older, as we have seen) may still have preferred printed newspapers, younger news junkies were drawn to the internet and its wide range of news sources – including online newspapers (PRC 2008b; Smith and Rainie 2009).

In 2007 there were four printed broadsheets: the *Sydney Morning Herald*, the *Age* and the *Canberra Times* (owned by Fairfax Media)[1] and News Limited's national broadsheet the *Australian*. Although not technically a broadsheet in size, Fairfax's *Australian Financial Review* should also be counted among these because it attracts an elite audience and has a broadsheet approach. The development of the *Australian* in 1964 and the *Australian Financial Review* (which began as a weekly in 1951 and became a daily in 1963) marked an important stage in the development of more specialised political and business reporting in Australia. In its early years, the *Australian* took an innovative approach that set a standard for 'serious' reporting of national affairs and, despite its more erratic reputation over the past decade-and-a-half, its national approach changed the nature of political reporting in Australia (Tiffen 2009).

Traditionally, broadsheets have been associated with a creed of journalistic professionalism that disdains sensationalism and demands that issues be reported fairly, in a balanced manner and with a concern for accuracy over and above any dramatic features of the story. This creed has lofty democratic aims, but it is also a commercial strategy, attracting a lucrative elite audience that is then on-sold to advertisers. In the ad industry magazine *AdNews*, Fairfax boasted that: 'Only the taxman has more ways of targeting Australia's wealthy' than its broadsheets (Fairfax 2003). News Limited promoted the *Australian* to advertisers as 'a powerful brand which delivers ... [an] affluent, well educated audience ... [that] earned a collective $57.6 billion in the last 12 months ... [and] collectively owns and drives 45 000 luxury cars' (Newsspace 2009a).

Table 3.1 confirms that those who read election news in broadsheets in the 2000s were disproportionately wealthy, educated older men. Australians over 50 were particularly overrepresented.[2] With its financial news focus attracting a younger (male) audience, the *Australian Financial Review* was an exception; but for all the other broadsheets, more than 42 per cent of their readership was over 50 – including nearly half of the *Australian*'s audience. The broadsheet audience was dominated by men, ranging from 76 per cent of *Financial Review* readers to 63 per cent for the *Australian* and 56 per cent for the *SMH*, but this discrepancy was less marked at the *Age* while the *Canberra Times* attracted 50 per cent women.

Over three-quarters of *AFR*, *Australian* and *Age* readers were university educated (and 73 per cent of the *SMH* audience) compared to 41 per cent of the national population. Not surprisingly, the *Financial Review* had the wealthiest audience – its readers were four times as likely as the general population to earn over $70 000 per annum. At the other end of the spectrum, although the *Age*'s audience was still unusually wealthy, it was less so than the other broadsheets because it had more white-collar workers and fewer managers/professionals. For all the other broadsheets, their readers were twice as likely as the average Australian to be managers/professionals and to earn over $70 000.

Free-to-air television

Broadsheet readers tend to be very light commercial media users and some do not watch or listen to commercial broadcasting at all. For example, the *Australian Financial Review* reported that 62 per cent of its readers only watched commercial television lightly or not at all and this was even more marked for commercial radio, with 86 per cent of AFR readers listening only lightly or not at all to commercial stations (AFR 2009:3). Instead, when they turned to television or radio, broadsheet readers favoured public broadcasters, particularly the ABC.

The ABC is the other major domain of what is described as 'quality' journalism in Australia. In the 2000s, it was fully state-funded, employed over 700 journalists, had a nation-wide multimedia approach and the most detailed editorial policies of any media organisation in Australia. Its mission is a non-commercial one described in the *ABC Charter* as being to provide programs that are of an 'educational nature' or 'contribute to a sense of national identity and inform and entertain ...' (ABC 2009). On free-to-air television, ABC1 broadcast influential news and current affairs programs such as *Lateline, The 7:30 Report* and *Four Corners*.

Australia's other 'public' broadcaster, the Special Broadcasting Service (SBS) is a 'multilingual and multicultural' broadcaster that uses a different economic model: a mixture of both public and private funding. SBS began to take limited commercial advertising in 1991. For 15 years, ads were only shown in between programs, but after 2006 were also broadcast during programs, leading to debate about whether the growth of advertising on SBS was leading to more populist programming.

At the end of the 2000s, the ABC and SBS were gaining audience share as the commercial free-to-air television channels were losing it (AFC 2009). In 2008, the ABC achieved its highest audience share 'since people meters were introduced' (Scott 2009a) and SBS's average primetime audience had risen by 17 per cent since 2004 (Dale 2008). For some, it might be tempting to view this as a backlash against the rampant commercialisation of news and current affairs on commercial channels. As we shall see, there does seem to be an element of truth to this when it comes specifically to the elite audience and its viewing of news and current affairs. But the audience growth could also be interpreted very differently: as the result of public broadcasters imitating more popular fare rather than leading a backlash against it. For example, most of SBS's primetime growth in 2007–08 was due to programs such as *Top Gear* and *Top Gear Australia* (which see presenters test driving and appraising cars as well as including some comedy, car stunts and celebrity appearances) and *Mythbusters* (in which urban myths and legends are tested). These programs were hardly ones that reflected SBS's special multicultural remit as 'a network established to serve minorities'.

More significant in explaining the audience shifts, though, was the larger context of change in television audiences. Although the public broadcasters were winning a greater share of the television audience, this was a larger slice of a smaller and diminishing pie. Television audiences declined – especially among the young (see Chapter 4). Older Australians continued watching television in large doses, with Australians over 55 watching an average of 4 hours and 17 minutes per day, compared to those under 25 who averaged just 2 hours and 9 minutes per day (Screen Australia 2008). Because public broadcasting audiences were generally older (Table 3.1 and Bean 2005), they retained more of the remaining television audience in the 2000s and were less affected by audience losses than their commercial rivals.

Programs that were focused on 'serious' news and political content had an especially older audience. Australians over 55 made up only 24 per cent of the population in 2007,[3] but all of the elite public broadcasting news and current affairs programs shown in Table 3.2 had much higher proportions of older viewers (OzTAM 2007a:1–2). For most programs – including *Parliament Question Time, The 7:30 Report, ABC News, Four Corners, Insight, SBS World News* and *Lateline* – more than half their audience was over 55. In 2007, the commercial channels also broadcast programs that they promoted as a more detailed, 'serious' presentation of news or an insider's look at political events. These commercial offerings attracted younger audiences than the public broadcasting programs, but they were still disproportionately watched by older Australians.

Table 3.1 suggests that ABC and SBS news and current affairs programs attracted significantly fewer female viewers than males, but the ratings evidence (in Table 3.3) builds up a more subtle, nuanced picture of the television audience and how it was changing. While men dominated the audiences for programs such as *Parliament Question Time, World News* and *Meet the Press* in 2007, the gender gap was not as marked as in other elite

Table 3.2 Age of elite television news and current affairs program audiences, 2007 (percentages)

	Channel	Over 55 years
Population		**24**
Parliament Question Time (PM)	ABC	66
The 7.30 Report	ABC	63
ABC News	ABC	60
Great Debate	ABC	56
Four Corners	ABC	56
Insight	SBS	54
World News	SBS	53
Lateline	ABC	53
Polling night broadcast	ABC	46
World News Australia Late	SBS	44
60 Minutes	Nine	44
Meet the Press	Ten	41
Sunday	Nine	38

Note: average mainland capital city audiences.

Sources: OzTAM data supplied to the author and OzTAM 2007a:1–2.

Table 3.3 Gender of elite television news and current affairs program audiences, 2007 (percentages)

	Channel	Male viewers
Population		**50**
Parliament Question Time (PM)	ABC	62
World News Australia Late	SBS	57
World News	SBS	56
Meet the Press	Ten	56
Great Debate	ABC	52
Lateline	ABC	51
Polling night broadcast	ABC	50
The 7.30 Report	ABC	49
Insight	SBS	49
Sunday	Nine	49
ABC News	ABC	48
Four Corners	ABC	48
60 Minutes	Nine	48

Note: average mainland capital city audiences.

Sources: OzTAM data supplied to the author and OzTAM 2007a:1–2.

media and some television programs even attracted more female viewers than men. *The 7:30 Report, ABC News, Four Corners, 60 Minutes, Sunday* and *Insight* all averaged more female viewers. Two of these programs were hosted or co-hosted by women: *Sunday* co-hosted by Ellen Fanning and *Insight* hosted by Jenny Brockie.

Studies have shown that men and women tend to go to different places for their news. Women rely on television more than men (Denmark 2005; PRC 2006). In the 2000s, this intensified because more men were turning off television news than women (Young 2009b). When television was the most sought-after medium at home, men traditionally had control of the television remote (Ang 1995:218); however, in the 2000s, in households with the internet, men were spending more time online than women and were using the internet more for news (ABS 2007b; Norris 2001a:68, 72; PRC 2006). Older women had especially low rates of internet use (ABS 2007b). In other words, as television's status declined and it was increasingly seen as the second-rate media option in the home, women were gaining better access to it.

Free-to-air television was in 99.7 per cent of homes in Australia (Screen Australia 2008). It had a reputation in the 1990s and 2000s for being an egalitarian medium as a result. Television attracted what Kenneth Newton (1999:587) has called 'the economically inactive (especially the old, the chronically ill and the unemployed) – who watch a lot of television'. Of course, not all of these viewers were watching news or watching public broadcasters, but the availability of television meant the opportunity was there. While the ABC/SBS news and current affairs audience was still more likely to be university educated than the general population and to have an income over $50 000, it was closer to the norm on these variables than almost all of the other elite media shown in Table 3.1. Public television did have a more representative audience than broadsheets, public radio or elite news websites.

Shifts in television viewing

Fewer Australians were watching television news and current affairs in 2007 than in 1991. Ratings declined significantly (see Chapter 4) and, oddly enough, leading the desertion from television news was the news-loving

Table 3.4 Most-watched programs for AB audience (managers, administrators and professionals), 2001 and 2007

2001 Top 10 programs			2007 Top 10 programs		
Program	Channel	Total AB viewers	Program	Channel	Total AB viewers
1 60 Minutes	9	254 000	Australia Votes 2007	ABC	217 000
2 World Crisis America Under Attack Evening 1 Day 1	9	252 000	ABC News	ABC	171 000
3 National Nine News (Sun)	9	245 000	ABC News (Sun)	ABC	169 000
4 Great Debate 2001	ABC	209 000	Media Watch	ABC	149 000
5 Budget Special 2001	ABC	199 000	The Leaders' Debate	ABC	147 000
6 ABC News	ABC	189 000	Four Corners	ABC	143 000
7 Seven News (Sun)	7	188 000	Budget Special 2007	ABC	140 000
8 National Nine News (Sat)	9	184 000	Australian Story	ABC	139 000
9 ABC News Special	ABC	183 000	60 Minutes	9	137 000
10 Seven News (Sat)	7	180 000	Seven News (Sun)	7	135 000

Note: average mainland capital city audiences.

Sources: OzTAM data supplied to the author and OzTAM 2007a:1–2.

elite audience. Table 3.4 shows the news and current affairs programs that 'managers, administrators and professionals' watched most in 2001 and 2007. This is the group known in marketing-speak as the most prestigious and lucrative 'ABs': it includes lawyers, politicians, academics and business managers. Although this group was still interested in elections and budgets in 2007, their viewing of these events and of television news and current affairs generally had decreased sharply (and despite a growth in population). By 2007, when they *did* switch on television for news, the ABs had also come to overwhelmingly rely on the ABC. Their top eight programs (and 15 of their top 20) were all on the ABC.

The elite audience especially deserted commercial television between the 2001 and 2007 elections with the biggest audience drops for Channels Nine, Ten and Seven but also for SBS World News which, in early 2007, had changed format as SBS merged its primetime news bulletin and sports news programs into a new one-hour bulletin with advertising breaks. The switch-off for some of these commercial programs was considerable – over 50 per cent of the audience for *Meet the Press* and the axed *Sunday* and *Nightline* programs (Table 3.5). The ABs were not always so averse to commercial programming – in 2001, their top three most-watched programs

Table 3.5 Shifts in audiences for elite television news and current affairs programs between 2001 and 2007

Program	Channel	Loss/gain of viewers	Audience change (%)
Meet the Press	10	−19 000	−73.0
Sunday	9	−44 000	−60.2
Nightline	9	−35 000	−54.7
60 Minutes	9	−117 000	−46.1
National Nine News (Sun)	9	−92 000	−37.6
World News	SBS	−13 000	−30.2
Seven News (Sun)	7	−51 000	−27.1
Four Corners	ABC	−18 000	−11.2
ABC News	ABC	−18 000	−9.5
World News Australia Late	SBS	−3 000	−7.9
The 7.30 Report	ABC	−11 000	−7.6
ABC News (Sun)	ABC	−	0
Lateline	ABC	+6 000	+10.9
Insight	SBS	+7 000	+18.4

Note: average mainland capital city audiences.

Sources: OzTAM data supplied to the author and OzTAM 2007a:1–2.

were on Channel Nine. The switch-off seems to have been at least partly a response to programming shifts that occurred as part of a fierce ratings battle between Channels Nine and Seven. In the late 1990s and early 2000s, the commercial channels were battling over a shrinking television audience that had come to consist of a greater number of older, female viewers. The networks did not believe these viewers were interested in 'heavy' news and current affairs (see Chapter 4).

In order to win over what they saw as a more apolitical, older female television audience, the commercial channels axed or significantly altered some of their more politics-heavy current affairs programs. For example, in 2006, the *Sunday* program changed to a more informal, panel-style approach dubbed '*Sunday Lite*' by critics. *60 Minutes* shifted to a formula focused less on world news and politics and more on celebrity interviews, family and lifestyle (see Turner 2005). In 2007, *60 Minutes* broadcast stories on mortgages, IVF, headaches, divorce, a boy struck by lightning, fears about children on the internet, gay dads, the Harry Potter movies, American celebrities JLo, Nicole Richie, Beyonce and Christina Aguilera, 'submissive wives', babies switched at birth, cancer and sperm donation. That the program producers felt they were broadcasting to an audience dominated by older viewers was evident in the way they addressed their viewers. For example, in a *60 Minutes* story on 'Generation Y', the reporter commented to viewers: 'love them or hate them, probably the latter, they're *our kids* and *we* indulged them.'

As commercial stations changed their approach to news, many in the elite audience who still wanted the 'hard news' approach stopped watching and this included turning off programs such as *60 Minutes* (originally an elite audience favourite) as well as *Meet the Press* and *Sunday* (which were specifically targeted to those wanting an insider's in-depth view of politics) (Tables 3.4. and 3.5). When the audiences for these elite news and current affairs programs are compared between 2001 and 2007, it is apparent that the ABs were switching off these programs more than any other occupation group. It's unlikely they suddenly became uninterested in news, but rather it seems they were increasingly using other media – especially the internet and pay TV 24-hour news channels.

This meant that people in the para-professional group (including teachers, clerks, salespeople, nurses and real estate salespeople) grew as a proportion of the audience for these programs between the 2001 and 2007 elections. People in these occupations are often unable to access the internet at work because either their working conditions do not enable it (nurses and teachers, for example) or they travel a lot during the day (real estate salespeople, for example). And some in the para-professional group (for example, teachers) are also more likely to be home by 6.00 pm, which is important for tuning in to primetime news.

Radio

During the Keating government (1991–96), and especially during the Howard government (1996–2007), radio interviews became a dominant feature of both election campaigning and political reporting more generally. Commercial talkback (discussed in Chapter 4) was particularly significant, but public radio also played a key role through its own version of talkback and its focus on news commentary and interviews with politicians. ABC Radio National, an especial favourite of the elite media audience, targets 'a politically literate demographic' with a formula that is 'unapologetically upmarket, sophisticated and highly produced' (Faine 2005:174).

Radio National's *AM* current affairs program is often nominated as one of the key 'agenda-setting' political programs (see Chapter 8). ABC News Radio has a different format around 24-hour news that, it argues, is 'factual, independent and opinion-free' (ABC 2008). It tends to be heavily monitored by newsrooms and journalists.

The direct listening audiences of Radio National and News Radio are small, whereas ABC local radio reaches a very large public audience through a network of 51 regional and nine metropolitan stations across Australia. These stations are often among the most listened to in their respective markets (NMRA 2008). They broadcast a mix of news, current affairs, talkback, entertainment, sport, music and rural issues. As Jon Faine notes (2005:175), the emphasis on politics 'varies from station to station, city to city and shift to shift' depending on presenters, programs and their focus.

Just as the ABC television audience was older, better educated, more affluent and male-dominated, these features also held true for the elite ABC radio audience (Table 3.1). The public radio audience was *even older* than the broadsheet and public television audiences. Over 55 per cent of listeners of Radio National, News Radio and ABC local radio in Sydney and Melbourne were over 50. These stations clearly had minimal appeal for the under-35s (a group the ABC caters for through a dedicated youth radio network, Triple J, that targets 18–24s). Consistent with the evidence about news junkies, Table 3.1 also confirms that men were more likely to listen to ABC radio and especially to the form that was most dedicated to news; 66 per cent of ABC News Radio listeners were men.

Pay TV

Dedicated news junkies are also an appreciative audience for 24-hour news channels. In 2007, the only local 24-hour television news channel was Sky News on pay TV. Since it began in 1996, Sky steadily sought to position itself as *the* politics channel of Australia. It used comprehensive live coverage of the 2004 federal election through a dedicated election channel to build its profile, but 2007 was really its 'CNN moment'. During the six weeks of the election campaign, Sky broadcast 24-hour coverage, seven days a week. Not all of it was original content – 24-hour broadcasters rely heavily on repetition – but Sky did have a series of major coups during the election, including hosting the only leaders' debate and being the first channel to call the result (see Chapters 8 and 9). On polling night, Sky Active had seven dedicated election channels, including a channel each for 'Howard', 'Rudd', 'Reaction' and 'Tally Room'. Sky News was therefore a political junkie's dream and its audience included politicians and their advisers as well as journalists who monitored Sky for breaking news and updates.

Sky's audience may have been influential, but it was small. In 2007, 31 per cent of Australians subscribed to pay TV (ASTRA 2008) but, overall, only about 0.5 per cent watched Sky (OzTAM 2007b). Political junkies switched on more during the election and, in the final week of the campaign, Sky's audience share more than doubled from just four months earlier (OzTAM 2007b, c). However, on polling night Sky's audience was still only about 8 per cent of the ABC's audience – around 90 000 viewers compared to the 1.1 million watching on the ABC (Ricketson 2007). Because the 24-hour news format is designed around repetition, its audience 'dips in and out'. We do not know average viewing times in Australia, but in the UK, British Sky News viewers tune in for only seven minutes *a week* on average (Edgecliff-Johnson 2007).

Pay TV was a fairly new medium in Australia in the 2000s and one often associated with young people. Compared to the other elite news media in Table 3.1, Sky was unusually good at reaching viewers aged 35 to 49 (third only to the *AFR* and *Crikey*). People in this age group were adults (aged 19 to 33) when 24-hour news channels came to prominence with CNN's broadcasting of the Gulf War in 1991. But overall, Sky's focus on national politics still attracted an older audience. Forty-eight per cent were over 50 in 2007 (more than for the *Age*, the *Sydney Morning Herald* and the *Australian*) (Table 3.1). This older news channel audience is not a phenomenon confined to Australia. In the US, the average Fox News viewer is 59 years old and for CNN is 60 (Farhi 2003:34). This again reflects the older profile of the politically interested elite audience.

The internet

It is no coincidence that the elite group who were watching less television news and current affairs were also the group with the best access to the internet. In 2007, households with an income of $2000 or more per week 'were three times more likely to have broadband compared to households on less than $600 per week' (ABS 2007b). Many in the AB demographic not only had good home internet access but also had access at work during the day and the relative autonomy to be able to use the internet to follow news. Neither the newspaper circulation figures nor the television ratings could therefore tell the whole story about the elite audience and its use of news media. There were, for example, some in the elite group who were still watching television news and current affairs programs but who did not show up in the television ratings figures because they accessed the programs *via the internet* instead. This was a very small proportion in 2007, but it was growing.[4]

Newspaper circulation and readership figures in the 2000s did not include people visiting newspaper websites for news. There were reports that the number of people reading online newspapers doubled just between 2007 and 2009 alone (Hyland 2009a). Newspaper companies were claiming very large amounts of web traffic (APC 2008, below and Chapter 10). The adult population in Australia was 17 million (ABS 2008a), which puts into per-spective claims in 2007 that the *SMH* had over 3 million 'unique browsers' a month increasing to 4 million in 2009 (APC 2008), or that Fairfax's websites (which also included radio as well as newspapers) received over 12 million unique visitors a month (Fairfax Media 2008a). There are many difficulties inherent in measuring website audiences and how many visitors are truly unique. For example, someone reading the *SMH* online at home at breakfast and then later at work during their lunchbreak would be counted twice as two unique visitors and when monthly 'unique browser' figures are used instead of daily figures, there is also the potential for duplication because visitors to the website who delete their web-browsing cookies during the month are counted as new browsers when they return.

These problems with audience measurement make it very difficult to accurately pinpoint how many people were shifting to the internet for news, but we do know their broad demographic profile. The elite media audience tended to gravitate to the internet and was something of a natural fit for online news, given their superior access to the technology and desire for detailed, multiple sources of news, especially text-based news. As a result, elite audience members were spreading out across many different places online. Sometimes they were accessing already trusted local news providers such as the ABC or their preferred broadsheet online. Other times they were going to international content, such as CNN online or the BBC or overseas broadsheets such as the *Guardian* or the *New York Times.* News aggregator sites that were specially designed for news junkies became more popular. These sites harness content from a range of sources and tailor it into one homepage. For political news, aggregators included *Real Clear Politics,* the *Political Wire* and *Google Reader.* There were also news and journalism websites that linked to news reports or performed some original reporting of their own, not to mention political-specific sites and many political blogs – both international and local (see Chapter 10). Within Australia, there were a number of politics blogs focused on federal politics. Measuring the audiences for these is also difficult but, overall, the evidence suggests that their audience numbers were modest and that blogs were used as a primary news source by only a small percentage of people (see Chapter 10).

Despite the internet's association with youth, American research has found that people who go online specifically for political news are 'older than internet users in general' (PRC 2008a). In 2007, the profile of someone who read a political blog on a daily basis was a male who was wealthier than average, had college or postgraduate education and was aged over 35 (Hindman 2008; PRC 2008a). In the US, 39 per cent of daily political blog readers are over 55 (Graf 2006:4). As a Pew Research Center report noted in 2008: 'seniors who go online are at least as likely to regularly read blogs about politics and current events' (PRC 2008a:26).

News websites tend to have a broader audience than politics-specific *blogs,* but they were not attracting audiences that were hitherto uninterested in traditional elite news. In the 2000s, in almost all cases, Australians who were using the internet to visit dedicated news websites (such as online newspapers and ABC online) were the same news-hungry audience who read newspapers. In 2007–08, there were only 0.2 per cent of Australians who went online to a news website who did *not* also read a newspaper (RMR 2007–08). In other words, there was no indication that the internet had attracted a different audience from that which sought traditional elite news.

Table 3.6 profiles the audiences of three elite news websites to demonstrate this point. The websites are the *Australian,* the *SMH* and the *Age* and information is taken from Table 3.1 so that the printed and online audiences for these broadsheets can be directly compared. The internet audiences were younger, but even more elite than the printed broadsheet audiences

Table 3.6 Comparison of audiences for online and printed newspapers, 2007–08 (percentages)

	Population (14 years+)	Australian Printed	Australian Online	SMH Printed	SMH Online	Age Printed	Age Online
Men	49	63	69	56	62	52	64
Women	51	37	31	44	38	48	36
Have university education	41	75	74	73	76	75	77
Personal income under $15k	33	15	23	21	20	23	20
Personal income $50k+	26	51	48	45	51	41	49
Personal income $70k+	14	36	31	29	32	22	29
Professional/manager	18	42	42	35	43	33	45
White-collar worker	19	20	20	22	23	28	25
14–17	7	1	3	3	3	4	2
18–24	12	9	18	10	15	10	15
25–34	17	15	21	16	26	16	29
35–49 years	27	28	31	27	30	27	31
Over 50 years	38	47	27	45	26	49	23

Source: data supplied to the author by Roy Morgan Research (Single Source Australia, July 2007–June 2008).

(Table 3.6). Online the broadsheets' websites were attracting even more men, including 69 per cent for the *Australian* and 64 per cent for the *Age*. Visitors to the *SMH* and *Age* websites were richer than the printed editions' readers, more than twice as likely to earn over $70 000 than the general population and to be professional or white-collar workers. The interesting exception was the *Australian* website. Its online audience had precisely the same proportion of professionals/managers and white-collar workers as for its printed edition and only 1 per cent less who were university educated. However, because the *Australian* online had visitors who were younger (especially in the 18- to 24-year-old group), they were less wealthy than the printed edition readers.

The other two websites shown in Table 3.1 are the ABC and *Crikey*. Along with Ninemsn (see Chapter 4) and the *SMH* website, the ABC website was one of the most-visited news websites in Australia. In 2007, one in four Australians (26 per cent) claimed to have accessed the ABC website (ABC 2007a:37). *Crikey* had a smaller audience (about a seventh of the size for the online *SMH* in 2007–08).[5] In terms of gender, education and wealth, the ABC and *Crikey* websites both had a similar audience profile to that of a broadsheet reader. Their audiences were male-dominated (63 per cent men), three-quarters were university educated and they were more than twice as likely as the average Australian to have a high income. *Crikey* website visitors were a particularly elite audience, second only to those of the *AFR* in terms of high income and university education. And this is how *Crikey* promotes its audience: 'crammed with highly intelligent, influential decision-makers' including a large number of subscribers in Parliament House, government departments, law firms, academia and banks or working as journalists (Fitzgerald 2008:375).

To sum up the evidence: on the internet, politics-specific online content tends to attract the political junkies while elite news websites attract a broader audience, but one that is still firmly within the realms of the elite. The audiences for elite news websites such as *Crikey*, the *Australian*, the *SMH*, the *Age* and the ABC were still an elite audience; they were just a younger elite. In pre-internet days they would very likely have become dedicated broadsheet (printed) readers and public broadcasting audiences, but they were now using the internet. Except for their youth, the divisions seen in other elite media still applied. In fact, they were even more emphasised. Men and 'those with high levels of income and education tend[ed] to be the most intense online news consumers' in an even more marked way than with traditional media (Smith and Rainie 2009).

Conclusion

The audiences for politics-heavy news media in the 2000s differed depending upon the format, but were generally dominated by men aged over 40 who were tertiary educated, well paid and in managerial or professional jobs. They were older, richer and better educated than the general population. This profile of the Australian elite audience fits both with the profile of the political junkies discussed in the previous chapter and with the overseas research on elite audiences (Lewis, Cushion and Thomas 2005; Ofcom 2005). American studies have found that 'African-Americans' and 'people from non-English speaking backgrounds' are also underrepresented in the audiences of elite media (PPEJ 2009). We do not have the data available to test this, but there is no reason to suggest that racial and ethnic inequities would not also be present in Australia.

So whatever their virtues in terms of presenting 'serious' news and detailed information, the 'quality' news outlets – especially those focused on politics – did not have much appeal for women, the young, and people who were unemployed or had low incomes or low education levels. This presents a serious dilemma for those who value the 'quality' journalism approach for its ability to create an informed citizenry, but recognise that the outlets which use that approach are not very effective at reaching – at least in a direct way – the citizens who would seem to be most in need of the benefits that greater political participation can bring.

Chapter 4

THE POPULAR PUBLIC SPHERE

While most Australians are not particularly interested in politics, they are interested in news. In 2001, half the adult population were spending at least one hour a day watching, listening to or reading news and current affairs (ABA 2001b). By 2008, over 80 per cent were still reporting that they would catch up with the news during their day (Phillips et al 2008). Even at the end of the 2000s, news and current affairs programs continued to top the television ratings in Australia, which was unusual by international standards. Taking just one ratings period as an example – April 2009 – demonstrates this. The most-watched television program in Australia was *Seven News* at primetime and four out of the top 10 were news programs. By contrast, in the US and UK no news program ranked in the top 20 in the same period (BARB 2009; OzTAM 2009; Zapit.com 2009).

General news, sport, entertainment and music were the types of news Australians said they preferred, with 'political analysis' ranked last (Phillips et al 2008). The more popular news products that attracted the largest audiences reflected these preferences. Sparks has argued that tabloid news journalism:

> devotes relatively little attention to politics, economics and society and rela-
> tively much to diversions like sports, scandal, and popular entertainment . . .
> the personal and private lives of people, both celebrities and ordinary people
> [receive much attention whereas] . . . relatively little [is devoted] to political
> processes, economic developments, and social changes (Sparks 2000:10).

Table 4.1 Characteristics of popular news source audiences, 2007–08 (percentages)

	Population (14 years+)	Newspapers						Radio stations			Internet websites			
		Herald Sun	Daily Telegraph	Courier-Mail	Advertiser	West Australian	Mercury	2GB (NSW)	2UE (NSW)	3AW (Vic)	Ninemsn	News.com.au	Google News	Yahoo!7
Men	49	52	56	55	55	55	48	54	56	49	48	62	63	54
Women	51	48	44	45	45	45	52	46	44	51	52	38	37	46
Some secondary/tech school education	18	20	15	15	22	21	18	13	15	22	12	9	12	8
Have university education	41	37	34	46	40	40	38	41	39	34	54	63	64	59
Personal income under $15k	33	31	29	21	30	25	31	28	28	30	27	19	29	25
Personal income $70k+	14	12	12	20	13	23	10	23	21	14	16	28	21	16
Professional/manager	18	16	17	23	19	24	18	22	20	19	27	43	30	26
White-collar worker	19	21	20	23	18	19	20	15	14	18	29	23	21	23
Skilled worker	8	8	9	8	8	9	6	8	8	6	8	7	6	7
Others*	15	16	16	14	14	14	14	9	11	13	10	8	11	13
Not employed	40	38	38	32	42	35	35	47	46	44	25	19	33	31
14–17	7	4	4	3	3	4	4	0	1	2	7	3	8	2
18–24	12	11	11	8	8	10	10	2	1	3	23	16	22	19
25–34	17	14	16	14	11	13	13	9	8	5	21	33	23	32
35–49 years	27	27	27	28	24	26	28	23	27	29	30	31	22	25
Over 50 years	38	45	43	48	54	47	46	66	64	62	20	18	25	22

Note: Newspaper figures relate to readers (not buyers) of weekday newspapers. 'Have only some secondary/tech school education' means not completed year 10. The 'Have university education' category includes combination of two categories, 'Some/now at university' and 'Have diploma or degree'. Website audiences refer to news sites visited in the last four weeks by survey respondents.
* including semi-skilled/unskilled.

Source: data supplied to the author by Roy Morgan Research (Single Source Australia, July 2007–June 2008).

A limited approach to political news has obvious appeal for the many citizens who say they are not interested in politics, but what about that segment of the population – identified in Chapter 2 – who *were* interested in political news but pursued it through the tabloid and commercial media, even though the elite media included more politics content?[1] This could be for a range of reasons. They might find the elite media boring, inaccessible, pretentious or in other ways at odds with their own life experiences. They might have a view of politics that is better reflected in the popular media; they might just prefer entertainment-focused media or want a summary only. As one news executive I spoke to pointed out: 'surfing the internet for news and selecting from different sources is not what [everyone] wants, or [has] time, to do.'

The *way* in which politics stories are reported in popular media outlets is obviously important. One of the factors that influences this is the way news executives view their audiences' relationship to politics. Interestingly, lack of political interest is often interpreted by news producers at popular outlets as not just the result of viewer apathy, but also of viewer disdain. For example, one news producer said that for many viewers politics was a 'turn-off... People get bored with it [and] they tend to think all politicians are crooks.' Former Seven news chief and former executive producer of *Today Tonight* Peter Manning (2007) has similarly argued that the audience of *Today Tonight* and *A Current Affair* is 'bored with [politicians] and doesn't believe them'.

News executives in the popular media have also sought to shift the definition of 'politics' from the formal to the informal politics of the everyday, a definition that fits very well with the news values of popular media. One news producer I spoke to argued that their audience was not interested in politics as 'party in-fighting [like] some stoush in the left wing of the New South Wales ALP but politics as something that impacts on everyone – then there is a real interest.' The CEO of Australia's largest publisher of tabloids, News Limited's John Hartigan (2009), said that 'most people in my view are well and truly bored with the politics of politics' and want content that 'inspires, surprises and delights... more humour, more escapism.' Before we can explore this and other claims about popular media in Chapter 5, we need to understand more about these audiences. This chapter follows the broad format used in the previous one, with Table 4.1 outlining the demographic profiles of audiences while the rest of the chapter elaborates on what the table shows.[2]

Tabloid newspapers

In 1977, Rupert Murdoch argued that newspapers needed to 'achieve a real breakthrough with [our] young readership [or] we will die along with our customers' (quoted in Windschuttle 1988:40). But in the 2000s, the printed tabloid newspaper audience remained, like broadsheets, dominated by readers over 50. This was especially the case for the *Advertiser* (54 per cent), the *West Australian* (47 per cent) and the *Mercury* (46 per cent) (Table 4.1). The internet, of course, did not help this and there was speculation that younger citizens would, in future, see printed newspapers as relics of a bygone era, a way of getting news akin to travelling by horse and cart (*The Economist* 2008).

All of the tabloids except the *Mercury* in Tasmania also had audiences that were disproportionately male, with the *Daily Telegraph* the highest at 56 per cent (Table 4.1). However, within these parameters of an older (male) audience, tabloids had a larger audience than broadsheets and one that was more representative of the general population. The *Herald Sun*, the *Mercury* and the *Advertiser* reached a high proportion of people on low incomes. People who had less than year 10 secondary education also tended to read tabloids. The *Herald Sun* readership closely resembled the national population in terms of occupation and, along with the *Daily Telegraph*, it had the audience with the highest proportion of semi-skilled and unskilled workers.

Audiences did vary, though, because tabloids that have a monopoly in one-newspaper markets (where there is no state-based broadsheet) tended to attract more affluent readers by default. In particular, the *Courier-Mail* in Queensland and the *West Australian* reached quite an affluent audience compared to the other tabloids (and a more educated one, too, in the case of the *Courier-Mail*). In the only two markets where there *are* state-based broadsheet competitors – New South Wales and Victoria – the presence of a broadsheet competitor means that the newspaper audience tends to divide very starkly in terms of education, occupation and income. Compared to broadsheet readers, tabloid readers are far less likely to have been to university and more likely to have only minimal secondary education, to earn under $15 000 and to be unemployed or blue-collar workers.

Free commuter newspapers

The ageing profile of newspaper readers and significant declines in circulation had become major problems for newspaper companies in the 1990s and they began to try new strategies to attract readers. One of these strategies was to develop commuter newspapers targeting young people, inner-city workers and university students, given away free from train stations, shopping centres and other city locations. These free papers were launched in many countries, especially in Europe, but also in the US, Canada, South America and Asia. *Metro* in Sweden was the first to be distributed via public transport in 1995. The rationale behind these papers was not only the advertising possibilities, but also the likelihood that they would encourage young people to get into the habit of reading a newspaper so that, in the future, they would buy one.

In Australia, both major newspaper owners launched free commuter newspapers at the same time and place – in Melbourne in February 2001. Fairfax led with *Melbourne Express* and, a day later, News Limited launched *mX*. Both papers were designed to be read in about 20 minutes, 'the length of the average train trip', and focused on colour, brevity, pictures, fashion, celebrity gossip and entertainment (Stoney 2001:239). However, this was a competition for a small market that could not sustain two papers. *mX's* shorter articles and more glossy format were ultimately more successful and Fairfax's version closed six months later. After conquering Melbourne, News Limited then launched *mX* in Sydney in 2005 and in Brisbane in March 2007. Anyone travelling by train in these three cities at peak hour during the 2007 election would have seen passengers reading these free tabloid papers.

These papers are particularly interesting because they reflected how newspaper companies viewed news audiences and the future of news. News Limited described its *mX* audience as 'young, time starved individuals who are increasingly difficult to reach using traditional media', 'a captive audience' for advertisers and 'part of the "idle thumbs" generation [of] technophiles' (Newsspace 2009c). Tim Stoney argued that the papers deliberately imitated the qualities of television (brief and visual with large photographs) in order to attract younger audiences. They tried to be irreverent rather than serious. *mX's* world news section was headed: 'Boring but Important'. Stoney (2001:242–3) characterised the approach as 'a string

Table 4.2 Characteristics of free commuter newspaper audiences, 2007–08 (percentages)

	Population (14 years+)	mX (NSW)	mX (Vic)	mX (Qld)
Men	49	56	52	57
Women	51	44	48	43
Some/now at university	9	19	19	18
Have diploma or degree	32	52	47	42
Personal income under $15k	33	25	34	23
Personal income $70k+	14	17	14	16
Professional/manager	18	32	30	36
White-collar worker	19	26	29	26
Skilled worker	8	6	2	10
Others (incl semi-skilled/unskilled)	15	13	10	10
Not employed	40	23	28	18
14–17	7	4	7	4
18–24	12	34	31	35
25–34	17	35	29	23
35–49 years	27	18	21	24
Over 50 years	38	10	13	15

Note: Figures relate to weekday editions.

Source: data supplied to the author by Roy Morgan Research (Single Source Australia, July 2007–June 2008).

of facts linked together by pretty pictures' and 'a format that reduces news to Trivial Pursuit answers'.

The readership of commuter newspapers was still dwarfed by that of the main tabloids, but their news formula did attract 18- to 34-year-olds in a way that conventional newspapers did not. They still appealed more to men than women, but most interesting of all was the fact that the *mX* audience was *not* the traditional tabloid audience – it was the young elite (Table 4.2). They did not yet have high incomes, but *mX* readers were much better educated than paid tabloid audiences and many were university students or those with degrees or diplomas. Traditionally this audience would have become broadsheet readers, but were now picking up a free quick-scan tabloid-style newspaper.

Commercial radio

Television and newspapers were the media that Australians turned to most for election campaign news (see Chapter 2). However, because so many

Australians consumed radio in such large quantities, it was undoubtedly a method by which many heard some form of political news, whether in news bulletins, in interviews on talkback or even through comedy program hosts discussing political events. Almost eight in ten Australians listened to commercial radio every week and they listened 'on average for 2 hrs 25 mins each day' (CRA 2007:2; 2008). Listeners tended to be loyal to their particular radio station (CRA 2009). This applied especially to talkback listeners.

Talkback

Talkback (also called 'talk radio') focuses on news, interviews and calls from listeners, although music, advertising, promotions, sport and entertainment are also part of the mix. Talkback has existed in Australia since the late 1960s, but it grew in the late 1990s and early to mid 2000s, especially in Sydney and through 2UE and 2GB (Tebbutt 2006). It became an especially important medium for political communication in the 2000s with regular appearances by politicians and especially by John Howard (Ward 2002a; Chapter 8).

The talkback phenomenon was especially strong in Sydney, although Laws also reached larger audiences because his program was syndicated 'to more than 60 stations across Australia' (Ward 2006:375). So great was Laws' perceived influence that Paul Keating famously argued: 'Forget the Press Gallery in Canberra. If you educate John Laws, you educate Australia.' 2UE program manager John Brennan similarly claimed that Laws and Alan Jones were 'the two most powerful men in the country, after the Prime Minister' (Adams and Burton 1997:2). But there were also suspicions that their political power and influence were more self-styled and exaggerated than real (e.g. Hamilton 2006a; Masters 2006).

Its advocates see talkback as a democratic medium that allows the general public to have a say and to question their representatives in a way that few other media allow but, in commercial terms, talkback is designed to attract an attentive, loyal audience for advertising. In 2009, Fairfax Media promoted its talkback stations (including 2UE and 3AW)[3] as being especially valuable for advertising. It claimed:

> live reads [by hosts] are 'perceived' by the listener as an endorsement of the product by their favourite personality . . . we are not limited by simply filling gaps between music . . . Our advertisers form an integral part of the show . . . Talk Radio attracts listener loyalty . . . fewer [advertising] spots are

required to generate frequency... [this] ... develops trust. This trust then
turns to purchase intention (Fairfax Media 2009).

The 1999 and 2004 'Cash for Comment' scandals showed how this trust
could be abused when hosts failed to disclose to their audiences that their
seemingly spontaneous and sincere comments were actually pre-scripted
advertisements for which they had been paid (ABA 2000).

Interestingly, talkback radio seemed to reach approximately the same
proportion of Australians who read tabloid newspapers – in 2006, there
were estimates that about 24 per cent of Australians were tuning in (Cincotta
2007; see also Denemark 2005:222). The AES study in 2004 found a similar
proportion of regular talkback listeners (24 per cent) who were listening
every day, most days or once or twice a week (Bean et al 2005). But only
a minority used talkback as their *main* news source (Denemark 2005:222)
and only between 5 and 10 per cent were listening every day or most days
during the 2001 and 2004 elections. Around half the electorate did not tune
in to talkback at all (Bean et al 2005; Bean, Gow and McAllister 2002).

The talkback audience generally consists of people who can listen to
radio attentively during the day. These include retirees, builders, drivers
and motor mechanics; people who have the radio on while they're driving,
or in the background as they do the housework or gardening. Like tabloids,
those who listened to talkback stations in the 2000s tended to be older than
average. 2GB and 2UE especially had older, male-dominated audiences in
2007 (Table 4.1).[4] However, because talkback is such a local medium, 3AW's
audience was noticeably different from that of the Sydney stations: it had
more women listening and its audience had lower education levels and lower
incomes.

Table 4.1 gives an average of the talkback stations' overall audiences across
the day; in Table 4.3 we can look more specifically at particular programs
that figured most prominently in political communication – Alan Jones,
John Laws and Neil Mitchell. These programs certainly attracted an older
audience, with the majority of their listeners aged over 55. However, unlike
tabloids and the elite media, talkback attracted more women than men. In
2007 Mitchell, Jones and Steve Price all had a higher proportion of female
listeners than was present in either the general population or the overall
audience for these radio stations. Laws' audience was the exception; he had
more male listeners and this was unusual for talkback programs. Adams

Table 4.3 Characteristics of commercial talkback audiences, Sydney and
Melbourne, 2007 (percentages)

	Sydney			Melbourne		
	Sydney population	Alan Jones (2GB)	John Laws (2UE)	Melbourne population	Ross Stevenson (3AW)	Neil Mitchell (3AW)
Men	50	48	59	49	45	43
Women	50	52	41	51	55	57
Education – upper secondary	24	29	23	26	39	36
Education – trade/diploma	27	33	30	23	21	23
Education – Degree	24	9	11	24	15	13
Household income $15–$50k	17	27	20	19	23	27
Household income $50k+	53	35	48	49	49	37
Household income $70k+	43	28	33	37	37	25
AB (managers, administrators and professionals)	29	17	15	28	23	18
C1–C2 (para-professionals and tradespeople)	23	20	23	20	22	21
DE (drivers, machine operators, labourers and factory hands)	5	3	15	7	7	6
10–17	12	3	2	11	2	0
18–24	12	1	0	12	1	2
25–39	26	5	13	26	8	7
40–54 years	24	25	31	24	28	28
Over 55 years	26	66	54	27	63	64

Notes: data are from Survey Four 2007, which covered the period 25 March–28 April and 6 May–9 June 2007. Categories
for 'men' and 'women' refer to listeners 10 years plus. Unlike those of OzTAM, Nielsen Media radio ratings include teachers
in the AB category.

Source: Nielsen Media, data supplied to the author.

and Burton (1997:242–6) showed in 1997 that female listeners constituted
a majority for most morning talkback hosts around the country.

The audiences for all of the commercial talkback programs shown in
Table 4.3 were less educated than the general population, especially in
Sydney, where only 9 to 11 per cent of the talkback audiences had a degree
compared to 24 per cent of the population. They were also poorer – especially
for Jones' and Mitchell's programs. Jones was especially known to remark on
this and to characterise his audience as 'battlers' on 'Struggle Street'. In many
cases, audience members were on low incomes because they were retired,
but those who *were* working were more likely to be para-professionals or
tradespeople rather than managers or professionals. Laws' program was
different – it attracted a younger audience compared to the other programs,

significantly more male listeners than female, and it was the only one in Table 4.3 to have a higher proportion of DE listeners (drivers, factory hands and labourers) than was found in the population. Laws' program was known to be especially popular with male truck drivers.

As the main talkback hosts aged in the 1990s and 2000s, so did their audiences (Table 4.3; Adams and Burton 1997:242–6). The proportion of listeners under 40 dropped between 1997 and 2007, while the proportion over 55 rose by 8 per cent for Jones and 5 per cent for Laws. Worse for the hosts, their overall audience declined and the golden age of talkback seemed to wane, especially after 2007 when Laws retired one week after the election and Jones posted his weakest ratings in three years. In the month before the election was called and the first week of the campaign, almost 100 000 listeners switched off 2GB (Javes 2007). John Howard – a talkback regular and staunch defender of Alan Jones – was then defeated in the election. In 2008, Jones was off air for periods due to ill health. Continuing audience declines and a changed political environment led some to question whether the talkback formula that had been developed so successfully by John Brennan at 2UE and 2GB in the 1990s was finally 'dead' (Dyer 2008a).

FM radio

While talkback attracted an older audience, commercial FM stations – such as those on the Austereo and Nova networks which focused on music, sport and comedy – had a large reach among Australians aged 24 to 39. Many of the 'top 40' FM stations sound alike because commercial radio is 'a very conservative industry' in Australia (Miller and Turner 2002:147). Politics is not a major focus of these programs and, during his 11½ years as Prime Minister, John Howard rarely appeared on FM radio. Four months before the 2001 election he conducted interviews on two Brisbane FM radio stations and, during the campaign, appeared on Triple-M, but these events were rare. Howard stuck mainly to appearances on the AM circuit and especially, as we have noted, talkback. However, Mark Latham in 2004 and Kevin Rudd in 2007 did appear on FM radio. Particularly in Rudd's case, this was interpreted as part of his strategy for communicating with young people 'on their territory' (along with the internet and television comedy shows) as well as showing Howard up for being out of touch for his failure to do so.

In the phoney campaign leading up to the 2007 election, Howard continued to avoid FM radio, although the then Treasurer Peter Costello appeared
on Sydney's highest-rating FM show – the *Kyle and Jackie O* program on
2Day FM – where he was quizzed on the cost of grocery items. By contrast,
Rudd appeared regularly on FM stations, including Nova in Sydney where
he was given an electric shock. During the campaign, Rudd conducted more
than 40 FM interviews. Howard made only one appearance, on the Fox FM
Matt and Jo Show, after the hosts broadcast a running segment on their
failed efforts to get Howard to appear, which focused especially on their
daily phone calls to Howard's press secretary David Luff.

FM stations attracted a very different audience from that of talkback radio
and other more news-focused media, and Rudd's emphasis demonstrated
an awareness of how this could work to his advantage. Radio stations such as
2Day FM (in Sydney) and Fox FM (in Melbourne) attracted over a million
listeners in 2007. These stations were popular among younger audiences
and especially among those in the first-time voting age bracket of 18 to 24.
Sixty-four per cent of Fox FM's audience was under 25 years and half of the
audience for Nova Sydney and Nova Melbourne was aged 18 to 24 (NMRA
2007b). These stations were also reaching many in the next generation of
voters – those aged 10 to 17.

Commercial free-to-air television

In recent years, television's extraordinary dominance over Australians'
leisure time has waned. Ratings have declined and young people especially
are spending less time watching television and more time on the internet
and with computer and electronic games (RMR 2009b; Screen Australia
2009). In 2009, headlines proclaimed that the internet was, for the first
time, overtaking television as the most-used medium in Australia (Dudley-
Nicholson 2009). But this was misleading. The research actually showed
that the average Australian was still spending more than double the amount
of time in front of television that they did on the internet, and that radio was
their next most-used medium. The only people who were using the internet
more than television were two specific, and relatively small, groups: 14- to
24-year-old 'heavy internet users' and young elites – people under 35 who
watched no commercial television (RMR 2009a).

Television has such a formidable place in Australian culture that it is unwise to overlook its continued influence. For most Australians, their interest in news has been pursued through television and especially through commercial television. Although public broadcasters have gained audience share, in 2008 the three commercial channels still had a combined share of 77 per cent of the free-to-air television audience. At the time of the 2007 election, television was the most universally available medium and, in a typical week, the average Australian adult spent nearly 22 hours watching it (Screen Australia 2009). As we noted at the beginning of this chapter, news is one of the most-watched program genres in Australia. In an era that some have dubbed 'the age of the image', the seeming ability for viewers to 'see for themselves' has lent television a heightened credibility, to the extent that it is often nominated as the most trusted news medium (RMR 2008).

News and current affairs

Blue-collar workers tended to rely heavily on commercial television for news in the 2000s. Table 4.4 contrasts their free-to-air television news and current affairs preferences with those of the ABs in 2007.[5] They were not as interested in election coverage or budgets as the ABs. When they did watch election coverage, blue-collar workers strongly preferred commercial channels; 18 of their top 20 most-watched news and current affairs programs were broadcast on commercial channels. Channel Seven's polling night coverage was the

Table 4.4 Most-watched news and current affairs programs, free-to-air television, 2007, by occupation group

Managers, professionals and administrators (ABs)		Labourers, factory hands and tradespeople	
Program	**Channel**	**Program**	**Channel**
1 Australia Votes 2007	ABC	60 Minutes	9
2 ABC News (evening)	ABC	Seven News (Sun)	7
3 ABC News (Sun)	ABC	Today Tonight	7
4 Media Watch	ABC	A Current Affair	9
5 The Leaders' Debate	ABC	Seven News	7
6 Four Corners	ABC	National Nine News	9
7 ABC News Budget Special	ABC	National Nine News (Sat)	9
8 Australian Story	ABC	Seven News (Sat)	7
9 60 Minutes	9	Seven News Election Special: Your Call 07	7
10 Seven News (Sun)	7	An Interview with Princes William and Harry	7

Sources: OzTAM data supplied to the author and OzTAM 2007a:1–2.

one they turned to most in 2007. Seven had promised in its advertising an entertaining approach to calling the election results, and that it would not be 'about boring pollies in suits or wonky headed computer geeks' (Chapter 12).

But Australian television audiences were declining overall. Between 1991 and 1998, over 200 000 viewers in Sydney alone switched off primetime news, while the drop in current affairs audiences was even more marked (Casimir 1998:4). A number of factors were involved in these audience declines. Australians were working longer hours, which meant that not all could make it home for 6 pm news each night (ABS 2003). Also, the genre of news, but especially current affairs, lost some of its gloss and credibility. There were scandals surrounding particular stories and, between 1994 and 1997, the satirical program *Frontline* (ABC) lampooned the whole format of commercial current affairs, including the egos and unethical practices involved.

Pay TV began in the mid 1990s, which saw up to 80 000 people watching pay TV at primetime instead of the free-to-air channels (Meakin quoted in Casimir 1998). More Australians also began to have a home computer and internet access. In 1996 only 2 per cent of Australians could access the internet at home, but just two years later this had jumped to 16 per cent (ABS 1997:12–13, 1999:1). By the time of the 1998 election, 3 million households had a home computer and 1.1 million were hooked up to the internet (ABS 1999). If only one person in each of these households was spending time on the computer instead of watching television, this was more than enough to put a dent in television ratings.

The ratings decline intensified between 2001 and 2007. People were not only watching sport, movies and sitcoms on pay TV, but also watching DVDs, doing online shopping, emailing, doing social networking, texting, and using MP3 players, digital cameras and games consoles. Table 4.5 shows the ratings for the five largest capital cities. The table includes not only commercial news and current affairs programs, but also morning and breakfast programs. Between 2001 and 2007, these programs became key ways in which the commercial channels targeted particular audiences by shifting the concept of 'news' from specific news bulletins broadcast at a set time to a more fluid concept, with news spread throughout light entertainment programs that included breaking news updates as well as news-related chatter, commentary and interviews.

Table 4.5 Audience growth or loss for commercial television news and current affairs programs between 2001 and 2007

Program	Channel	Average audience loss (viewers)	Audience change (%)
Meet the Press	10	145 000	−67.4
Ten Late News	10	211 000	−43.0
Sunday	9	170 000	−42.4
Today	9	170 000	−39.5
Ten 11.30am News	10	70 000	−32.9
Nine Morning News	9	72 000	−32.6
Nightline	9	122 000	−32.1
Seven Late News	7	71 000	−25.3
Seven Morning News	7	32 000	−19.7
National Nine News	9	258 000	−17.5
Ten News at 5pm	10	167 000	−16.5
A Current Affair	9	221 000	−16.0
60 Minutes	9	236 000	−14.2
Today Tonight	7	(+96 000)	+7.2
Seven National News	7	(+201 000)	+14.3
Sunrise	7	(+316 000)	+77.3

Note: average mainland capital city audiences.

Sources: OzTAM data supplied to the author and OzTAM 2007a:1–2.

The battle between Channels Nine and Seven muddies the waters somewhat in interpreting Table 4.5. For decades Nine had dominated in news ratings, with Seven coming a strong second and Ten a distant third, but between 2001 and 2007 *Seven News* ascended. In this period, Seven started winning the primetime news slot against *Nine News*; *Today Tonight* was winning against *A Current Affair*; and *Sunrise* was winning the competition with *Today* (see below). These programs therefore saw some audience gains at the expense of Channel Nine but, overall, the larger context for news and current affairs viewing is still obvious. Between 2001 and 2007, news audiences declined significantly – and not just at primetime but for morning, late news and current affairs programs. Most programs lost over 70 000 viewers and some lost over 200 000.

The biggest drop in television news viewing was among the young. As we have noted, young people have traditionally not been as interested in either politics or news as older people but, when they did access news, television was their main source. Now people under 40 were watching less television than they were in the 1990s and, when they did switch on, they

Table 4.6 Audience growth/decline for the most-watched news and current affairs programs between 2001 and 2007 (percentages)

	Channel	0–17 yrs	18–24 yrs	25–39 yrs	40–54 yrs	55 yrs+
National Nine News (Sun)	9	−42.6	−28.4	−27.9	−15.1	+3.8
A Current Affair	9	−44.7	−21.4	−30.0	−22.5	+7.4
National Nine News	9	−47.8	−28.8	−33.6	−23.4	+5.4
Seven News (Sun)	7	−33.3	−36.8	−22.3	+2.9	+20.0
60 Minutes	9	−39.7	−18.6	−32.0	−20.8	+12.4
National Nine News (Sat)	9	−47.7	−40.9	−36.7	−23.0	+15.9
Today Tonight	7	−25.7	−17.2	−18.1	+11.1	n/a
Seven News (Sat)	7	−36.0	−40.8	−30.2	−11.3	+7.5
Seven News	7	−17.9	−17.5	−6.6	+18.6	+26.5
Ten News First at Five	10	−37.5	−38.8	−25.2	n/a	n/a
ABC News	ABC	n/a	n/a	n/a	−12.6	+20.2
Late News	ABC	n/a	n/a	n/a	n/a	+9.2
Average loss/growth		**−38.0**	**−29.1**	**−27.3**	**−10.3**	**+13.2**

Note: average mainland capital city audiences. 'N/a' means the program was not in the group's top 10 most-watched.

Source: data supplied to the author and OzTAM 2007a:1–2.

were not turning to news and current affairs in the way that they used to (Screen Australia 2008; see also Burton 2000 and Sternberg 1998; Ward 1992). Table 4.6 shows changes in viewing patterns, by age, for the top 10 news and current affairs programs watched by various age groups in 2001.[6] Only the over-55s were watching more television news and current affairs. The viewing of these programs by all other groups declined dramatically between 2001 and 2007 – by 38.0 per cent for the under-17s, by 29.1 per cent for those aged 18 to 24, by 27.3 per cent for those aged 25 to 39 and by 10.3 per cent for those aged 40 to 54. While younger Australians had always watched these programs in smaller numbers, in 2001 there *was* a younger audience for these shows that, by 2007, had declined dramatically.

The over-55s were the key remaining loyal audience for television news and current affairs by 2007. Viewing by this group went up 13.2 per cent, which was in line with the group's growth in population (ABS 2008b). As we noted in the previous chapter, the other groups that were still watching television for news were women and para-professionals including teachers, clerks, salespeople, nurses and real estate salespeople. As the television audience declined and shifted to an ageing middle-class female demographic, this had a major impact upon news and current affairs programming. The programs that rated well in 2007 were doing so because they were capturing this demographic. For example, Seven's flagship 6 pm news was Australia's highest-rating television news program in 2007; 52 per cent of its audience was over 55 and three-quarters (74.8 per cent) was over 40. An illustration of the extent to which this audience has become *the* key audience for television is the way it has shifted Channel Ten's strategy. In the 1990s, Ten began to specifically target a younger audience aged under 40 (Braithwaite 2007; Green 2001) but, because of the changing demographics of television audiences, Channel Ten had to expand its target audience in the late 2000s to include older viewers aged 25 to 54 (Schulze 2009).

Breakfast programs

Because breakfast programs appealed to the older female television audience, they were one of the few types of news programs to increase their ratings in the period 2001–07 and the commercial channels began to put more emphasis on these programs. Like talkback and its presentation of news, the long-form, chatty style of news presentation by trusted hosts (mixed with commercial endorsements) was seen to appeal to older people and to women at home alone. It has been said that this form of presentation especially appeals because 'nothing [is] worse than an empty house' (Dyer 2008b).

Seven's *Sunrise* program had already existed in several different forms and timeslots but, in 2002, the pairing of Melissa Doyle and David Koch sparked a program revamp to make the show more focused on consumer stories and celebrities and to make it more 'family friendly'. The program included news shown every 30 minutes along with interviews, weather and traffic. In 2003, *Sunrise* began to pick up ratings against *Sunrise*'s rival on Channel Nine, the *Today* program. *Today* had been broadcast since 1982, although it too underwent many modifications to programming, hosts and timeslots. In 2007, *Sunrise* won the ratings battle, averaging 149 000 more viewers than *Today*. As Table 4.7 shows, both *Today* and *Sunrise* achieved their growth by attracting older female viewers. By 2007, around 60 per cent of their audience was female. *Sunrise* had a younger audience than *Today*, but both had high proportions of over-55s compared to the general population (24.1 per cent).

Sunrise proved to be especially important politically in the 2000s because Kevin Rudd used it when he was a shadow minister to build a public profile. For five years (2002–07), Rudd and Liberal MP Joe Hockey appeared in

Table 4.7 Characteristics of audiences for breakfast programs, 2001 and
2007 (percentages)

		55 years+		Female	
Program	Channel	2001	2007	2001	2007
Sunrise	7	19.4	32.3	50.0	61.1
Today	9	33.7	49.6	58.1	60.4

Note: average mainland capital city audiences.

Sources: OzTAM data supplied to the author and OzTAM 2007a:1–2.

a *Sunrise* segment that revolved around the two men and their friendly
political banter. Their segment ended six months before the 2007 election
after a controversy about a fake Anzac Day memorial service planned by the
show to coincide with peak early morning viewing times. Imitating *Sunrise*'s
formula, in 2007 *Today* began a regular Friday morning discussion between
Labor deputy leader Julia Gillard and the then Health Minister, the Liberals'
Tony Abbott.

Current affairs

Commercial primetime current affairs programs traditionally played a key
role in political reporting in Australia. When lengthy political interviews
were more common on these programs in the 1980s and 1990s, they were
seen as a key way for politicians to reach large popular television audiences.
This was not always to their advantage. For example, the infamous 'Birthday
Cake' television interview occurred with Mike Willesee and Liberal leader
John Hewson on *A Current Affair* ten days before the 1993 election. Hewson
could not answer in a straightforward manner whether the cost of a birthday
cake would go up or down under his proposed Goods and Services Tax. His
complicated, laboured answer on national television was interpreted by
some as a key moment in his subsequent defeat.

With a declining audience base and the migration of the elite audience
to the ABC, Channel Nine's *A Current Affair* and Channel Seven's *Today
Tonight* changed format dramatically in the 1990s (Turner 2005:18–21).
Like morning television programs, they sought an older female audience
with news targeted to their perceived interests and more apolitical stance.
Neighbourhood disputes, small-time con-artists, crime and social dysfunc-
tion became far more prevalent, but so did stories about consumer products, health and lifestyle, including stories on supermarkets, petrol prices,

Table 4.8 Characteristics of audiences for commercial current affairs programs, 2001 and 2007 (percentages)

Program	Channel	55 years+		Female	
		2001	**2007**	**2001**	**2007**
Today Tonight	Seven	38.4	47.5	55.9	56.9
A Current Affair	Nine	36.9	47.5	55.1	55.5

Note: average mainland capital city audiences.

Sources: OzTAM data supplied to the author and OzTAM 2007a:1–2.

diets, celebrities, 'miracle' cures and cosmetic surgery. In 2001 both programs had a high proportion of female viewers, but by 2007 the proportion of their audiences who were *older* females had significantly increased (Table 4.8).

Current affairs programs such as *A Current Affair* were originally associated with investigative reporting, providing background and context to news stories, and interrogation of political issues. However, as their audiences changed, politicians began to be increasingly seen as a 'ratings killer'. In 1998, when he was host of the program *A Current Affair*, Ray Martin had declared that: 'Anyone who suggests that you get ratings by having the Prime Minister or Leader of the Opposition on is a dope . . . Australians don't want that . . . they don't watch . . . ' (ABC 1998). However, political content did not disappear entirely – in 2007, for example, *ACA* host Tracy Grimshaw gave both John Howard and Kevin Rudd a pop quiz that included a question about the current interest rate. When Howard answered incorrectly, he responded with visible annoyance. Howard and then treasurer Peter Costello also did a rare double interview on *Today Tonight* to showcase their productive partnership amid rumours of their personal animosity.

However, occasional stories aside, the political focus was much diminished from earlier decades. On the *ACA* website in 2009, for example, the story categories were 'health, money, lifestyle, consumer [and] general'. There was no category for 'political'. This attracted (as it was designed to) a different audience from viewers of elite media representations of politics. As former *Today Tonight* executive producer Peter Manning (2007) observed, there was basically 'no overlap' between the audience of a program like *Today Tonight* and the audiences of elite media such as 'the *Age*, the *Australian*, the ABC or SBS'.

Pay TV, digital television and the internet

Pay TV

Pay TV may have become a key method for the 1 per cent of dedicated political junkies to access 24-hour news, but the rest of those who had pay TV in Australia in the 2000s did not tend to use it for this purpose. They used it instead for watching the normal free-to-air channels (this accounted for 53 per cent of pay TV viewing) as well as sport, movies, television sitcoms, lifestyle programs, documentaries and children's content spread across 60 channels (OzTAM 2007c).

Digital television

Digital television also, slowly, allowed greater choice on television for those unable to afford pay TV. After the digital spectrum was switched on in January 2001, over 30 new digital free-to-air television channels became available. Many were entertainment-based, including Channel Ten's 24-hour sports channel and most of them came into effect after the 2007 election. SevenHD was the only free-to-air commercial television channel to be available in metropolitan areas during the campaign and – like the other commercial HD channels when they began – it consisted of minimal programming and very little exclusive content. Also diminishing its impact was the fact that less than half of Australians had the equipment required to receive digital television at the time (ACMA 2007:82).

The take-up and use of digital television in Australia in the 2000s was stunted by a range of factors, including the impact of government policies designed to protect the interests of major media players, but the fragmentation of audiences that it and pay TV represented was proving to be an unstoppable force. The 2000s was an era that heralded the development of more and more ways of occupying people's leisure time, including through technology and devices that did not exist or had only minimal penetration 20 years ago. This had a major impact upon political communication and on news journalism, because it meant that neither media owners nor politicians could so easily identify a mass audience and target it in one place. Nowhere was this fragmentation more visible than on the internet, where people were spreading across a wide range of activities and sites.

The internet

Even if television still reigned supreme as a news medium for the average Australian in 2007, there was also no doubt that more people were using the internet more frequently than in 2001. The key question is whether they were using it for 'news'. If we use this term in the sense of traditional news formats and news journalism, the evidence shows that most people were not using their time online to specifically go to 'news' sites. People – especially younger people who were far more likely to be online than older Australians – tended to use the internet for emailing, socialising (including using social network sites) and entertainment as well as shopping, doing homework or research, playing games, downloading music, paying bills and looking for jobs (RMR 2007–08).

When it came to getting news from the internet, the medium was still tending to attract a specific audience – young, educated and affluent white males. This elite audience is, of course, familiar to us from Chapter 3 and many factors of the digital divide influenced this, including the cost of home PCs and internet connections as well as the leisure time and access required. Those who said they specifically went to news websites were still disproportionately male, university educated, professionals or managers with high incomes (Table 4.9). As the internet becomes more popularly available, we may expect this situation to change and a growing number of females, older people and the less affluent to use it for news. However, we cannot take this for granted as we have also seen that – talkback and some television programs aside – males tend to dominate the audiences for news media. Even when *mX* newspapers are given out free, for example, males tend to pick them up more.

In 2007, the most popular news websites Australians visited were Ninemsn, Google News, News Limited's aggregate website (news.com.au), the *Sydney Morning Herald* online, the *Age* online and the ABC. We examined the last three as sites favoured by the elite audience in Chapter 3. The more general news audience – especially younger Australians – were more likely to go to Ninemsn, Google News, Yahoo!7 and news.com.au.

Ninemsn began as a joint venture between PBL Media (owners of Channel Nine and other Australian media assets) and Microsoft. Because Microsoft owned Hotmail, one of the world's most-used webmail systems, Australians who had a Hotmail email account were led to Ninemsn automatically when they closed their email. This helped make Ninemsn one of

Table 4.9 Characteristics of audiences for online news websites, 2007–08 (percentages)

	Population (14 years+)	Accesses online news sites
Men	49	57
Women	51	44
Have university education	41	61
Personal income under $15k	33	23
Personal income $50k+	26	40
Personal income $70k+	14	23
Professional/manager	18	32
White-collar worker	19	24
14–17 years	7	4
18–24 years	12	14
25–34 years	17	24
35–49 years	27	31
50–64 years	22	20
Over 65 years	16	7

Note: Figures are rounded, so male–female does not equal 100% as proportions were 56.5% to 43.5%.

Source: data supplied to the author by Roy Morgan Research (Single Source Australia, July 2007–June 2008).

the most accessed news sites in Australia more by serendipity than deliberate choice. Yahoo!7 was another joint venture between an Australian media company and an American IT company – in this case between the Seven Network and Yahoo! Inc. Just as Ninemsn used Channel Nine content, Yahoo!7 included content from Channel Seven news bulletins. News.com.au is News Limited's Australian site and it includes news headlines, access to News Limited's Australian newspapers (all of which are tabloids except for the *Australian*) plus Fox Sports, CareerOne, MySpace and CarsGuide.

Google News was quite different from these other websites, which all began from traditional media companies. Part of Google, the world's largest search engine, it was a news aggregator drawing on content from other news providers and acting as a search engine across many news services. Google has been described as the world's largest advertising medium 'posing as a search engine'. It has also been called a 'parasite' by existing news companies that dislike not only its hold on online advertising but also how it profits from the journalistic content made by others (Hartigan 2009; Chapter 10).

Like commuter newspapers, all of these four sites focused on brevity, visuals and a more tabloid selection of news in 2007. However, because of

Table 4.10 Comparison of audiences for online and printed tabloid newspapers, demographic profiles, 2007–08 (percentages)

	Population (14 years+)	Daily Telegraph		Herald Sun	
		Printed	Online	Printed	Online
Men	49	56	64	52	61
Women	51	44	36	48	39
Have university education	41	34	58	37	59
Personal income under $15k	33	29	21	31	23
Personal income $50k+	26	27	52	27	41
Personal income $70k+	14	12	31	12	20
Professional/manager	18	17	37	16	34
White-collar worker	19	20	23	21	30
14–17	7	4	3	4	4
18–24	12	11	12	11	15
25–34	17	16	27	14	24
35–49 years	27	27	33	27	33
Over 50 years	38	43	25	45	24

Note: figures are rounded so male–female does not equal 100% as proportions were 56.5% to 43.5%.

Source: data supplied to the author by Roy Morgan Research (Single Source Australia, July 2007–June 2008).

the nature of the digital divide, even these websites attracted an audience that was quite elite compared to that for other popular media (Table 4.1) and – except for Ninemsn – were still dominated by young males. News. com.au attracted the wealthiest audience, with more professionals and managers, higher incomes and the highest proportion of university degrees and diplomas. Ninemsn and Google News had the highest proportion of visitors aged 18 to 24. News.com.au and Yahoo!7 had older audiences – especially in the 25–34 age bracket, but diminishing considerably after the age of 50.

Like free commuter newspapers, the popular news websites attracted fairly elite audiences. This also extended to those who read online tabloids. They were a very different audience than for printed tabloids. Online tabloid readers were even more likely to be men, but also more likely to be university educated, nearly twice as likely to be affluent (earning $70 000 plus) and to be professionals or managers (Table 4.10).

The online news environment posed many challenges to the traditional media companies, but there were particular challenges in capturing the general audience. While elite media audiences often feel quite strong loyalty to their favoured outlets, survey and statistical evidence suggests that the general internet user wants 'their news straight and they want it quick;

they're not much bothered who brings it to them' (Katz 2000:9). While the political junkies have a dedicated interest and a particular news specialism that can be identified and catered to, the general news audience includes 'news grazers' who are 'less dedicated to news' but 'check in on [it] from time to time' and have an 'eclectic news diet' (PRC 2004). While the elite audiences' preference for detailed textual information has been well served online, the technology in its first two decades limited the extent to which the general audience's preference for audiovisual forms of journalism could be accommodated. It was only towards the end of the 2000s, especially since broadband internet became popularly available, that audiovisual content became more widely available on websites.

Conclusion

When it comes to reporting politics, media have different formats, styles and priorities. They attract different audiences as a result. Blue-collar workers tend to prefer commercial television, tabloid newspapers and commercial radio. Younger Australians are more likely to get their news from commuter newspapers, commercial FM radio and websites such as Google News. The politically interested tabloid, talkback and commercial current affairs audience is older, with men preferring tabloid newspapers and internet news sources while women prefer radio talkback, breakfast shows and current affairs programs on commercial television. As with elite media audiences, these audiences did not just pre-exist as some fully formed entity but were created and cultivated in particular ways by media companies. One of the ways popular media distinguish themselves from elite media and cater for a broader audience is by using a different form of address with their audiences and delivering different types of content. It seems that this can have important effects when it comes to their audiences' knowledge about, and attitudes towards, politics and society.

Chapter 5

ELECTIONS AND AUDIENCES

Looking at media audiences and their preferences gives us one part of a larger puzzle about why politicians expend such effort in reaching media audiences: why do they believe these efforts can make a difference to election results? To get to the heart of this, in this chapter I address four themes around political learning, attitude formation, voting behaviour and media effects. I focus on four main questions: (1) How much do Australians know about politics? (2) Are some media better than others at informing people? (3) Do audiences choose media outlets that accord with their partisan views? – and, finally, putting all of this evidence together – (4) What impact can media content really have during an election?

All of these individual questions about political learning, political attitude formation and media effects have spawned a vast literature and many different theories both in Australia and beyond. This is because, in the study of audiences, untangling causes, effects, correlations and associations is notoriously difficult. To take an example, if someone who reads the *Age* newspaper is more likely to vote Labor, is this because they have been influenced by its 'left-wing' content (see Chapter 11 for allegations of this nature), or is it because they were already a Labor supporter and selected the *Age* in the first place because its content seemed to fit well with their pre-existing views?

Relationships between media content and political attitude formation are complex. There are many factors involved in an individual's political

84

attitude formation, including the strong influence of education, occupation, gender, class, ethnicity, country of birth, religion, values, age and personal knowledge and experience. An individual does not come to media content as a 'blank slate' waiting to be filled. Nor do they gain information from just one source during an election. Over a five- or six-week campaign, people are exposed to hundreds, if not thousands, of persuasive appeals through the media. These include not only news but also political ads, comedy show sketches and a vast range of other forms. Sometimes people may be highly attentive to these messages but at other times they may only be paying selective attention. For example, they may have the television news on but be eating dinner or doing the dishes or using their laptop at the same time.

Many people will also have experiences of the election outside the media. They may have some personal contact with politicians during the campaign, either in person or through the politicians' letters, phone calls or, increasingly, emails and text messages. During the campaign they may discuss the election with their workmates, friends or family. These personal discussion networks can be highly influential in how people use the political media and evaluate the news it presents. If they go to their local school to vote on polling day (as many Australians do), they may chat with one of the amiable, pamphlet-waving party supporters who cluster at the school gates. All of these experiences can 'mediate and filter media messages, sometimes reinforcing them, but often diluting, deflecting, or even destroying them' (Newton 2007).

Media reporting is not consumed in a vacuum, nor is it entirely homogeneous or stable. For example, to continue with the example of the *Age*: if it was as pro-Labor as its critics allege, why did it endorse the Coalition in 2004 in its eve-of-election editorial and again fail to advocate a vote for Labor in its 2007 editorial (see Chapter 11)? Even within one media outlet, content is multifaceted, fluid and sometimes contradictory. Different parts of a newspaper, for example, can promote conflicting accounts of the same events including, very deliberately, the op-ed page where different polemical columnists use their contrasting views to provoke debate. What impact a news report, a newspaper editorial, an op-ed piece or any other media text can have upon a person's level of knowledge, their political views or their voting decisions is the central question of media effects research.

Political interest, knowledge and participation

According to research performed in the 1990s by political scientist Ian McAllister (1998:8), the majority of Australians 'know little about politics and possess minimal factual knowledge about the operation of the political system.' But those who are the most interested in politics are also the most knowledgeable about it (PRC 2007; Tranter 2007; Weaver and Drew 2006). This is hardly surprising because, of course, one of the outcomes of being interested is a greater tendency to seek out political news and information. Having background knowledge also makes new information easier to understand and retain (Miller and Krosnick 1997).

We know from the two previous chapters that the desire to seek out news is not held equally by all. Social conventions around news use and political interest influence the way in which news is made and promoted. As a result, news interest tends to correlate with people's socioeconomic position, with women, the young and the poor feeling less 'need' for news (see Chapters 3 and 4; also Putnam 1995). It is not surprising, then, that the Australian research on political knowledge has found that it is older people, men, those with tertiary education and managers who know the most about Australian politics (Tranter 2007).

In studies of political knowledge men almost invariably perform better than women. There is some speculation that this may be due to the fact that women taking tests are more likely to admit when they do not know an answer, whereas men more often hazard a guess and may sometimes select the right answer as a result. However, it seems that the most important factor in these results is the variable of interest. Paying attention to national politics 'is strongly correlated with age, and, at every age level, men are more likely than women to be highly attentive' to politics (Saad 2005; see Curran et al 2009; Jones and Pusey 2008; Tranter 2007).

A lack of interest in politics also helps explain why, on these types of tests, young people often 'know the least' about politics (PRC 2007). Ethnicity also seems to matter. In tests of Australian political knowledge, people born in Australia knew more about politics than those born overseas (Tranter 2007). In American studies of political knowledge, whites regularly perform better than African-Americans (PRC 2007).

These findings are of significant concern because, just as political interest and knowledge are linked, so too are political knowledge and participation.

Research has shown that the more knowledgeable a citizen is, the more likely they are to participate in politics (PRC 2007; Weaver and Drew 2006:25). In countries with voluntary voting this is an especially serious problem, because it means that those who abstain from voting tend to be the least interested and least knowledgeable. These also tend to be people 'with low levels of education; who experience residential instability; are new migrants; are members of an ethnic minority; are young, unemployed or otherwise socially or economically marginalised' (Young and Hill 2009:75–6).

This makes 'voluntary' voting an activity dominated by the more politically interested (and thus socioeconomically better-off), especially when there are barriers to registration and voting, such as when elections are held on a work day, as in the US and UK, making it difficult for blue-collar workers to attend a polling booth. By contrast, in Australia, even those who consider themselves to be politically indifferent or feel they don't know a lot about politics are still required to vote. Electoral administration has been designed to facilitate this and achieves it in a manner that has led Australia to have voter turnout rates for registered voters that are the envy of the industrialised voluntary voting world (94.8 per cent in 2007).

However, while Australia's turnout rate is extremely impressive, the actual enrolment of voters is not as universal as the law requires. When we look at who fails to enrol to vote, the same links between interest, knowledge and participation that impede people from voting in voluntary voting systems are still visible. In 2009, the Australian Electoral Commission revealed that more than 1.2 million eligible people were missing from the electoral roll and non-enrolment was particularly high among the young, with one in five Australians aged 18 to 24 years missing (Hudson 2009). There are also a significant number of Australians who cast invalid ('informal') votes. At the 2004 election, over 639 000 Australian voters failed to have their votes counted. Many of these entered a number '1' only, or a tick or cross for their preferred candidate, but this did not meet the requirement for a valid vote because voting for the House of Representatives requires that voters number every candidate on the ballot in order of preference. The major predictors of this type of accidental informal voting are English language competency, education levels and socioeconomic disadvantage – the same factors that impede voters in voluntary systems (Young and Hill 2009).

Compulsory voting cannot ensure 100 per cent registration nor can it, on its own, bridge the links between opportunity, interest, political knowledge and participation. What it has done, though, is ensure that more people who might otherwise abstain from politics register and cast a vote. As a result, Australia has a far more socioeconomically representative turnout of voters than is seen in any other comparable country (Tiffen and Gittins 2009:44). This, combined with the use of single-member, geographically defined electorates and the fact that the two major parties' loyal supporters tend to be evenly distributed (and therefore cancel each other out), has inadvertently led to one of the defining features of Australian politics – that 'swinging voters' in marginal seats determine election results.

Softly committed voters and the uncommitted

Before the 2004 election, the Liberal Party's federal director, Brian Loughnane, warned a meeting of party members that only 3776 votes needed to change in key marginal seats for the government to lose (quoted in Young 2004:43). Voters who are open to changing their vote from the previous election are most often called 'swinging voters' or 'switchers', although they might be more accurately characterised as 'softly committed', because few 'swinging' voters are swinging in a complete political vacuum.[1] These voters have long been crucial to Australian election results, but they have become more crucial as they have grown in number. In 2002, John Howard observed:

> When I . . . was active in [election] campaigns in the early 60s, I used to think the Australian electorate divided on a sort of 40, 40, 20 basis – 40% always voted Labor, 40% always voted Liberal and we had 20% that would move around in the middle. I now have the sense that we divide on a sort of 30, 30, 40 basis.

Swinging voters do not have strong partisan views – they have been described as being 'at the centre' of the political spectrum and, in Liberal Party research, as believing that:

> there is little between the two parties. Thus ideology . . . is of little consequence. What is of consequence . . . [to the swinging voter] is the way he [sic] thinks the application of an ideology will affect him personally or his family (quoted in Young 2004:48).

A Labor Party internal report from 1986 warned similarly that:

> contrary to popular myth, [swinging voters] are *not* discerning upper middle
> class professionals who carefully reason their vote. They are basically igno-
> rant and indifferent about politics. They vote on instinct for superficial, ill
> informed and generally selfish reasons (quoted in Mills 1986:3).

Unflattering views of swinging voters were not just held inside the political
parties. Political scientists also considered swinging voters to be 'not the most
rational of voters' and to be less committed basically 'out of apathy' (Jaensch
1995:138–9). They are described as 'people who know little about politics
and government, care less and may well vote only to avoid the prospect of
a fine' (Bennett 1996:166). Disdain for their perceived ignorance is long-
standing, with one political scientist in the 1960s arguing that swinging
voters were 'politically vacuous and illiterate' and 'a tremendous danger'
because they were vulnerable to scare campaigns and making 'unreasonable'
decisions based on trivia (Crisp 1965:131).

Because swinging voters are considered one of the least politically interested groups and one whose knowledge of politics is impoverished, it is
significant that they are associated with particular media. In the early 1980s,
the ALP's research suggested that politically uninterested swinging voters
were:

> essentially the products (and supporters) of mass market commercialism,
> gaining their political information from Mike Willesee or his equivalent [in
> 2007, *A Current Affair* or *Today Tonight*], the tabloid newspapers and the
> occasional commercial news bulletin (quoted in Mills 1986: 22).

Are some media 'better' than others at encouraging politically knowledgeable citizens?

There is a determined view that some media are better than others at
imparting political news and information. Printed newspapers have long
been considered the most informative and identified as key sites for rational
public debate (Habermas 1989; Putnam 2000; Schudson 1998). Studies of
political learning supported this view with findings that newspapers were

correlated with high levels of political knowledge (e.g. Druckman 2005; Robinson and Levy 1986). Reading a broadsheet in particular has been 'strongly correlated with mobilization'; that is, with people knowing more about politics, being more involved in it and believing that their involvement matters (Newton 1999:597–8).

Interest is clearly a factor that helps explain these results – the effort required to obtain and read a newspaper (especially a broadsheet) suggests that these readers are likely to be more than normally interested in public affairs. People who prefer print also generally have higher socioeconomic status and better formal education. Their backgrounds and jobs may give them greater incentive to be interested in this type of content as well as a better ability to memorise the sorts of facts that social science researchers use as indicators of political knowledge. However, even with all of these qualifiers, newspapers were still perceived to have some special qualities relating to their nature as a printed textual medium. Newspapers and print were celebrated (some might even say glorified) for having a capacity for detail and complexity and a way of demanding high concentration from readers that other media – such as television – could not achieve (e.g. Postman 1985).

As a result, television was much maligned in early studies for its 'irrational' focus and its propensity to focus on images over issues, style over substance and personality over policies. Critics of television noted that, compared to newspapers, television had much less space for detailed news (especially political news, which was not popular fare in commercial news bulletins) and was dominated by visuals that precluded issue-based analysis. Also, unlike readers of newspapers, unless the broadcast was taped, television viewers had no control over the pace at which they had to receive and then process information (Druckman 2005; Postman 1985; see also Semetko and Valkenburg 2000). In the 21st century some of these criticisms were rendered less relevant, as there was more space available for longer, more specialist news (through 24-hour news channels, for example). In an era of cable and digital television, personal video recorders (PVRs) such as TiVo and Foxtel IQ and online sharing of television content (through YouTube and the channels' own webpages, for example), individual consumers had far more control over the timing and pace of television content.

Later studies were much more open to 'the value that television ha[d] to viewers – and to democratic processes generally' (Grabe and Bucy 2009:77) and found that television even had some advantages that other media lacked. People not actively seeking political news were found to 'learn more from television' than from print, and television was especially good at reaching 'groups that tend to lack political information, such as young people, immigrants and less interested citizens' (Chaffee and Frank 1996:28, 48) as well as women, the less educated and, in the US context, African-Americans (Prior 2007:84). In other words, television seemed to lead to a wider dissemination of political information among those who would previously have avoided it.

What seemed to matter most for political learning was not so much the *medium* – an hour-long political documentary on public television, for example, might contain more information on politics than a tabloid newspaper – but the *content* and *information* delivered. Newton (1999:592) summarised the research findings thus:

> The more general [entertainment] television people watch, the less they know about politics . . . [but the] more people watch television news, the more they know about politics and the higher they rate their own interest, information and understanding of politics.

Researchers also found that there were differences between those who 'fell into the news' – who just happened to watch it because the television was on – and those who actively sought it out. Those who 'fell' into watching news seemed less able to interpret and understand it (Newton 1999). There were also important distinctions *between* different news programs. As common sense would suggest, the issues that were covered and how they were reported made a difference in terms of viewers' knowledge levels (Jerit 2009). Researchers found that a 'serious, in-depth treatment of news . . . [can] inform and mobilise, whereas a superficial and sensational treatment may induce malaise' (Newton 1999:581).

Television news and its advantages for learning seemed to apply mainly (or in some studies, only) to *public broadcasting* news. The audiences of public and commercial channels exhibited real differences in their knowledge levels (Holtz-Bacha and Norris 2001; Norris 2000). In the UK, Norris (1997a:218) found that viewing public broadcasting news was associated with higher levels of information during an election campaign, whereas commercial broadcasting news generally was not. A more recent study by

Curran et al (2009) examining television news in Denmark, Finland, the US and the UK also found that public service television fostered greater knowledge in public affairs. In Australia, studies have also pointed in this direction, with public broadcast viewers found to be more politically knowledgeable than commercial viewers (Jones and Pusey 2008).

Researchers had been grappling with the nature of television for five decades, but in the 2000s they also had to start to try and understand how the different characteristics of the internet impacted upon how political information was provided and received. This process is still in its infancy (e.g. see Eveland, Marton and Seo 2004; Hindman 2008; Prior 2007). However, one of the key initial questions has been whether, as the internet has expanded the options for news and information, it has also improved levels of political knowledge.

On this point, it is interesting that the Pew Research Center (2007), which has undertaken a regular study of current affairs knowledge in the US over the past 20 years, found in 2007 that '[despite the rise of the internet and] the fact that education levels have risen dramatically over the past 20 years, public knowledge ha[d] not increased accordingly.' Pew studies also highlighted the significance of the *content* of media rather than its *form*. Where older studies of political knowledge found that broadsheet readers were by far the most politically sophisticated, in recent Pew studies the most politically knowledgeable citizens have still had the same broad demographic characteristics; however, they use a variety of media, including traditional media but also online newspapers and political satire programs on cable television such as *The Daily Show* and *Colbert Report* (PRC 2007).

Preaching to the converted? News use and partisan preferences

The theory of 'cognitive dissonance' suggests that people have 'a drive that propels them to avoid information that is disagreeable with their attitudes or beliefs and, conversely, to seek out information that supports those views' (Shaw et al 1999). This doesn't always apply. Many people *do* listen to opposing views. News junkies especially have wide news tastes and may even deliberately seek out contrary views. In general though, according to the cognitive dissonance theory, people do not like being in a state of doubt, so they look for information that supports rather than undermines their existing beliefs. They also tend to be uncomfortable when their beliefs are challenged, especially on issues connected with their economic welfare, physical safety or strongly held values. Based on cognitive dissonance theory, it is not surprising that many people suspect that some media outlets in Australia have a left- or right-leaning stance and an audience to match.

I examine media content and claims that some media outlets are biased (either ideologically or towards a particular party) in Chapter 11. In this chapter, however, we need to examine the political preferences of news audiences and how these relate to attitude formation and media effects. The evidence I can put forward on this is based on survey data collected by Roy Morgan Research between July 2007 and June 2008, asking people about their voting preferences and media use. This was a period when Labor was in the ascendancy before an election win, so support for Labor was quite high.[2]

Broadsheet readers usually score highly on political knowledge tests but research has also found that those who have the best understanding of politics also tend to have the *strongest* party identification (Albright 2009; Lazarsfeld, Berelson and Gaudet 1944). According to Table 5.1, this is also true in Australia where broadsheet audiences are, on the evidence, a quite partisan bunch. There are relatively few who are undecided, unsure or unwilling to reveal their voting preference in surveys (compared to other media users).

Table 5.1 First preference voting intention for broadsheet newspaper audiences, 2007–08 (percentages)

	ALP	Liberal	Nationals	Greens	Other	Can't say
Population (14 years+)	**47.8**	**31.0**	**2.6**	**7.1**	**3.4**	**8.0**
Canberra Times	60.7	23.8	0.2	11.6	1.9	1.8
Age	53.9	22.9	0.9	16.1	2.4	3.8
Sydney Morning Herald	52.3	26.8	1.2	10.5	2.7	6.5
Australian	47.3	33.8	1.5	10.0	3.6	3.9
Financial Review	42.9	39.9	1.4	8.1	2.4	5.3

Note: 'Other' includes 'Democrats', 'One Nation' and 'Independent/Other'.

Source: data supplied to the author by Roy Morgan Research (Single Source Australia, July 2007–June 2008).

The broadsheets can be divided into two quite distinct partisan group-ings. The *Financial Review* and the *Australian* had a higher-than-average Liberal audience, but the other three broadsheets had more Labor and

Green voters than the general population. Labor support was especially pronounced among the *Canberra Times* readership (12.9 per cent more than the survey sample), but also among the *Age* and *Sydney Morning Herald* readers (4–6 per cent). For the *Canberra Times* there are some regional and media market factors at play because it is the only metropolitan daily newspaper in the ACT, a traditionally Labor-leaning constituency.

But overall, the broadsheet audience in 2007 was quite left-leaning, if we define this as support for the Greens, because all of the broadsheets – including the *Financial Review* and the *Australian* – had more Green voters than were present in the general population. There were twice as many Green supporters in the *Age* audience than in the general population. At the other end of the spectrum, the *Financial Review* was clearly the newspaper of choice for conservative voters. The *Australian* was not as easy to characterise. Although it also had a higher-than-normal proportion of Liberal-voting readers and has faced allegations of conservative bias (see Chapter 11), its audience still disproportionately favoured the Greens (albeit not to the extent of some of the other broadsheet audiences).

Table 5.2 First preference voting intention for ABC radio audiences in Sydney and Melbourne, 2007–08 (percentages)

	ALP	Liberal	Nationals	Greens	Other	Can't say
Population (14 years+)	**47.8**	**31.0**	**2.6**	**7.1**	**3.4**	**8.0**
ABC 774 (Melb)	49.1	30.3	1.4	11.5	2.8	4.9
ABC 702 (Syd)	51.1	27.3	0.3	11.2	2.5	7.5
ABC News Radio (Melb)	52.2	24.9	0.8	13.8	3.2	5.1
ABC News Radio (Syd)	53.5	23.2	1.3	10.6	3.7	7.7
ABC Radio National (Melb)	53.3	20.7	3.0	17.4	3.5	2.1
ABC Radio National (Syd)	52.7	18.9	3.3	17.5	3.4	4.3

Source: data supplied to the author by Roy Morgan Research (Single Source Australia, July 2007–June 2008).

The elite ABC radio audience – News Radio and Radio National – was even more left-leaning than the broadsheet audience. These two stations had a pronounced lack of Liberal voters in their audience (Table 5.2). This was especially so for Radio National in Sydney. (Only 18.9 per cent of listeners were planning to vote Liberal compared to 31 per cent in the survey sample.) This is a reflection of the Sydney radio market where, because there are several conservative talkback radio stations available, the radio audience is more polarised than in Melbourne.[3] Because conservative listeners in Sydney can opt for an overtly conservative station, this leaves the Sydney Radio National audience more dominated by Labor and Green voters. However, there is more to it than this, because the left-leaning audience holds true across both cities, with Radio National audiences in both Sydney and Melbourne twice as likely to vote for the Greens than the average: an even more Green-leaning audience than for the *Age*. By contrast, the audiences for local ABC stations more closely resembled the general population, with local ABC listeners in Melbourne and Sydney – especially Melbourne – very close to the general population in terms of their support for the Liberal Party.

Table 5.3 First preference voting intention for tabloid newspaper audiences, 2007–08 (percentages)

	ALP	Liberal	Nationals	Greens	Other	Can't say
Population (14 years+)	**47.8**	**31.0**	**2.6**	**7.1**	**3.4**	**8.0**
West Australian	40.5	43.5	1.0	7.3	3.3	4.4
Herald Sun	47.1	38.0	1.9	4.3	2.4	6.3
Examiner	48.7	37.7	0.0	7.7	0.6	5.3
Adelaide Advertiser	46.0	37.1	0.5	4.2	4.6	7.6
Daily Telegraph	49.0	35.2	2.6	3.6	3.2	6.5
Courier-Mail	50.5	33.5	3.8	5.0	2.1	5.1
Mercury	52.4	28.0	0.0	13.7	2.0	3.9
mX (Qld)	43.5	25.2	0.0	23.8	5.0	2.5
mX (Vic)	52.4	23.4	4.2	11.5	3.2	5.3
mX (NSW)	58.6	20.5	0.0	10.2	3.3	7.3

Source: data supplied to the author by Roy Morgan Research (Single Source Australia, July 2007–June 2008).

The tabloid audience was a much more conservative audience, with the notable exception of free commuter newspapers (*mX*) (Table 5.3). The younger readers of *mX* were very different from the other traditional tabloid readers – a deliberate outcome of a strategy to attract new and younger readers. *mX* readers more closely resembled broadsheet readers; they were far more likely to vote Labor or Green than the readers of other tabloids. All of the other traditional tabloids (except the *Mercury*) had a higher proportion of Liberal voters in their audiences than in the general population – especially the *West Australian*, the *Herald Sun*, the *Examiner*, the *Advertiser* and the *Daily Telegraph*. But they also had – with the exception of the *West Australian* – Labor-voting readers in similar, or even slightly higher, proportions to the general population.

Like the *Canberra Times*, the *West Australian* is something of a special case: a monopoly newspaper serving an area that had unusually strong political preferences in 2007, in this case for the Coalition. A number of factors influenced this in 2007, including economic prosperity in Western Australia and the Liberal campaign message that the mining boom would be put at risk by a vote for Labor, but also the behaviour of two union officials that made headlines in WA during the campaign. At the election, the vote for Labor in WA was 6.6 per cent less than the national average (AEC 2007b). Regional factors in political preferences also help explain why, unusually for tabloids, the two Tasmanian newspapers – the *Mercury* and the *Examiner* – had higher proportions of Greens voters than the average population. The Greens have a strong support base in Tasmania, where the party developed in the 1970s.

If tabloid audiences were more conservative than the population, they were perhaps somewhat less so than we might expect, given claims of a Murdoch-owned tabloid press advocating right-wing views (and not just in Australia). As in the UK, it may be that the Australian popular press is 'more right-wing than its readers' (Curran 1998:86). Some commentators claimed this was a factor in 2007 and that News Limited papers misread the change in political mood that had led to a shift in support for the ALP and remained, in Rodney Tiffen's analysis (2008:25), 'systematically biased against Labor in [their] news judgements and framing of stories' during the election.

Table 5.4 First preference voting intention for talkback radio audiences (Sydney and Melbourne), 2007–08 (percentages)

	ALP	Liberal	Nationals	Greens	Other	Can't say
Population (14 years+)	**47.8**	**31.0**	**2.6**	**7.1**	**3.4**	**8.0**
2GB	28.4	58.5	0.5	1.4	2.6	8.6
3AW	38.5	48.6	0.6	3.2	1.6	7.6
2UE	41.3	45.5	0.4	1.6	2.6	8.6

Source: data supplied to the author by Roy Morgan Research (Single Source Australia, July 2007–June 2008).

Compared to the tabloid audience, commercial talkback listeners were a more staunchly conservative audience. Table 5.4 shows that 2GB, 2UE and 3AW listeners were at least 14 per cent more likely to vote for the Liberals than the general population. Of these, 2GB's audience was by far the most conservative and a staggering 27.5 per cent more likely to vote Liberal. Audiences for all three stations were highly unlikely to vote Green. The commercial talkback audience was, as many commentators pointed out, a

Table 5.5 First preference voting intention for television news and current affairs audiences, 2007–08 (percentages)

	ALP	Liberal	Nationals	Greens	Other	No answer
Population (14 years+)	47.8	31.0	2.6	7.1	3.4	8.0
Current affairs						
A Current Affair	45.4	38.6	1.0	4.8	2.6	7.6
60 Minutes	47.9	35.4	0.7	5.9	2.7	7.4
Today Tonight	48.5	34.5	1.0	4.8	3.0	8.2
Q&A	45.5	34.0	3.1	8.0	2.9	6.5
7:30 Report	48.8	31.5	2.9	8.0	3.3	5.5
Sunday	50.4	31.4	0.8	7.0	3.1	7.3
Four Corners	49.2	31.3	2.7	7.3	3.4	6.1
Meet the Press	51.9	30.7	0.8	6.7	2.4	7.5
Insiders	52.2	28.9	2.6	7.9	3.1	5.3
Lateline	54.3	25.8	1.9	9.8	3.1	5.1
Evening news						
National Nine News	46.8	37.7	0.9	4.2	2.6	7.7
Ten News	48.4	36.0	1.1	4.8	3.2	6.5
Seven Nightly News	48.9	35.5	1.1	3.7	2.5	8.4
ABC News	48.3	32.0	2.7	8.0	3.1	5.9
SBS World News	53.5	26.0	1.6	10.3	2.9	5.7

Note: News program figures relate to weeknight audiences for primetime programs.

Source: data supplied to the author by Roy Morgan Research (Single Source Australia, July 2007–June 2008).

key conservative heartland in the 2000s and an audience that John Howard diligently courted during his tenure (Ward 2002a).

To examine television audiences, in Table 5.5 I have combined the elite and popular television news and current affairs programs because there are so few commercial current affairs programs (and so few news programs overall) that it makes more sense to analyse them comparatively. The television news and current affairs audience is much less overtly partisan than the newspaper and radio audiences examined above. However, there are still some important differences between commercial and public audiences. Australians who supported Labor were more likely to turn to the ABC for their current affairs, while supporters of the Coalition chose Channel Nine. Elite current affairs programs such as *Lateline, Insiders, Sunday* and *Meet the Press* had a higher proportion of Labor voters, while Coalition voters were more attracted to commercial channels, especially Channel Nine. *A Current Affair* attracted the most politically conservative audience.

Commercial news bulletin viewers were more likely to vote for the Coalition than the general population, but they also included proportions of Labor voters that closely mirrored the general population. *SBS News* was the only news bulletin to have a more markedly partisan audience, with high proportions of Labor and Green voters. Despite allegations that the ABC was serving a left-wing constituency, the audience for *ABC News* looked very similar to the general survey population and *The 7:30 Report* also had similar proportions of Coalition and Labor supporters to the general population. The public broadcasting program with the lowest proportion of Labor voters (and the highest proportion of Coalition viewers – including Nationals voters) was *Q&A*. This is interesting because it was a program that was designed to showcase ideological diversity in the wake of pro-Labor bias allegations levelled at the ABC in the 2000s (see Chapter 11). *Q&A* had well-known conservatives on the panel and the ABC had made a determined effort to find Coalition supporters for the studio audience.

An earlier survey on television viewing and voting intention had been conducted in 2003–05 and there were some interesting changes by the time of the 2007–08 survey (RMR 2005). Partisan gaps between audiences had narrowed. The Channel Nine news and current affairs audience was still more conservative than the general population, but this had diminished. This may reflect changes of ownership at Nine following the death of Kerry Packer. Nine's new owner (from 2007) was a private equity firm more focused on profits than on political influence of the type that Packer exerted through his media assets. The shift may also reflect general pressures to be more centrist and to aim for a more mid-market audience at a time of diminishing returns and diminishing audiences. The ABC audience had also converged more in the middle since the earlier survey. This could reflect programming changes made by the ABC (especially following all the bias allegations in the 2000s), but probably more strongly reflects how the elite media audience (who were generally more supportive of Labor) had been moving away from television (as explored in Chapter 3).

Media effects and election outcomes

In Chapter 2, we noted that very keen politics followers were particularly interested in the 1993, 1998 and 2007 elections (Table 2.4). Now that we know more about the partisan composition of the keen elite media audience, it suggests one reason why those particular elections may have been of interest. These were the only three elections since 1990 when Labor garnered more than 50 per cent of the two-party preferred vote (although it still lost in 1998) (AEC 2007a). Because the elite media audience consists disproportionately of Labor supporters, it makes sense that they would switch on more for an election when their preferred party was doing well and had a chance of winning. This partisan factor may also help explain why there was a large jump in ratings for watching polling night programs in 2007 when the Labor-leaning elite audience was particularly interested in the result.

However, there is also a broader ideological dimension related to media use and interest levels. Tranter found that, while there was little difference in knowledge levels between those who voted for the major parties in Australia in 2004, there *was* a difference in terms of ideological commitments, and those 'who place[d] themselves on the Left of the political spectrum [were] more knowledgeable than the Right...' International studies have found similar patterns and have concluded that this was again related to the link between interest and knowledge. Those on the Left tend to be 'more politically interested and active than the Right...' (Tranter 2007:86, 77). Those on the Left also tend to favour the media outlets that studies have found are linked with higher levels of political knowledge (broadsheets and public broadcasting).

It is very likely that similar links would also be evident for the audiences of elite media websites. In the US, research has found that 'liberals dominate the audience for politics online' and high-frequency visitors to political websites are 'more than twice as [likely to be] liberals [than] conservatives' (Hindman 2008:23). Even a cursory scan of the key political blogs in Australia suggests that there are more left-leaning blogs than right-wing ones (see Chapter 10).

Before we jump to any conclusions about a 'left-wing' media, we should note that the tendency for hard-news consumers to be left-leaning reflects some very broad social factors, especially level of education. People with university education tend to be socially more liberal and are also more likely to choose broadsheet and public broadcasting news formats. It is also far too simplistic to see the elite audience as consisting entirely of left-leaning partisans. There were some elite outlets that attracted a high proportion of conservatives, including the *Financial Review*, the *Australian*, *60 Minutes*,

Meet the Press and the now defunct *Sunday* and *Business Sunday*. Even among the newspaper readerships with the highest proportions of Labor and Green voters, one in four readers still planned to vote for the conservative parties.

We should also note that the elite audience is vastly outnumbered by the large general audience. This audience is not only much larger but also less partisan and, in theory, therefore more open to external influences. It also includes more of the all-important swinging voters. Therefore, *if* media content is 'biased', it is conservative bias in the popular commercial media outlets that would affect far more people and probably with much greater impact. This seems an important point, given that the general news audience did have more conservative social and political views.

In the 2001, 2004 and 2007 elections the results were determined by an average of 4 percentage points (AEC 2007a). Close margins mean that neither major party 'can afford to assume that election campaigns are irrelevant' (Tiffen 1989:144). As we have seen, the effects of election campaigns are not uniformly felt, but neither do they have to be because there are politically strategic voting blocs – especially swinging voters in marginal seats. If we consider media effects in this way – in terms of voting preferences – election campaigns seem to have the *least* effect on voters who are the *most* politically engaged (Albright 2009; Lazarsfeld, Berelson and Gaudet 1944; see Ward 1995).

Relatively few citizens pay close attention to political news, 'but those who do tend to be older and more strongly partisan, and therefore . . . less susceptible to shifting their political attitudes' (Saad 2005). Political junkies who most actively use the media for political news tend to be loyal partisans who have determined their vote well in advance of a campaign, and who then tend to interpret media content in ways that reinforce their existing predispositions (Denemark, Ward and Bean 2007:90, 107; Lazarsfeld, Berelson and Gaudet 1944). When people know something about the news, have first-hand experience of it, or have well-established attitudes and opinions, then the mass media may have little influence. John Zaller (1992) has even argued that those who follow politics most closely tend to filter out information that conflicts with their partisan predispositions.

However, influence occurs across a wide spectrum. Even staunchly committed partisan voters, who are unlikely to change their vote on the basis of media reports during a six-week campaign, may nonetheless be influenced by media reports in terms of what they assess to be the most important issues facing the nation as well as how they evaluate politics, the leaders, parties and election policies. A 'rusted on' partisan may stick with their party but still influence politics by advocating a different leader, or stating that their party should pay more attention to a particular policy area, for example.

Most people, however, do not have well-formed attitudes on more than a handful of political issues (Delli Carpini and Keeter 1996). And on the issues that people know little about, care little about, have little first-hand experience of, or find it difficult to make up their minds about, then the mass media may have more influence. The traditional view is that those who know less about politics are more likely to be influenced by media content because they have less information to draw upon to assess it, less strongly held views and less partisan cues (Lazarsfeld, Berelson and Gaudet 1944).

This is the classic reasoning behind party appeals aimed at swinging voters who are considered 'politically ignorant' and liable to vote for 'superficial' reasons. However, in a later thesis Converse (1966) found that, rather than the 'politically ignorant', it was 'moderately sophisticated voters' who were sometimes the most susceptible to persuasion in election campaigns because they paid 'enough attention to campaigns to be fairly heavily exposed to persuasive messages but lack[ed] the sophistication to be able to resist' (Zaller 1989:181).

In the 2001–07 elections, aside from the usual swinging voters, three main examples were given of important groups of 'softly committed' voters who seemed to make a difference to the election result. Significantly, not everyone agreed that these groups actually existed in psephological terms or that they had as large an impact as was claimed, but they nonetheless entered campaigning folklore about the election outcomes.

One of the groups was 'Howard's battlers' who were, allegedly, a blue-collar and usually Labor-voting block who instead supported Howard and the Liberals between 1996 to 2004 only to desert them – mostly over *WorkChoices*, according to the most prevalent narrative, in 2007. (For views on the 'battler' phenomenon see Brent 2004; Goot and Watson 2007.)

Another group of concern for Labor were inner-city progressive, normally Labor, voters who shifted to the Greens, especially in 2001 in response to Labor's position on the *Tampa*.

Finally, there was a group that were said to especially worry Liberal strategists in 2004 and 2007. Dubbed the 'doctors' wives', these were people on the top of the income ladder who could normally be counted on to vote Liberal but who were moving to the Left over non-economic issues, especially the Iraq War, refugees, David Hicks' incarceration and the environment.

During an election, parties have to reach many different groups: their loyal supporters, those who might desert them, those voters who are only 'softly committed', the undecided, the uninterested and especially those in marginal seats. Some groups clearly take precedence over others, as they are judged more strategically significant to the outcome. But even if the parties could somehow identify, locate and reach all of these voters, this still brings us back to the central question of media effects research: just how does media content influence people's political attitudes and behaviour?

After decades of studies, there is no grand, single theory that can explain this and it is likely there never will be. Academic research into media effects has generated theories and findings that have ranged markedly from serious concerns in the 1920s that media content had an immensely powerful influence on citizens, to a later position – especially prevalent in the 1950s – that media effects were only of minimal significance in explaining important decisions such as voting choices, and that other factors relating to socialisation and background were more important (Klapper 1960; Lazarsfeld, Berelson and Gaudet 1944). Since the 1970s, the pendulum has swung back to a more mid-way position, which suggests that media effects can be significant, especially since socialisation cues – such as class, partisanship and voting as your parents do – have broken down.

Media are now widely judged to play a key role in political socialisation and learning, but this is not as simple as content being transmitted from sender to receiver and then swallowed whole and unaltered. Media effects depend upon availability, choice, content and the characteristics of the person who is accessing media content. Overall, it seems that multiple messages penetrate differently into the electorate depending upon media content and the voters' level of awareness and responsiveness (Zaller 1989). However, what the studies of the past four decades have documented is that, given the right conditions, there are some specific ways in which media content influences audiences.

Framing, priming and agenda-setting

The basic finding of *agenda-setting* research – and this finding has been replicated extensively since the 1970s – is that the more prominent an issue is in the news, the greater is the impact of that issue on political attitudes. Agenda-setting theory is neatly encapsulated in the oft-quoted statement by Bernard Cohen that: 'The press may not be successful much of the time in telling people what to think, but it is stunningly successful in telling its readers what to think about' (quoted in Iyengar and Kinder 1987:2). In other words, the media are very effective in directing attention. Studies have shown that, if you ask people which are the most important issues at stake during an election campaign, the issues they identify will generally match up with those accorded the most media coverage (McCombs and Shaw 1972). This theory is so widely known that some media outlets proudly claim the mantle of 'agenda-setters'. (This is tested in Chapter 8.)

But, as early media theorists suspected and politicians have always known, media outlets can have more influence than merely placing an issue on the agenda. The term *framing* is used to draw attention to the fact that how people think about an issue can depend upon how it is framed by the media, including the language and images media reports use. Frames 'highlight some bits of information about an item . . . thereby elevating them in salience . . . making them more noticeable, meaningful, or memorable to audiences'. Reporting elections as if they were a 'horse-race' is an example of an organising frame; several others are illustrated in Chapter 9. The frame used in media reports can determine whether people 'notice and how they understand and remember' an issue or problem (Entman 2002:392, 393). For example, through selection, omission, placement, choice of words and visual images, media outlets can (inadvertently as well as deliberately) promote a particular definition of a problem as well as its cause and recommend remedies.

Finally, *priming* theory suggests that media content can alter the criteria by which we make our judgements. We can be primed to consider certain issues when evaluating parties, leaders or policies, for example. We may not alter our core values and beliefs as a result of media coverage, but it can lead us to alter the relative weight we give to various considerations and this can influence our final evaluation. A key study by Iyengar and Kinder (1987) found that voters evaluated political leaders in terms of topics they had recently noticed in the news. For example, where a voter might normally assess the party leaders in terms of their experience or intelligence, if the issue that dominated media coverage was terrorism, this could prime them to instead assess them in terms of who was toughest, was most resolute or had the strongest defence policy.

Conclusion

There are strong connections between political interest, knowledge and participation and these are, in turn, strongly linked with media use, education, wealth and status. A person's background matters when it comes to knowledge about public affairs and the motivation and self-efficacy to participate in political life, but so too does their use of different media. The research findings have been strikingly consistent in that, when it comes to politics, broadsheet readers and public broadcast viewers are better informed and more likely to participate. This may well be because their background and skills would have meant they would do well on knowledge tests and participate more than usual, regardless of whatever media they chose. However, we cannot discount that there might also be a level of *benefit* in using the 'hard news' or elite media sources. Just as there is a demonstrable benefit in accessing education for social and economic mobility, perhaps news journalism is also a form of information and knowledge that has tangible outcomes.

Media have an influence not just on individuals' levels of knowledge and participation but also on the conduct and outcome of elections. The extent of media influence differs between individuals and is contingent on a range of variables, but the parties campaign on the basis that these effects occur and that they matter a great deal. The parties have key constituencies of voters that they must reach during an election campaign, but media outlets also have particular audiences that they need to cater for during an election and this informs how they produce the news. Some audiences are highly knowledgeable and interested; some are partisan with strongly held values; and some just want to avoid political news as much as possible. How news workers conceive their audiences – and what needs and preferences they perceive those audiences to have – are important factors in how they produce news.

Part II

WHERE DOES ELECTION NEWS COME FROM AND WHAT IS IT ABOUT?

Chapter 6

CREATING ELECTION NEWS: JOURNALISTS

Politicians use media to communicate to voters with the aim of persuading them. However, media outlets and media workers are not merely a conduit for these messages or a neutral arbiter of them; they are also actors in their own right with their own strategic purposes and messages to communicate. This is not the same as saying that political reporters are 'players' who have specific political agendas to pursue (although this is a claim that is sometimes made). Rather, this is a much broader point: that news workers are not separate from political events but are central to them. This chapter looks at the role that journalists, especially, play in election reporting.

While journalists are often portrayed as observers and recorders of politics, in reality they often cause news to happen rather than just report it. For example, by ringing sources and asking for quotes on possible events, they can set those events in motion. When they repeatedly draw attention to a leader's poor opinion polls, they help create an environment that is ripe for a leadership challenge. They also have a crucial role to play in who the parties select as leader, because a leadership aspirant's media skills are viewed as a key criterion of their electability. Election campaigns are really the ultimate manifestation of the centrality of the media. As Tiffen (1989:127) has pointed out:

> There is an unacknowledged irony in news coverage of election campaigns: the media maintain the pretence that they are reporting a campaign which exists independently of them, when in fact the primary purpose of those campaign activities is precisely to secure favourable news coverage.

Because television was the key medium for Australian politicians from the 1980s to the 2000s, it profoundly shaped the events it reported. Television needs visual images and colourful events – 'No pictures, no story' is a television motto – so politicians set out to provide a steady stream of fresh images during an election campaign. They may be shaking hands with voters at a shopping centre, wearing a hospital gown and visiting patients, announcing their environment policy in a forest or sitting with schoolchildren in a classroom reading them stories. These events are not recorded just because the television cameras happen to be there; they are entirely designed for television: they happen because of the medium's instigation. Photographs taken for newspapers are also similarly staged or contrived. Even the most powerful political leaders in the country will often comply with instructions to make something more visually interesting or to recreate an event for photographers.

Journalists usually have a professional conception of themselves as independent, neutral and detached observers, but we know from studies of how news content is made that their accounts of political events are laden with value judgements and subjectivities. This is not necessarily about political 'bias' so much as it is a general result of the way that journalists invariably transform messages in the process of newsgathering and reporting because they select events and information, they structure and frame them and they construct interpretations. By performing these functions, journalists occupy a powerful role.

Australian journalists

Despite their perceived power, there have been relatively few studies of Australian journalists. One of the largest to survey their backgrounds was performed by John Henningham in the 1990s. He found that journalists were more likely than other Australians to come from middle-class homes and to have 'a more privileged upbringing than the population in general' (including private schooling), and that the industry was a 'white Anglo-Saxon occupation' dominated by men (Henningham 1998a:338). Women journalists were fewer in number and generally had lower rank and lower pay (MEAA 1996). By 2005, female journalists still comprised only 37 per cent of Press Gallery journalists (88 compared to 153 men) (Fitzgerald

2008:14). Women also remained underrepresented in media management and positions with decision- and policy-making power.

Traditionally, political journalism was a high-status specialty, especially in the 1970s and 1980s, but as other types of news grew in prominence and commercial value – including sports, lifestyle and entertainment – the status of political reporting diminished. Reporters on some other beats could command larger audiences and salaries and young journalists were 'increasingly [using] Canberra as a stepping stone to the big job in Sydney or a foreign posting' (Oakes in Price 1999). In the 1990s, when they were compared with other journalists, political reporters – especially in the Press Gallery – were still an elite within an elite, though; better paid and even more likely than their colleagues to be privately and tertiary educated (Henningham 1995:325). Their attitudes to their work also differed from those of their colleagues. They were more likely to express a deep interest in news and current affairs and indicate a desire to serve the public by 'righting wrongs or exposing corruption'. They were also more committed to an advocacy role for journalists including being critical, investigative and interpretative rather than 'just reporting the facts' (Henningham 1995:326, 328).

In terms of their political views, journalists in general and Press Gallery reporters specifically are more likely to consider themselves left-of-centre than the population at large although, compared to American journalists, Australians were much more likely to choose a middle-of-the-road position (Henningham 1995:322; 1998b). This general finding, the tendency for journalists to be left-leaning, has been replicated in a number of studies both in Australia and overseas. As one noted, there is 'ample evidence . . . that people who work in the media are relatively liberal' (Gaziano quoted in Henningham 1995:322). This is related to several factors, but especially to education.

Until the 1970s, the standard entry path to journalism was via a cadetship and in the early 1960s only 5 per cent of Australian journalists had a degree, but by the 1990s over half had studied at university (Henningham 1998a:336). That figure would be even higher in 2007, with 'the majority' of Gallery journalists having a Communications or Arts degree (Fitzgerald 2008:18). As researchers in other countries have noted, these patterns resemble the 'profile of other professionals' in the sense that 'like most people with a social science or humanities degree, journalists tend to be socially more liberal than the general population and to have a keener

sense of social responsibility' (Graber 2006:87). The shift in their education base meant that journalists, by the 2000s, closely resembled the elite
audience in terms of their characteristics and preferences and it also led to
important debates about whether the occupation had changed from a trade
or craft, learnt on the job, to a profession.

Journalism has important features that indicate its professional nature,
including a strong sense of purpose as a public service. However, journalists
do not enjoy the autonomy in their working lives that other professional
occupations have (Schultz 1998). Those in the traditional professions –
such as lawyers, doctors and academics – collectively and individually
make more of the important decisions about what work they do and how.
These other professionals developed, over a long period of time, exclusive control over the services they provided by holding a tight monopoly
over entry through training and licensing. The number of practitioners is
limited in these areas (because entry is based on student intake numbers
and positions available) and this drives up salaries and prestige.

The older professions instituted professional and ethical codes and
established a set of skills and knowledge that 'belonged' exclusively to their
profession. They also controlled resources crucial to the conduct of their
field of work (such as access to medical equipment; the ability to represent
a defendant in court or to provide examinations that could be accredited
towards a degree). As a result, no-one can just set up shop as a doctor,
lawyer or academic. By contrast, many people can (and do) write, gather
facts and put forward opinions and call themselves journalists, especially
in the digital era.

The working environment of journalists

One of the key factors that affect the working environment of journalists
is the extent to which they are free from restrictive laws, censorship and
editorial pressure from the State. Journalists in Australia work within a
relatively free media environment. There is no explicit constitutional protection for freedom of the press (as in the US), but significant High Court
judgments in the 1990s pointed to an implied right of free political speech
in the Australian Constitution. The relative freedom journalists have is crucial, because it means they can report on political matters and investigate

powerful actors without undue influence from the State. However, this does not mean they face no limitations on their work, and some of those they face relate to the way they work in organisations with chains of command. As Ian Ward (1995:102) notes, journalists:

> may see themselves as independent and independently-minded professionals, but the great majority in fact work in highly bureaucratic organisations, where their superiors will have the final say in whether (and how) their stories appear.

Especially important are the editors, producers and senior reporters who choose stories, assign reporters to cover them and who ultimately accept, reject or alter what other journalists submit. Socialisation and informal communication within these hierarchies is also important. Ward (1995:104) notes that:

> reporters, for instance, need not be officially instructed on the political line they should take in reporting election stories. They will quickly learn what is appropriate from the way in which sub-editors run, cut, rewrite or 'spike' their copy.

Although most journalists entering the media industry today have tertiary education, much is still learnt on the job and through socialisation. In newsrooms there is a craft element to journalism, focused on mastering the technical parts of the job. These include writing (or speaking) in clear language and conveying all the important parts of a news story within limits of time or space and by deadline. There remains a strong sense that journalism is learnt 'by doing' and, as Graber (2006:89) notes, this means that 'colleagues and settings strongly influence newspeople.' This influence is not always positive or benign. Some analysts suggest it drives journalists to write for each other rather than their audiences and others note that journalism is highly competitive. Journalists are in competition with each other and they compete not only between rival outlets but also within organisations.

Newsrooms are considered to be highly stressful working environments, not only because of the degree of supervision, competition and peer scrutiny but also because of the nature of the work with its constant demands and deadlines, creativity harnessed into institutional demands and long and unsocial working hours. In recent years, changing technology and work patterns, multiskilling and digitisation have added to this. The new media environment:

> requires journalists to write, handle images, audio and video [and] ... goes beyond redesigning news for a new platform, demanding intensive interview techniques ... sometimes asking the same question for different technologies (MEAA 2008:18).

Increased workloads, a lack of training and 'promotions without pay rises' are said to have contributed to 'lower newsroom morale' (MEAA 2008:12–13). In the commercial sector, as advertising revenues and audiences diminished in the 2000s, there were reductions in staff, centralisation and other cost-cutting measures.

Media ownership and economic factors

Ownership and editorial interference have long been considered major pressures on journalists. In the 2000s, there was an argument that ownership no longer mattered as much as it once did, because we had moved on from the days of the powerful press barons and many current owners were more concerned with economic success than wielding political power through their media assets. Yet others noted that large media businesses such as News Corp/News Limited were still tightly controlled and run as a family business with a high degree of proprietor intervention.

Editorial interference in journalists' work is not always overt, nor does it always relate to partisan aims or political agendas (as discussed in Chapter 11). Ownership differs in significant respects from the old press baron model, but it still has a major impact on how Australian journalists, most of whom work for commercial organisations, do their jobs. Colourful stories of owners giving 'riding instructions' (instructions on political slant) to their editors do exist (and are discussed in Chapter 11), but the more common forms of proprietor intervention come through newsroom organisation. This includes which priorities and interests determine the scope and character of news coverage for that outlet, which areas of reporting are given most resources and support, what the organisations consider they can afford to cover, relationships between marketing and content and whether subeditors are allowed to rewrite copy without reporter approval.

For journalists in both commercial and publicly funded media, economic facts circumscribe their day-to-day activities. In commercial organisations, news is a means to an end. It is a way to attract audiences and journalistic choices are constrained by this. Because the advertising rates that the media company can charge are determined by its circulation or ratings and the social characteristics (especially the disposable income) of its audience members, the news must have sufficient appeal to deliver the right audience to advertisers. In a newspaper, most of the space is actually taken up by advertising – not news – and while, in television news, advertising is a smaller proportion of the total, the advertisements have a significant impact on pace, structure and content of the news. In public broadcasting organisations such as the ABC, a fixed budget constrains newsgathering resources.

Ultimately, all media organisations – commercial, publicly funded and even small alternative outlets – have to constrain the costs of producing and distributing news. This is a less entertaining fact than stories of Murdoch haranguing editors on the phone, but ultimately it is economic circumstances that are likely to constrain newsgathering and reporting more deeply and routinely. These include the underlying commercial profit motive of most media organisations, as well as newsroom organisation and the technical constraints of news reporting that impact upon all.

Before we move on from economic factors, we should also note that there are strong economic links between the media and the powerful political figures that they scrutinise. Media companies donate money to the parties. For example, in 2007–08, Australia's largest commercial radio company Austereo donated over $100 000 in air-time to both the Labor and the Liberal parties; Village Roadshow (which owns Austereo) gave the ALP over $290 000 and the Liberals over $197 000, Network Ten gave $75 000 to both parties and PBL Media gave Labor $50 000 and the Liberals $20 000. The money flow also works back the other way. Parties pay media companies during an election to have their arguments put forward through political advertising. Government advertising is also a major stream of revenue for commercial media organisations, especially television companies but also newspapers (Young 2006; Young 2010).

Media policy and consolidation

Media policy has shaped the nature of the Australian media and the working environment of journalists. Law changes on media ownership in 1986–87 triggered a turbulent period of multiple ownership changes and poor management, with some networks going into receivership because of debts. As a result, the *Broadcasting Services Act 1992* reflected policy more focused on economic viability and efficiency and also allowed greater industry self-regulation. These changes strengthened the position of the three commercial broadcasters; this has been an ongoing theme in media policy development in Australia, where policies have tended to be highly favourable to established major owners (Chadwick 1989).

Before the 2007 election, the Howard government made major changes to media laws which came into effect seven months before the election. The key plank of the changes was to water down restrictions on cross-media ownership that had been put in place by the previous Labor government. To stop greater media ownership concentration, Labor had prevented newspaper owners from owning either radio or television assets in the same market, and vice-versa. Journalists at Fairfax had been among the most enthusiastic supporters of these cross-media ownership requirements, because they prevented a Kerry Packer takeover of Fairfax. However, in the new media environment of the early 2000s, Fairfax CEO Fred Hilmer (2002) argued that the rules needed to be scrapped if Fairfax was to obtain the critical mass it needed to survive in the world of global media. In general, journalists were not so keen on the changes, though. In one poll, over 80 per cent opposed the new laws on the grounds that they would lower the quality and diversity of news coverage (RMR 2006).

After the new laws relaxing ownership restrictions were proclaimed, a round of asset-buying and merging ensued. Fairfax, one of the largest employers of journalists in Australia, then merged with Rural Press – which reduced the number of major newspaper owners by one – and entered into a complex deal with two other media groups that netted it several radio stations, including talkback stations 2UE and 3AW. The asset-buying was widely viewed as a pre-emptive move to enlarge Fairfax so it could avoid being bought out by any other large player, but it was an expensive strategy that contributed to Fairfax's $2.3 billion debt. Trying to adjust to a changing media environment, Fairfax undertook a 'strategic reorientation of the company' (Fairfax Media 2008b:3), developing into a multimedia company that included radio, websites, agricultural magazines and music, moving away from newspapers as its core business and instituting a round of redundancies and other cost-cutting measures. But declining advertising revenue and the impact of the global financial crisis saw Fairfax's shares drop to a 15-year low in 2008, leading to speculation about its long-term future (Maiden 2008; Mayne 2008).

A reduced number of media owners was the outcome of the 2006–07 law changes. This was the continuation of a process of ownership consolidation that had been occurring for decades and had led Australia to have 'the most concentrated press ownership among established democracies' (Tiffen and Gittins 2004:182). By 2007, only three newspaper owners – News Limited, Fairfax Media and APN News – owned every Australian newspaper except one metropolitan (the *West Australian*) and two regional dailies (APC 2008:1–3). News Limited and Fairfax controlled more than 90 per cent of newspaper circulation between them (Gardiner-Garden and Chowns 2006). In commercial broadcasting, there are also a limited number of owners. There are six main operators of commercial television in Australia and the most popular radio stations (those that reach over 10 per cent of the population) are owned by ten main operators. Putting aside its broader impact on diversity and choice, this makes a very narrow employer base for journalists in Australia. It constrains job opportunities and job security, but it also limits the degree to which they can take risks or challenge traditional orthodoxies in their newsrooms.

Competition and cooperation in difficult times

The business model for news organisations changed dramatically in the 2000s. The greater choice of media and leisure activities (especially the internet) saw the old media organisations face new competition for their audiences' attention. This might not have been so damning (smaller, niche audiences can still be profitable) but for the fact that, at the same time, they were also losing advertisers to cheaper and more effectively targeted means of advertising, especially on the internet (see Chapter 10).

Large media companies were still highly profitable but, by the time of the 2007 election, were experiencing leaner times than when newspapers had a monopoly (or duopoly) on classified advertising and a television licence was considered a 'licence to print money'. Increased commercial pressures, lower profits and an uncertain future saw a search for cheaper models of journalism. Sky News exemplified the approach. It did not seek a mass audience, but was a niche news provider. It drew a lot of its content from elsewhere and its content was packaged and repackaged, used and reused. It had a very small number of staff doing many different tasks, including work that journalists do not traditionally perform. At Sky, reporters did their own make-up, paid for their own clothes, wrote their own scripts, edited their own videos and even operated automated cameras with their feet.

Diversification was another strategy employed by organisations, including moving into entertainment as well as news. There was also increased cooperation between the remaining large media companies. Organisations that were fierce competitors were now sometimes partners – for example, PBL and News Limited as partners in pay TV operator Foxtel (along with Telstra). Sometimes they were linked – Murdoch purchased a small share in Fairfax in 2007 – and sometimes they were allies with shared aims, as when they were promoting relaxation of media laws or looking to cooperate over erecting paywalls for their internet content (see Chapter 10).

Professionalism

As Curran (1998:89) notes, within journalism there is a strong element of professional belief about what journalism is, how it should be and how it can best serve society and 'this public interest component transcend[s] organizations ... [and] provides a potential counter balance to press control' either by owners or the State. Journalists may not have obtained the autonomy of other professions, but they did develop strong professional values. Many journalists were highly committed to the notion of a 'watchdog' role for the media and to serving and enlightening their communities. There are political journalists in Australia who are renowned for their thoroughness, fairness and accuracy over long careers.

Journalists 'take their professional reputations seriously' (Ward 1995:109) and journalistic norms and values are a key to understanding their work. Objectivity has been one the most central values of journalism: that news will be reported accurately, fairly and independently. This is viewed as especially important to political reporting and elections (see Chapter 11). However, journalistic norms tend to exist in journalism training, self-conceptions and socialisation within workplaces, rather than being written down as a letter of the law in formal documents. The closest thing to a professional journalism code in Australia is the MEAA Code of Ethics, but it applies only to journalists who are members of the MEAA (not to non-members or editors, managers or owners) (Alliance Online 2009).

The Code and its penalties are also somewhat ambivalently applied. It seems that no recent breach of the Code has been used to dismiss or expel an MEAA member and there is no record of fines being handed out in recent years.[1] Ambivalence would hardly be surprising though, given that this is a union – an organisation normally aimed at protecting members and their entitlements and job conditions – which has placed itself in the position of sanctioning and penalising members for poor professional conduct. That it saw a need to take on this role reflects the lack of a defined entry route for journalism, the lack of a central body overseeing the entry or accreditation of journalists, and the possibility that ethics may not be a high priority within media organisations that have other aims.

This does not mean that journalists are unaccountable. There are a number of players involved in monitoring their activities – some more actively than others – including the Australian Press Council, the courts, their peers, the *Media Watch* program on the ABC, lawyers, academics and audience members. Journalists are aware of, and anticipate, scrutiny and complaint. There are many stories of politicians ringing journalists (or their editors) to complain about what they perceive as unfair treatment. Some have made their complaints publicly. In the 2000s, as journalists posted their content online, they began to experience instant feedback with audience members posting comments, corrections or critiques. Increased scrutiny of their work has also been made possible by means of news archives, databases and search engines that have increased the ability of people to check and compare journalists' reports over time or with other sources.

But it is not only new technology that is leading to more opportunity for complaints. Conformist pressures on journalistic norms and values – including notions of what is proper and relevant – broke down in the 2000s. The definition of what was 'in the public interest' was increasingly fluid. In 2002, Laurie Oakes revealed an affair between Cheryl Kernot and Gareth Evans, based on his view that the matter was in the public interest after she omitted it from her 'tell-all' book. In 2004, the marital infidelities of Ross Cameron, the member for Parramatta, were widely reported. There were many other examples of reporting what once would have been considered private matters from both state and federal politics. Previously sacrosanct 'off-the-record' conversations between politicians and journalists were also judged to be reportable in some circumstances. For example, two months before the 2007 election, three senior Press Gallery journalists reported that Peter Costello told them at a private dinner two years earlier that he had planned to challenge John Howard and, that if he lost, would go to the backbench and carp at Howard until he destroyed his leadership.

Newsgathering

Selection

One of the most crucial roles that journalists and media managers play is making judgements about which issues to report and which to leave out, as well as about a story's placement, priority, emphasis and prominence. Some stories are so 'big' that they have to be covered – natural disasters, wars, the death of an 'A list' celebrity, for example – but for most a decision has to be made about whether they should be omitted or included and what degree of attention they deserve. A national election is clearly a big story that cannot be ignored, but the extent of its coverage can vary a great deal between news outlets.

On any given day of an election campaign, there are multiple events and stories that could be told. Journalists have to decide which candidates are newsworthy, which campaign activities and statements should be covered and with what level of detail. Most events will have to be ignored or down-played due to limitations of time and space. Yet news organisations generally perpetuate a myth that the news they deliver – whether election news or otherwise – is somehow complete. In the 1990s, the 30-minute Channel Nine television news bulletins headed by Sydney anchor Brian Henderson and Melbourne anchor Brian Naylor were promoted with the slogan 'I know everything I need to know 'cause Brian told me so.' Henderson would sign off by saying '. . . and that's the way it is.' The *New York Times'* motto is 'All the news that's fit to print' and my local radio station introduces its two-minute news bulletin with the promo: 'Complete news and information for Melbourne'.

Journalists' decisions about what is 'newsworthy' are crucial to how news is selected and what reaches an audience. But when they are asked about such decisions, many find it difficult to articulate how they assess newsworthiness, sometimes referring to gut instincts or 'just knowing' (e.g. see Tiffen 1989:67). For their part, academics are fond of pointing out that all news is 'constructed', but this notion only gets us so far. Journalists may construct news, but they do so from real events and existing material. They don't have an infinite choice, they don't make up material (with rare exceptions such as Jayson Blair of the *New York Times* in 2003) and there are some stories they can't ignore.

The stories they are most likely to judge worth telling involve *conflict* (violence, war, disaster, scandal), are in *proximity* (close to home geo-graphically, but also to the concerns of audiences), are *timely* (have just occurred or are out of the ordinary) but also have a degree of *familiarity* (the audience is already familiar with events or they relate to well-known people or situations) (Graber 2006:100–1). Stories are particularly attrac-tive if they are 'dramatic, immediate, sudden events, stories with human interest angles and stories that can be constructed around personalities' (Manning 2001:63).

Telling stories

Journalists make decisions not only about what story to tell but also about how to tell it, including what words to use to describe it and what images to publish or broadcast with it. To make news accessible and comprehensible, part of their skill is to 'take occurrences which may be different from one another and fit them into a framework which is already understood and anticipated' (Ward 1995:112). They incorporate new facts and events into a familiar social context or framework that helps audiences make sense of them. Comparisons, metaphors or historical examples may be used. Events may be personalised or simplified. Actors may be introduced in familiar terms, even to the point of drawing on stereotypes. Two different actors in the story may be represented as being sharply polarised.

It is no coincidence that news is described using the terms 'news *reports*' and 'news *stories*'. 'Reporting' tends to suggest that an event has been faith-fully recorded in a disinterested manner, whereas the term 'story' draws attention to the narrative structure that news items have. To engage the audience and make it meaningful and comprehensible, a story has a narra-tive; actors are allocated backgrounds, motives and causes; responsibilities are apportioned and implications are drawn. But one of the most important aspects of media framing is not about how a particular story is framed, but about how *all* news stories are reported as significant and worthy of the audience's attention.

Just as political actors try to persuade voters to vote for them, political reporters try to persuade their audiences that something important has happened and, more than this, that their account of what has happened is truthful and complete. They do this through a number of signalling devices including the use of authoritative sources, eyewitnesses, experts and on-the-spot reports as devices that signal its veracity. The presentation style of news formats also plays a large role in this. We have noted their slogans and promotions that signify their versions are 'complete'. There is also the serious music used at the beginning of a news program (or the ticking of a stopwatch for *60 Minutes*) as well as the tone of voice reporters and anchors use, they way they dress and their dry, formal language. All are designed to signify the significance, veracity and seriousness of 'the news'.

Sources

A large part of a journalist's job is to make contact with the organisations and individuals who most reliably create usable news. Journalists maintain detailed lists of quotable news sources who are accessible and authoritative and, for television, are preferably concise and visually appealing as well. Sources are important because most news stories 'recount what someone says occurred, not what actually happened' (quoted in Ward 1995:115). Sources do more than just add a quote, some colour or additional information to an already existing news report. The centrality of their interpretations and accounts can lead them to become 'primary definers' of issues and events (Hall et al 1978).

The sources who are most often quoted in news reports are politicians and people employed by government. This is true not just for political reporting specifically but for news stories generally (Herman and Chomsky 1988; Manning 2001). This is because government, politicians and political parties are powerful, well resourced and well organised. Government spokespeople are seen as highly credible and authoritative, which is a major advantage, but they also have the training, experience, skills and motivation to provide news reporters with a steady stream of reliable, cost-effective and credible stories, quotes and visuals. Contrary to the way journalists usually represent them, spin doctors are not always intrusive or obstructive or bullying. They are often very helpful to journalists. Media advisers provide material in an accessible and attractive form and they provide information that would often be otherwise difficult for the journalist to get. They subsidise a lot of media work, for example by staging events and picture opportunities that provide valuable material for news stories.

Politicians are obviously going to be a key source for election stories; in political reporting, this relationship between politicians and journalists is crucial to how news is reported. Older accounts of the relationship, based on the watchdog model, saw it as irrevocably adversarial but today, with a better knowledge of newsmaking processes, there is an increasing awareness that it is highly cooperative as well (Blumler and Gurevitch 1981). The two groups need each other to achieve their objectives and their close links and mutual reliance preclude the relationship from becoming *too* adversarial. The nature of the Canberra Press Gallery leads journalists, politicians and their staffers to work in the same workplace and to socialise together. Relationships can be friendly, and more so than is sometimes publicly acknowledged or than the watchdog model of journalism would recognise. This has led some commentators to be concerned that the relationship is too close and has led to 'capture' – where journalists come to see the world as their sources do, becoming 'insiders' when they should be 'outsiders' observing from a distance.

However, this is also a relationship where politicians can never be off-guard, where journalists have a professional drive and strong incentives to monitor them, to scrutinise and ultimately to catch them out in any wrong-doing. There are many unspoken and often flexible agreements about what can and cannot be done and many politicians have felt betrayed by reporting which they felt broke those unspoken agreements. As we have noted, the ground rules are more contentious today than in the past as competitive pressures, shifting social and behavioural norms and changed reporting frames (including the reporting of politicians as celebrities) are changing the ground rules and leading to conflicting interpretations of what is fair.

Journalists are not entirely reliant on government and politicians. They have other contacts including think-tanks, NGOs, lobbyists, academics and commentators. But their heavy reliance on government and political sources leaves them vulnerable to manipulation by those sources and politicians are well aware of this. A report for Labor in 1982 even specifically advised:

Candidates should work towards becoming recognised as a news source for journalists. Pass on news tips, gossip items and offer to background journalists... After a while you will find that journalists will be coming to you for news and information (Walsh 1982:2).

In recent years, many commentators have been concerned that politicians and their media advisers have come to play too dominant a role in news-making. All of the major media organisations in Australia joined together in 2007 to launch Australia's Right to Know Coalition, citing concerns about media freedoms, including laws preventing public disclosure of information as well as police raids on news organisations seeking the source of leaked stories about government (ARTKC 2007). John Hartigan, chair of News Limited, claimed in 2009 that: 'In my 45 years in journalism, it has never been more difficult for a journalist to get and verify a news story than it is today' (quoted in Hyland 2009b).

Yet, as Mark Scott (2009a), ABC Managing Director, pointed out during the launch of the Coalition:

for many in the public, media excess is an issue generating more commentary than media freedom. Many would argue that the media [have] never been more intrusive, [have] never had more power.

Journalists are hardly naive innocents in the journalist–politician relationship. Just as politicians have a range of PR methods (outlined in Chapter 7), journalists have their own repertoire of techniques for extracting information from their sources including wining and dining politicians, keeping their secrets, using flattery and charm and using variants of lies, bribery, blackmail and threats. In retaliation for missed stories or false information, for example, they can deny a politician the 'oxygen' of publicity.

One of the few former journalists to write publicly about this is Niki Savva, who also worked as an adviser for Costello and Howard. Savva (2010:55) has recounted how, when working as a senior political journalist, if a backbencher refused to give her information about party meetings she never rang them or mentioned their name in a story again 'unless they had done something wrong, of course'. Savva even argues that journalists 'win hands down' over politicians when it comes to 'scheming and lying, plain old hypocrisy and dishonesty... apart from a few honourable exceptions.'

Journalists are neither victims nor villains. They have power but they also have vulnerabilities. Ultimately, at the heart of the journalist–politician relationship is an exchange. The journalist has an audience that the politician wants access to and significant power to grant or deny access and to interpret events in ways that will support or damage the politician's cause. The politician and their advisers have information, stories, quotes and visual material that the journalist needs. They also contribute ways to frame information and themes to structure the news with. Both groups bargain in the process. The relationship is alternately competitive and cooperative.

Election campaign reporting: rules, resources and realities

In some countries, journalists have to adhere to special rules for reporting elections. In France, the media cannot report opinion poll results on election day or the day before, due to fears about the undue influence these could have on the result. In Canada, opinion polls also cannot be published on the day of the election and if a media outlet publishes them during the campaign they must provide very specific details about how the poll was conducted so that voters can assess its validity (Elections Canada 2000). In Australia, there were no special restrictions on election campaign reporting in the 2000s, but this was not always the case.

Like their European counterparts, Australian legislators in the 1940s had serious concerns about the impact media reporting could have on election results and they went even further in their restrictions. From 1942 until 1983 the *Broadcasting Act* required a complete 'blackout' of electoral broadcasts in the last few days of a campaign. Radio stations – and after 1956, television stations as well – were forbidden to broadcast any election-related material for three days between midnight on the last Wednesday of a campaign and the Saturday polling day. This was intended so that voters could have a quiet period of reflection to deliberate their vote, but the expansion of electronic media and changing news cycles made the reporting blackout impractical. It came to be seen as overly restrictive and unworkable and was removed in 1983.[2]

Journalists expressed concern in the 2000s about sedition and anti-terror laws as well as other legislation that affected their reporting, but there have rarely been any attempts at overt media censorship in Australia, save in times of war. The removal of the election blackout, as well as the series of High Court decisions in the 1990s that found an implied freedom of political communication, strengthened the ability of the media to freely report elections. Internal guidelines on reporting elections are only in place in some organisations (those at the ABC are by far the most detailed) so, for most, it is only the usual factors that restrict media reporting, such as legal requirements around defamation, that apply. But although legislative frameworks provide relative freedom, the newsgathering processes during an election provide more practical challenges and limitations.

The sheer intensity and volume of work increases during an election and there is a great deal of pressure for journalists to report news accurately, objectively and quickly in multiple formats. Media workers covering an election work extremely long hours in high-pressure situations. Pamela Williams described how, during the 1996 campaign, reporters' deadlines 'ranged from half a dozen stories filed once a day [for newspaper reporters] . . . to half a dozen stories filed a dozen times a day for the radio reporters.' She described the pace of the journalists' work as 'breathtaking' (ABC Radio National, *Background Briefing*, 15 August 1999).

Conclusion

By 2007, newsgathering and reporting had sped up so that the concept of journalists filing for specific bulletins – as Williams described in 1996 – was declining. Previously reporters had all day to get the facts of the story for that night's evening news or the next morning's newspaper, but by 2007 they may have had only minutes to file for more frequent breaking news reports on radio, television and online. For example, newspaper journalists were no longer just writing newspaper articles; they were also writing material destined for the newspapers' websites and maybe even contributing audio or video and writing a blog or tweeting as well. There was no clear news cycle any more and no single deadline. Exemplifying this was the 24-hour news channel Sky News, which reported election news as it was happening, with no end and, when it was live or breaking news, without editing. The rolling news focus of online news websites as well meant there was a breaking news model that was far more evolved in 2007 than it was just six years earlier when the newspaper websites copied content from the morning's paper and rarely updated those stories.

By 2007, an exclusive or a scoop would no longer last a whole news cycle but instead could be displaced in a matter of minutes. Updates, live crosses and breaking news led the audience to be more accepting that the news they were getting was not necessarily the final version. The pace of reporting meant the greater possibility of mistakes being made, but there was also a greater ability to fix such mistakes than in the past when, if a newspaper was wrong, it stayed wrong all day. News organisations have always relied on other individuals and organisations to generate stories, but especially during an election campaign when the story *is* how the parties and candidates campaign. The changing news cycle meant an increased need for fresh stories and 'breaking news' that fuelled opportunities for politicians to exploit the increased need of the media for content at a time when media resources were stretched. It was not only reporting that had changed but also how politicians campaigned. Keen to oblige the news-hungry media, politicians took on a key role in providing content with campaigns designed for maximum media coverage.

Chapter 7

THE STARS OF THE SHOW: POLITICIANS AND CAMPAIGNING

The reporting of elections has been transformed not only by shifts in media, technology and journalism, but because the way elections are conducted – the substance of what journalists have to report on – has also changed. Greater media focus and faster news cycles presented both demands and opportunities for politicians in the 2000s. Describing his experiences in the UK, Tony Blair (2007) related:

> When I fought the 1997 election, we took an issue a day. In 2005, we had to have one for the morning, another for the afternoon and by the evening the agenda had already moved on.

A similar process occurred in Australia.

This chapter looks at how politicians campaigned and provided the raw material of election news. Politicians and their advisers went to great lengths to influence election news through campaign organisation and political PR techniques in the 2000s. These techniques might have been aimed at short-term objectives (setting the day's news agenda or winning a six-week campaign), but they also had much broader effects on political reporting and the nature of Australian democracy. To consider these effects, we need to look beyond the last decade to see how campaigning evolved in Australia from the early days of Federation to an era of electronic and then digital media.

Election campaigns: from Federation to the 1990s

Travel and public meetings

Face-to-face interaction with voters was crucial to early campaigning and this was obviously much easier when electorates were small. Pre-Federation, when there was a restrictive franchise and only a small number of (male) electors in each area, early political meetings were often held in pubs. Later, as numbers grew and women were accorded the vote, politicians took campaigns out to the suburbs, streets and houses to reach voters. Street corner meetings became a staple and were still widely held into the 1950s, with canvassers sent from house to house to gather an audience. The meetings only drew small numbers but, because the audience was 'constantly changing', 'in a morning [a candidate] might reach two to three hundred people' (Rawson 1961:151). Early candidates might give a 'stump speech' standing on a box or later, when the technology allowed, would speak into a microphone from the back of a ute that drove around town or set up a public address system in the street.

Unlike local candidates, who can focus on their own electorates, party leaders are emblematic of national leadership and have to run a national campaign. As Dean Jaensch (2001) has pointed out about the 1901 election: 'Travel was inescapable – it was the only way to canvass.' Jaensch describes how Free Trade party leader George Reid 'went to all states except WA... travelled by train and steamer and a buggy drawn by two horses... and spoke at every possible place he passed through.' Another legendary effort was Joe Lyons' 'marathon' campaign during the 1937 election when he travelled 9600 kilometres and 'held 43 meetings in 43 days' (Henderson 2001:167).

By the 1940s, local candidates found attendances at their public meetings had dropped off, something they largely attributed to the mainstream use of radio, which caused people to stay at home. Party leaders could still draw audiences to town hall meetings into the 1950s and 1960s, though. Night meetings were held at eight o'clock so that people could attend after work and were advertised beforehand in newspapers to encourage crowds. Meetings received prominent media attention – including live radio coverage and front-page newspaper reports the next day – which was a large part of their appeal for politicians.

Judith Harley (1990) recalled that at meetings in town halls and 'draughty school halls... [in the 1930s and 1940s] women were very involved... Housewives without jobs relished the opportunity to meet the candidate, listen to his [sic] speech and tell him about their concerns.' A good speaker at public meetings was expected to speak off-the-cuff, rather than read from notes, and to answer questions from the audience. The questions were usually the high point and many voters went, not only to hear candidates who were skilled orators, but also to 'have a verbal stoush with them' (Jaensch 2001). Political meetings were seen as a form of entertainment, the legacy of 'an era of open-air mass meetings whose all-male audiences regarded politics as a form of street theatre' (Bolton 2001:28).

Some politicians were famed for their encounters with hecklers. Menzies' meetings were often 'the liveliest' and 'rowdiest', 'punctuated by the removal of persistent interjectors' by police. They included '[h]ostile placards, thrown eggs, struggling policemen, howls from the floor, and sneers from the platform' (Rawson 1961:97–8). Menzies was skilful in his use of radio. As his meetings were often broadcast live, Menzies would sometimes make asides and comments into the microphone for his radio audience, which the town hall audience could not hear. Listening at home and hearing his 'strong, measured voice, with the clamour of hecklers around him, had the effect of drawing the listeners to him, evoking both sympathy and intimacy' (NAA 2009).

Television and campaigning

By the late 1960s television was, like radio before it, playing an important role in how people spent their leisure time. It was getting harder to gather crowds for political meetings in draughty halls, although Gough Whitlam was something of an exception to this. Like Menzies, Whitlam used wit and humour to draw his audience's attention and make a mockery of his detractors. He could still regularly draw crowds of between 500 to 1500, but these were only half what Menzies had achieved a decade earlier.

Television was also playing a growing role in how politics was communicated. In 1958, two Labor politicians (H.V. Evatt and Arthur Calwell) and two from the government (Harold Holt and William 'Billy' McMahon) had appeared on television for the nation's first television debate. From 1963, policy speeches began to be presented before the cameras. Television news and current affairs were also gaining greater importance. The ABC's

Four Corners had been around since 1961 and its other flagship current affairs program *This Day Tonight* began in 1967 (and ended in 1978). It achieved high ratings and became what Graeme Turner (2005:28) describes as 'a "water cooler" show – a program that entered into conversation at work and home to the extent you had to watch it in order to know what your friends were talking about.'

The 1969 election marked the end of the traditional public meeting-based campaign. Whitlam's speechwriter Graham Freudenberg argued that it was 'the last campaign that wasn't tailored mainly to television. It was the last campaign that depended upon the . . . eight o'clock public meeting . . . in whatever city or town we were speaking.' For the 1972 campaign, Labor unveiled a strategy unlike anything seen previously in Australia. It was based on detailed market research and opinion polling and focused extensively on television, including television advertising. The success of Labor's 'It's Time' campaign changed the nature of campaigning. Thereafter, campaigns were geared for the demands of television and public meetings took 'second place to the television campaign' (Freudenberg 2000:122, 152).

The focus on television meant a much greater emphasis on appearance and control. Even for an orator as skilled as Whitlam, his campaign team in 1972 worried that any dissent or hostility at meetings would be magnified on television. They advised him to dispense with the most popular part of the meetings – the questions from the audience at the end (Oakes and Solomon 1973:190). The questions stayed for the 1972 campaign, but it was only a matter of time before public events became much more controlled. They also drew smaller crowds. People had access to politics at home. Aside from television news and the ABC current affairs programs that began in the 1960s, the commercial channels also capitalised on a burgeoning interest in public affairs and initiated programs such as *A Current Affair* (Channel Nine from 1971) and programs hosted by Mike Willesee (on Channel Ten in 1974 and then on Channel Seven from 1975 to 1982). *60 Minutes* started in 1979. Aside from politics, of course, the other thing that television offered was entertainment, including popular programs such as *Homicide* and *The Graham Kennedy Show*.

By 1980, party stalwarts were counselling candidates that, if they wanted to hold a traditional public hall meeting with the leader attending, they would have to ensure the hall was full, as it was embarrassing when leaders showed up and attendance was low (Cohen 1980:31). The parties were increasingly aware that their 'campaigns were [being] won or lost on the national media, before a national audience, rather than in the face-to-face campaigning by the leaders' (Mills 1993:127). They were more focused on swinging voters and not the party faithful who braved the draughty halls. The 1987 Labor *Campaign Manual* now advised candidates that the main point of hall meetings was:

> to have an event which will attract media coverage . . . A meeting in which the speakers communicate only with those physically present (who will usually be strongly committed one way or the other anyway) is likely to be so much wasted effort (ALP 1987:19).

Travel remained a key part of the leaders' campaigns – aided by planes, buses and linked roads that made it much easier than in horse and buggy times – but television had become a very direct source of a leader's authority. Just as Menzies had used radio to great effect in the 1960s, Bob Hawke was particularly effective in using television in the 1980s. Campaign events – especially the parties' campaign launches – were now conducted as major events designed for television coverage. Hawke's 1983 policy launch at the Sydney Opera House was only topped in its display of unprecedented razzamatazz by his 1987 launch, again held at the Opera House where he arrived by barge from Kirribilli House.

Public meetings of some form or another still continued in the 1970s, the 1980s and even into the 1990s. In 1983, for example, Hawke drew 'thousands' to a lunchtime rally in Hobart where, according to Graham Richardson (1994:126), 'Lunchtime workers flocked to hear him, taking it in shifts according to their lunch hours'. Fraser and other Liberal leaders also continued holding meetings, most notably in 1993. During the 1993 election, Liberal leader John Hewson held a series of lunchtime street rallies in the final ten days of the campaign. The Liberal Party had indicated in advance where Hewson would be campaigning and this gave Labor time to organise protesters.

Television footage of protesters shouting abuse at Hewson (and of him shouting back) were damaging. Gone were the days when hecklers and dissent were an expected part of campaigning. Now newspaper headlines spoke of 'Wild Scenes' and chaos unbecoming for a potential national leader (Crouch 1993:4). Thereafter, more controlled appearances in shopping centres and schools as well as smaller staged events became the focus of campaigns.

Politicians and their advisers used these occasions as a chance to sup- ply a steady stream of visually interesting material for television. In 2007, Labor especially focused on this. Every night of the campaign, an ever- smiling Rudd was shown in an active and highly visual pose made for television. He was holding up a laptop, with his shirt sleeves up rolling dough, looking through a glass-bottomed boat, doing the hokey-pokey on the street, walking across a paddock, buying a train ticket, handing out sausages, eating a hot dog (with his tie casually thrown over his shoulder), sitting on a train, shovelling grass off the back of a ute on a farm, feed- ing sheep, holding up a massive stack of papers (with signatures opposing *WorkChoices*).

Parties, spin doctors and political PR

The effort of politicians to cast themselves in the best possible light is as old as politics itself. After the 1970s, Australian politicians became particularly dependent on professional assistance. This was partly a result of the need to respond to a much larger and more demanding media sphere. Senior politicians are deluged with requests for interviews and comments on a daily basis. But it was not just a reactive move. Politicians were also more focused on shaping media coverage than in the past. To that end, PR has become an institutionalised part of both campaigning and governance. The major parties rely extensively on teams of paid consultants including media advisers, advertising agents, speech coaches, image consultants, direct mail consultants and pollsters.

Media advisers are chosen quite specifically on the basis that they have an intimate knowledge of how the media work. Many have been journal- ists themselves, so they know the newsgathering processes involved and how best to exploit these. In the 1970s, journalists were very aware of, and quite contemptuous about, the new breed of advisers the parties were employing. They started to write them into their stories and seemed equally fascinated and frustrated by them. In 1972, Laurie Oakes (1972:5) reported that Liberal leader Bill McMahon 'has not stirred out of Sydney without at least sixteen people with him' including speechwriters, press officers and television experts. Another journalist declared: 'Mr McMahon clutches these people to his bosom like a security blanket' (Barnes 1972).

This was part of a shift, into the 1980s and 1990s, when political reporting became far more concerned with relaying the tactics being used by politicians and their advisers. Reporters were increasingly willing to share with their readers the behind-the-scenes aspect of the campaign. This included campaign strategies, findings from the parties' privately commissioned research and also which staff had been appointed to campaign headquarters and even how much they earned and how they were getting along with each other – in 1972, with 'some friction' in Prime Minister McMahon's camp, while Whitlam's staffers 'work[ed] smoothly together' according to the *Age* (Barnes 1972).

This focus on the behind-the-scenes of politics was not just occurring in Australia and it intensified as the parties became even more professionalised. Encouraged by the fascination of the media, Machiavellian 'spin doctors' became a pop-culture phenomenon in the 1990s and 2000s on television shows such as *Spin City* and *The West Wing* (US), *The Thick of It* (UK) and *The Hollowmen* (Australia). No Australian media adviser attained the dizzy heights of celebrity that Alastair Campbell, Blair's director of communications, reached in the UK, but neither would they wish to. PR is most successful when it is hidden. In Australia, a focus on the adviser would be seen as a sign of inappropriate self-promotion and poor media management that took attention away from the 'boss'. However, Australian advisers were, nonetheless, discussed more in the media in the 2000s. For example, over the Howard years broadsheet readers became quite familiar with Tony O'Leary, Howard's chief media adviser, for example, who was described as being 'fearsome', 'grumpy' and having a 'prickly' relationship with the media (Starick 2007).

The techniques

Politicians and their media advisers use a range of both overt and covert techniques to influence news reporting (Gaber 2000; Richardson 2002; Tiffen 1989). There are some obvious and basic techniques such as providing comments, sending media releases and information, ensuring suitable photo opportunities for the media and making sure journalists are in the right place at the right time. However, there are also more sophisticated (and covert) techniques such as giving strategic leaks to journalists, courting them privately and granting exclusives to selected journalists.

Box 7.1

Some political PR techniques

- To put journalists **'on the drip'** is to give them 'favoured access to Government [or party] stories in return for favourable emphasis' in the story (Suich 2004c)
- **'Firebreaking'** is the deliberate creation by a party or government of 'a constructed diversion to take journalists off the scent of an embarrassing story...'
- **'Kite-flying'** is what they do when they 'use the media to float proposals in order to test reaction'
- **'Laundering'** involves 'finding a piece of good news that can be released at the same time as bad news...'
- **'Burying'** a bad news story can be done by releasing a host of positive stories at the same time (Gaber 2000:12, 14, 16).

Although the concept of news deadlines was changing rapidly, politicians still routinely tried to time the release of information according to those deadlines that remained (the primetime news and morning newspapers were two of the most crucial). If they wanted to avoid detailed scrutiny of a new policy document, for example, they could provide a thick copy of it to reporters very close to their filing deadlines so that they didn't have enough time to examine it in detail. Or, to obtain maximum publicity for a good news story, they could get the party leader to announce it at an event timed to make the evening news. If, on the other hand, they wanted to minimise the impact of bad news, they might get a less newsworthy junior backbencher to announce it very late (possibly on a Friday night or on a weekend) or when another big news story was already taking up space.

Timing is important for all political PR but is especially vital during election campaigns, when all activity is geared towards polling day and parties have to ration their activities across a five- to six-week campaign so that there is always something fresh. Campaign events have to be timed for a range of media with different requirements. If an opponent makes a scurrilous accusation, it will have to be vigorously defended, and quickly, so that the news cycle does not move on without the rejoinder appearing.

Bill Clinton's 1992 campaign team used the slogan 'speed kills' to describe their media strategy.

Despite the increased salience of other media and outlets in the 2000s, politicians still kept the demands of primetime television news uppermost in mind when timing their major events, for all of the reasons outlined in Part I. Campaign launches and major policy announcements were held in the morning or afternoon so that they would meet all deadlines for the evening news. Conversely, when politicians were worried that an event might backfire – such as a shopping centre visit in a marginal seat during the last days of the campaign – the announcement was often held late in the day so any unscripted or embarrassing moments would not make the evening news.

Centralised control and staying 'on message'

In 1969, Labor did not start preparing its election campaign until six weeks before polling day. There was little in the way of centralised coordination. In the 2000s, in the era of the 'permanent campaign', the parties never rested. A new campaign rolled on when the last one concluded and was underpinned by long-term planning, including years of research and strategy development. Centralised control is a hallmark of the modern campaign. One of the most obvious markers of this is the requirement that candidates 'stay on message', sticking to their set theme and using their media time to reinforce a predetermined message.

This is one of the most well-known PR techniques that politicians use, but it is especially crucial during an election, when a party has so many individual candidates campaigning for office. In 2007, Labor had 177 candidates across Australia and the Coalition had 192, including Liberal and National candidates running against each other in a handful of seats. With so many people, there is always the potential for a candidate to say something that is inconsistent with party policy or that diverts media attention from the topic of the day. To get their candidates to stay on message, the parties establish themes for the day and predetermined responses. The odd maverick or gaffe aside, the major parties were very effective in the 2000s at achieving consistency between different party spokespeople.

They were effective because they had long experience at enforcing centralised control. As early as 1975, the Liberals started taking a coordinated, national approach to campaigning and this soon became standard for both major parties. This structure allowed them to enforce tight party discipline and suppress dissent in order to minimise divisions within the party. In 1980, for example, Labor's campaign management team gagged all but eight spokespeople from speaking on national issues so contradictions would not occur; in the Victorian branch, local members were threatened with expulsion if they made pronouncements on national issues (Weller 1983:71–3).

Since the 1980s, the major parties' campaigns have been run out of a campaign headquarters where the centralised planning occurs. On a typical day of the election, the campaign directors and their central teams begin work before dawn, taking over from a night-shift that has monitored the media overnight. The campaign team then looks over media-monitoring and polling results, works out strategies for steering the news agenda that day and fine-tunes scheduled campaign events.

Limiting coverage

The techniques used by politicians and advisers to prevent media coverage are just as important as those designed to secure it. They include withholding information, demanding that journalists' questions be provided in writing, ignoring questions or taking a long time to respond to them, using threats, bullying and intimidation, denying journalists access including as punishment for unfavourable coverage and making complaints about media coverage. One of the Howard government's more controversial techniques was the ruthless tracking down of leaks from the public service.

One of the key media management methods that politicians from both sides used was to limit and control interactions with the Press Gallery. There is a long history of this. For example, in 1975, the Liberal campaign team insisted on separate press conferences for print and electronic media in order to try and prevent television getting footage of aggressive questioning by newspaper journalists (Penniman 1977:201). In the 2000s, politicians tended to reduce the time they spent with the Gallery. In place of regular press conferences, doorstop interviews were held. (In a doorstop interview, the politician stops on their way in or out of a venue and makes brief comments to the waiting media.) Compared to a formal sit-down press conference, a doorstop allows less time for journalists to question the politician at length and makes it much easier for the politician to walk away when the questions become too difficult.

During the 2007 election, there was generally 'only one chance for a press conference each day' (Murray 2007). The rest of the leaders' commitments were radio or television interviews. This included talkback radio, but also breakfast television programs such as *Sunrise* and *Today* and, in 2007, Rudd's FM radio and *Rove Live* interviews. These 'soft' media appearances sidelined the Press Gallery and, journalists argued, allowed politicians to avoid the sort of questioning that experienced journalists could provide. However, given the audiences outlined in Part I, these appearances might also have expanded the audience for political news and information.

Political advertising and news

As elections became more competitive and more mediated, the parties became increasingly unwilling to accept that the media coverage they were going to receive would be determined by journalists and news organisations. They turned to paid advertising to get their message across. Australia has had very permissive laws on political fundraising and spending: unlike many other countries, it had no restrictions on election advertising spending in the 2000s and earlier. This laissez-faire environment led the two major parties between 1974 and 1996 to increase the amount they spent on advertising tenfold from $1.2 million to over $15 million (Young 2004:41). This blew out even more in the 2000s with major party spending doubling again between the 2001 and 2007 elections so that, by 2007, they were reportedly spending about $40 million each.

The US has similarly permissive laws on political advertising and there it also plays a very important role in election campaigns. In the US, one academic researcher, Gerald Sussman (2005:43), has even suggested that political advertising has now 'replace[d] news as the main conduit of political information'. More than this, he argues that, as political advertising increased, political news reduced and this was no accident:

> ... it is so profitable, TV stations have a perverse incentive to reduce news coverage of campaigns in order to force candidates to invest more money in political advertising. The business logic is flawless, with the result that news coverage of candidates ... [has] declined ... (Sussman 2005:68).

Even if the reduction in election news was not a deliberate economic strategy by media companies, because there were so many political ads during television news programs, it is possible that producers felt less responsible for delivering political news and information when they could see that politicians were using other means to get information to people. The producers also needed to think about the tolerance of popular media audiences for political content. When a commercial news bulletin has up to eight political ads spread throughout its ad breaks, its producers are probably less likely to want to devote a great deal of time to reporting the election for fear of saturating their audiences.

The advantages of a 'PR state' for campaigning

When they were in government in the 1990s and 2000s, parties boosted the resources of office in a manner dubbed the 'PR state'. They began creating large, well-resourced units to perform media-monitoring and other media management activities. This gave them a head start for elections, not only in promotion but also because a key part of campaigning is attacking one's opponent. The resources of government were now being used to dig dirt on opponents through media-monitoring designed to identify any blunders, inconsistencies or broken promises that could be used to haunt them during a campaign.

The notorious National Media Liaison Service (NMLS) set up by the Hawke government was dubbed 'ANiMaLs' by journalists for its ferocious approach to media management (see Ward 1995; 2006). The Howard government instead used a Government Members Secretariat (GMS) and more than 70 media advisers spread across ministerial offices (*Advertiser* 2007:12). By the 2000s, journalists were becoming vastly outnumbered. There were estimates of between 400 and 600 media advisers working across the main levels of federal government. How to classify the different groups makes tallying their numbers difficult, but in one estimate from 2007 there were over 660 'ministerial minders', press secretaries and departmental liaison officers compared to 241 Press Gallery journalists (Fitzgerald 2008:17, 14). This didn't include the many communication officers working across the public service and in statutory bodies.

Government advertising was another key advantage of office exploited to influence public opinion, including 'softening' the electorate on controversial policies before an election campaign even began. There was an unprecedented use of taxpayers' money for partisan advertising during the

Howard government including large-scale advertising campaigns on controversial policies such as the Goods and Services Tax and *WorkChoices* at crucial points in the electoral cycle. Over $1.7 billion was spent over the term of the government, including advertising spikes before the 2001, 2004 and 2007 elections (Young 2007). The sort of public opinion research that governments pay consultants to perform is also invaluable for trying to influence public opinion and plan election strategies.

Once an election campaign has begun, the government enters a caretaker period that limits its activities. However, all of the information and advice obtained in the course of government activities will not be conveniently forgotten just because an election was called. The government has to avoid making major policy decisions that would commit an incoming government but, during the campaign, the media will still call on government members to comment on domestic and international matters that arise at that time. Governments can still announce decisions made before caretaker period and ordinary matters of administration still need to be addressed and can provide a publicity boost.

The departisan 'product': policies, leaders and parties

It is not just how parties promote themselves – both in government and during elections – that has changed over time but also the substance of what they are offering to voters. In Australia, politics tends to gravitate towards the centre. This is partly the impact of compulsory voting which means, as we have noted, that elections are decided by voters who are neither ideological nor partisan nor even especially interested in politics (and would probably abstain from voting if they lived in the US or UK, for example). It is also a result of preferential voting, which has tended to nudge political parties to the centre because they have to try to obtain the preferences of voters who won't vote for them in the first instance.

Compounding these tendencies were decreasing party identification, decreasing formal political involvement and decreased class identification since the 1960s. All of these factors meant that, in the 2000s, the parties increasingly tried to appeal to voters at an apolitical level. Since the 1980s and the Hawke era especially, one of the ways the major parties did this was by trying to downplay their partisan identities and instead emphasising the party leader. For many apolitical voters, who the leader is matters a great deal. Labor strategist and power-broker Graham Richardson (1994:127) argued:

> Leadership is everything in a campaign. Sure the campaign itself must go well, your policies must be saleable, discipline must hold ... but in the end if the people won't cop your leader you won't win.

There is an ongoing debate among Australian academics about 'party convergence' – the extent to which the Australian parties have drawn closer together in their ideologies, policies and behaviour (e.g. see Marsh 2006). However, reflecting on how party convergence affected the reporting of politics, veteran newspaper journalist Peter Charlton (in ASPG 2003) argued, after over three decades reporting on politics, that:

> as the great ideological issues have been settled, the parties have drifted closer and closer together. The differentiation between the two is now much more difficult to make so that political commentators and political reporters are then reduced to reporting the sizzle, not the sausage – reporting the ephemera almost of politics ...

Compounding the focus on the ephemera and the day-to-day matter of campaigns was the way in which the parties released their policies in the 1990s and 2000s. In earlier eras, the leader had traditionally outlined their party's vision for the nation, and all of its major policies, at the beginning of the campaign. This was a result of Edmund Barton's opening the 1901 campaign with a 'policy speech', something that became a tradition of Australian elections thereafter. The 'policy speech' was taken to signal the start of the campaign and open up the policies for scrutiny and debate weeks ahead of the poll.

In the 1980s, policy speeches were transformed into televisual 'campaign launches' and by the 1990s the parties recognised that holding these early worked against them. It meant their opponents and the media had plenty of time to find even small errors in the detail or costings of policies. Also, releasing all of their major policies in one go meant that it was difficult to sustain media attention across the five or six weeks. By the 2000s, 'campaign launches' had become an anomalous term. Both parties held their 'launches' in week 4 of the 2001 campaign and pushed them out even later into week 5 for both the 2004 and 2007 campaigns. Policies were instead spread throughout the campaign and, to minimise scrutiny, key policies or controversial ones were released late.

The forerunner to this approach was Howard's release of Coalition policies very late in the 1996 election campaign, including release of the key tax policy only on day 22 of the campaign and then with details given out so close to media deadlines that journalists had to absorb a 40-page 'densely argued' document in '10 minutes'. As Charlton (in ASPG 2003) recounted, this meant 'sensible questioning was out of the equation . . . [let alone] time to pick up a telephone and call someone from Treasury and say, "Look, does it work?"' This late-release strategy was widely used by both parties in campaigns thereafter until, just as it was beginning to look like an entrenched strategy, the Coalition confounded Labor in 2007 by releasing their tax policy on the first full day of campaigning. Labor hurried to respond quickly, releasing theirs four days later.

It was not just the late timing of policies that came to represent the parties' less ideological stances and their more cautious approach to campaigning. The *content* of their policies was also significant and journalists variously accused the parties of running a 'small target' strategy between 1996 and 2007 – but especially John Howard in 1996 and Kim Beazley in 1998 and 2001. This strategy involved studiously avoiding setting out any big visions in case they became big targets, avoiding controversial issues and instead setting only modest policy goals.

The campaign trail: on the bus

As we noted in the previous chapter, the relationship between journalists and their sources has a significant bearing on reporting. One of the most important changes to election reporting has been changes in how travel is coordinated for the leaders and for the journalists travelling with them during the campaign. In the 1950s, the parties would provide the media with the leader's itinerary at the beginning of the campaign and newspapers would print it.

This became a problem, though, once there were more organised political parties and social movements, better telecommunications and much higher stakes involved in favourable television coverage. The 'wild scenes' at Hewson's 1993 meetings and the cost this inflicted on the Liberal campaign were taken as a salutary lesson by both major parties. Their open itineraries had become, in the words of Howard's former adviser Grahame Morris (2004):

> an open invitation for an angry mug to turn up to protest . . . [And people dressed as] a rat or a koala . . . [would] steal five seconds of a political party's 40 seconds of television time or shove the picture about health, education or the elderly out of the paper . . .

The events of 1993 were still fresh when the highly competitive 1996 election was held and both major parties put in place new logistical arrangements for the journalists travelling with party leaders. In providing transport, the parties took the opportunity to impose a level of secrecy about the leaders' daily schedules. Journalists on the campaign buses and planes following the leaders would be kept in the dark about where they were going and only given short notice of where they were being taken. This made it difficult for them to adequately prepare and even to organise camera crews to be on location. Once there, journalists would sometimes be provided with detailed policy documents only minutes before interviews were to be held or deadlines to be filed. Journalists dubbed this the 'magical mystery tour' (Williams 1997:242–3).

Over the next few election campaigns, the secrecy intensified. The leaders' advisers had begun by printing out itineraries for the next day and slipping them under journalists' hotel doors at around midnight once their 'print deadlines had passed' to stop them making them publicly known. By 2001, travelling journalists were instead sent a text message just before the bus left advising of its departure time, the place it was headed and the issue of the day. By 2007, they were only getting a text message about what time the bus or plane was leaving, no details about where it was headed, what the event was going to be or what the issue of the day was. Journalists could find themselves on the way to regional Queensland or suburban Tasmania, covering an environment policy launch or a housing affordability plan. This information was only provided once the bus was well on its way to the campaign event (Morris 2004).

The parties were trying hard to control information flows in an era of instant messaging when mobiles, texts, tweets and emails enabled the details of their events to be communicated very quickly to opponents who could disrupt them at very short notice. In the already harried atmosphere of election reporting, journalists found that the new methods made it difficult for them to seek out information other than what was being provided. It was also more difficult for them to scrutinise policies. By 2007, it had become 'routine' for the leaders to make policy announcements before the documents about those announcements were released to the media, thus 'denying journalists the chance to ask potentially embarrassing questions about the details' (Steketee 2007).

Off the bus

If 'capture' is thought to be an issue for those reporting on politics generally and those reporting from Canberra and Parliament House especially, it is even more relevant in the confines of a bus (or plane) across a six-week campaign. Some Australian journalists complained bitterly about the travel arrangements imposed after 1996, seeing them as diminishing their capacity to report. They described it as being like 'travel[ling] in a hermetically sealed bubble' (Steketee 2007), holed up with media advisers and other journalists away from all outside influences. This wasn't a new issue. Timothy Crouse's (1973) best-selling book *The Boys on the Bus* had detailed how much of a problem this was for American journalists covering the 1972 presidential election. The campaign bus was said to induce a form of 'Stockholm Syndrome' in reporters who, hearing the same speeches given over and over and being reliant on their 'captors' for information, lost perspective.

The complaints beg an obvious question that even fellow journalists ask: 'Why do the country's media, in the lead-up to an election, obediently attend stage-managed media events?' (Kermond 2004). The answer relates partly to the centrality of the leaders' campaigns to how elections are framed, as well as the shifting news cycles we examined previously. Competitive pressures also play a role. Outlets can't afford to miss a story that their rivals have covered. The pressure not to miss out on the obvious means that journalists 'don't have their editors' support to make the change' from the bus (Suich quoted in Kermond 2004). But another part of the answer is that some journalists did get off the bus – the senior ones.

The 'magical mystery tour' of 1996 led news organisations to rethink how they would cover future elections. Kingston (2001:xix) noted that, in the 1998 election, senior political reporters began to 'no longer travel with the leaders, instead ensconcing themselves in head offices, issuing orders to reporters on the road, and packaging election news from the vision and sound sent in.' Grattan (1998:40) confirmed that: 'In particular, the senior television correspondents [stayed] in Canberra, feeding questions to their more junior reporters on the road.' This has continued ever since. Senior reporters from most print and television outlets covering the 2004 election stayed in Canberra for most of the campaign, only attending the 'big set-piece campaign events, or spend[ing] a couple of days with each leader to get a feel for the mood' (Morris 2004).

Morris observed that 'The campaign news [was] more often than not provided by the political lesser lights (plus colour writers) and the heavy-weights pull[ed] it together from afar.'[1] This pattern of reporting continued in 2007. It led some commentators to suggest that the higher turnover of those on the bus and the youth and inexperience of reporters following the leaders meant they were less able to provide the tough questioning senior Gallery reporters had, and they were more susceptible to the PR techniques politicians used.

The senior reporters got off the bus just as transport and technology made campaigns easier to cover from afar. Once, reporters had been reliant on the campaign buses to stop and provide them with a place with phones and faxes where they could file their stories. In the 2000s, portable cameras, digital equipment, satellite and wireless ability to transmit audiovisual material back to base quickly made for faster and more efficient ways of reporting news. Stories were sent from BlackBerrys, mobiles and laptops using email or sometimes blogs and Twitter. In 2007, reporters could also rely on secondary sources more than ever before. It was possible to watch the campaign unfold from the office or at home by watching press conferences and other events live on Sky News, receiving information direct from the parties by SMS, email and RSS feeds – including their media releases and transcripts of their press conferences and media interviews as well as accessing websites and blogs, listening to news, interviews and pundits on radio and television.

We may see in Australia in the future what occurred in the US during the presidential elections of 2008. There was an even more diminished journalistic presence on the campaign buses and planes. News reporters openly questioned the value of following the leaders on campaigns, arguing that this was no longer 'where the information [was]', that the buses were 'just the façade of the campaign... quite limited, even superficial'. There was a sense that 'information and important decisions [were] being made elsewhere' (Farhi 2008a). This included events occurring behind the scenes as well as events occurring in the media and online.

Conclusion

When citizens change the way they connect with politics and the way they consume and attend to the media, politicians adjust their campaigns accordingly. In the first three-quarters of the 20th century politicians shifted from face-to-face campaigns to a significant focus on television. Politics was no longer such a drawcard and the parties no longer had mass memberships or armies of partisan foot soldiers available for local campaigns on the ground. They were facing a more competitive electoral contest in which voters were less bound by partisan or group loyalties. They needed a national and mediated approach to campaigning.

In the last decade of the 20th century, the parties could no longer rely on a 'mass media' approach to campaigning with all of their attention focused on primetime television news coverage, nor could they rely on the Press Gallery to be the sole conduit of their message. They wanted to reach people beyond news journalism and communicate with more targeted audiences including through talkback radio, direct mail, YouTube and FM radio. They were also willing to pay for political advertising in order to gain media access outside of news journalism. The frequency and 'winner-takes-all' nature of Australian elections had always created an intensity about them but, in the 1990s and 2000s, the intensity was visibly heightened. The signs of this included the expense devoted to election campaigns, the levels of professionalisation in the parties and their increased willingness when in government to use incumbency resources to electoral advantage.

Chapter 8

WHO CONTROLS THE NEWS AGENDA?

In 2007, over a thousand candidates campaigned for office – over 60 per cent of them from outside the major parties. Interest groups, social movements, lobbyists and members of the public also proposed a large range of topics and expressed many different views. Every day of the campaign, events were held in electorates across the country. Between them, the two major parties put out over 80 separate policies and their leaders conducted more than 200 media interviews and press conferences. From this kaleidoscope of material, what was judged to be 'newsworthy' and included in the final product of news is an important matter.

According to agenda-setting theory, by making decisions about what stories to cover and how much prominence and space to give them, the media have great power to influence the public agenda – what people find important, what they think about, discuss with others and use as a basis for their decision-making. But if this is true, as we saw in the previous chapter, it is tempered by the power that politicians and their advisers have to influence news content. This chapter considers what is reported in election news and where those selections stem from. It tests whether politicians have 'hijacked' the news agenda but also whether the Australian media, as they are often accused, tend to hunt as a 'pack', following the same stories and interpretations.

Agenda-setting

Since the 1970s, hundreds of studies have tested the theory of agenda-setting and found that, when the media focus on certain issues during a campaign, this leads the public to perceive those issues as more important than others (McCombs 2005; McCombs and Shaw 1972). Research on priming suggests this goes even further, as people then tend to use the most prominent issues as standards for how they evaluate governments, policies and election candidates (Iyengar and Kinder 1987; Iyengar, Peters and Kinder 1982).

Either the media are extraordinarily successful at working out what their audiences are interested in and reflecting this in their coverage or – and this is the more prevalent view – they are very effective at signalling importance and directing public attention. Studies analysing time series data found that public opinion lagged behind media coverage and followed the issue importance that the media prescribed (see McCombs 2005). News workers also tend to believe that the media lead public opinion. In a survey of Australian journalists in 2006, 71 per cent said that Australian media companies and owners had 'too much' influence in determining the political agenda (RMR 2006).

The news media signal importance by highlighting some issues while ignoring many others or granting them less space or priority. These signalling devices are so effective that we come to expect the most important news story to be on page one of a newspaper or to be the lead story in a news bulletin or on a webpage. Research has shown that people tend to know more about the topics that appear in these more prominent spaces and to judge them as the most important and worthy of their attention (Graber 2006:240; Schudson 1998).

Media attention does not only influence the public. When editors and news producers select topics and interview subjects, and order their news schedules, they are also influenced by what is in other media outlets. (In the academic literature this is called 'inter-media agenda-setting'.) In the 2000s, they were particularly influenced by newspapers. Despite circulation declines and economic woes, newspapers were still the largest injectors of new stories into the news cycle and they tended to be the first major influence on a journalist's day, whether read in print or online. Eric Beecher (quoted in Craig 1993:191) has noted that, although newspapers are read by fewer people, 'among those people always are television and radio news directors and executive producers. Where newspapers lead, television, radio and the politicians follow.'

Inter-media agenda-setting is not necessarily related to the popularity of an outlet. Top-rating television news programs are highly influential with the public but generally not with other news workers because they are largely reactive, recounting day-to-day events. The most influential media tend to either conduct original investigations or provoke passionate debate. For example, in the US the *New York Times* is a leading inter-media agenda-setter, signalling important issues for other news workers across the nation (Gilbert et al 1980; Golan 2006). In the UK, the tabloid *The Sun* with its over 9 million readers is often considered a political agenda-setter that breaks (and sometimes instigates) stories that other outlets are then obliged to cover.

In 2001, an ABA study surveyed 100 Australian news practitioners. The medium they nominated as the most influential on their work was newspapers – especially the *Australian* and the *Daily Telegraph* – along with the *AM* radio program, AAP news wires and talkback radio, especially in Sydney and particularly 2UE, which was broadcasting both Laws and Jones at the time (ABA 2001b:201). Talkback was undeniably important in 2001. Howard, then prime minister, was a regular on 2UE, appeared with Neil Mitchell on 3AW every fortnight, was on Brisbane 4BC once a month, on Adelaide 5DN with Jeremy Cordeaux and appeared frequently in Perth either on 6PR or 6WF. His opponents tended to follow suit.

News media outlets had little choice but to pay attention. Talkback had the key guests and it often broke news because politicians made announcements on air or gave newsworthy responses when questioned by hosts and listeners. Television cameras faithfully traipsed into radio studios to take images of the leaders' interviews for television news. Media advisers handed out transcripts of the interviews to journalists in lieu of press conferences or other material. This all encouraged the perception that talkback led the political agenda although, in reality, it too was subject to a circular process of inter-media agenda-setting. Morning radio usually fed out of what was in that morning's newspaper (Faine 2005) and some talkback hosts relied heavily 'on newspapers for much of their news and, in some cases, their views as well' (Solomon 2002:226).

So few media allowed for direct public feedback in the early 2000s that talkback came to be seen (despite its narrow audience) as a litmus test of how the public were responding to issues. Another factor magnifying its impact was the lack of diversity in Australian media. It was relatively easy for politicians and their advisers to set the news agenda by focusing on a handful of outlets. In New South Wales, media advisers called these the 'trifecta' and aimed for the 'front page of the *Telegraph*, a talkback segment with Jones or Laws and the Nine Network's 6 pm news' (Simper 1998:8). According to Errol Simper, they had a 'well-worn strategy' to set the news agenda:

> leak a story to the city's 440000-circulation *The Daily Telegraph*. If the item appeals to talkback radio... it'll be up and running by breakfast and well into the morning. If it generates enough passion the three commercial television networks will have to run it on their evening news bulletins. If there's substance there, genuine philosophical content, the ABC and... *The Sydney Morning Herald*, will be forced to mull it over.

For federal elections, the parties would add national media outlets to their 'wish-list' and, when they visited a particular geographic area, the biggest newspaper and radio programs in that area. However, the Sydney media would still remain vital no matter where they were because, in Australia, there is a decidedly East Coast-based news agenda (ABA 2001b; Butler 1998; Charlton in ASPG 2003). As Malcolm Farr (2002:14) has noted, Sydney and Melbourne are really 'the megaphone cities of Australia... [where] the big radio, television and newspaper companies have their head-quarters and flagship outlets. Say something there and it is heard around the country.'

The 2001 election is the ultimate example of agenda-setting in Australian election reporting. The campaign was heavily influenced by a strong message promoted on talkback and tabloid newspapers in Sydney and Melbourne which had a far-reaching impact on the news agenda.

2001: the *Tampa* election

The 2001 election was the first after the Howard government's introduction of the Goods and Services Tax. Capitalising on teething problems with its introduction, Labor had looked to be competitive earlier in the year. August opinion polls 'showed the parties neck-and-neck, with Labor still marginally ahead' (Warhurst 2002:10). But on 10 November the Liberal Party won the election comfortably, with an increased majority and the largest swing to an incumbent government for over three decades. The news agenda had a profound impact on the result. It was shaped by several incidents prior to and during the campaign, including the 9/11 terrorism attacks in the US – which occurred 24 days before the election was announced – as well as Australia's subsequent commitment to strikes on Afghanistan. However, an incident that had occurred five weeks before the election announcement was also critical.

On 26 August 2001, the Norwegian container ship the MV *Tampa* rescued 433 survivors from an Indonesian wooden ferry that was sinking off the north-west of Christmas Island. The survivors persuaded the *Tampa*'s captain to sail towards Christmas Island and Australian territorial waters. On 27 August, the Howard government refused the *Tampa* permission to enter Australian waters. Australian special forces boarded the *Tampa* to prevent passengers disembarking at Christmas Island, denying them the right to claim refugee status in Australia (see Solomon 2002 and Marr and Wilkinson 2003). This event dominated news coverage for over a week.

There were reports of callers jamming the switchboards of talkback radio to congratulate Howard on his tough stance. 'These people are not refugees, they're queue jumpers,' declared Alan Jones, whose 2UE breakfast show was then reaching 700 000 listeners. The detainment of 433 people – and unconfirmed predictions that up to 2000 more could be planning a similar voyage – led the *Daily Telegraph* to warn its readers of a 'human tide' and a 'wave of illegals' while the *Herald Sun* described a 'human flood'. The two major tabloids made their support for the government's actions clear. The *Daily Telegraph* said there was 'little question of . . . the validity of the Australian Government's decision' (28 August 2001:16) and that a 'firm stand [was] the only option' (30 August 2001:24), while its columnist Piers Akerman declared it was 'Tough medicine to discourage others' (28 August 2001:17). Somewhat less stridently, a *Herald Sun* editorial called the government's decision 'correct' (29 August 2001:18) (see also Chapter 11).

Political scientist Ian Ward (2002b:21, 22) argued that the *Tampa* was premeditated, a 'carefully researched . . . Liberal Party strategy [designed] to revive its flagging electoral stocks'. The Howard government had reportedly been planning an event involving asylum-seekers. Mike Seccombe (2001) reported that 'voters in marginal seats began getting Coalition mail-outs, a couple of months before anyone had ever heard of the *Tampa*, screaming that Labor was "soft on refugees".' In the previous election, Pauline Hanson's

One Nation party, with its anti-immigration platform, had won over a million first-preference votes. Party research even 20 years before had argued that swinging voters tended to be 'racist' and 'hardline about... refugees' (Rod Cameron report for ALP quoted in Young 2004:215). Most of those on the *Tampa* were Muslim, many from Afghanistan, which had a potent symbolism after the 9/11 attacks.

Aside from appealing to electorally significant voters and capturing their attention when they did not usually pay much attention to politics, another major advantage for the Coalition was that the issue exposed a split within Labor's support base. Labor's response to offshore processing of asylum-seekers was seen as too soft by some traditional supporters, who held a strong stance against 'queue jumpers' while Labor voters who were 'tertiary-educated, inner-city-dwelling, middle-class' were appalled by what they saw as an unprincipled capitulation to 'populist' xenophobia (Charlton 2002a:103).

In August, the *Tampa* had put the issue of asylum-seekers to the forefront of the news agenda. When a boat en route to Australia sank fifteen days after the election was called, drowning 353 asylum-seekers, this also ensured renewed coverage. But the Howard government also used a variety of news management techniques to ensure the issue stayed prominent throughout the campaign including leaks, information control and selective briefings. Most controversially, two days after the election was announced, the Immigration Minister Phillip Ruddock told the media, in a claim later proved to be false, that asylum-seekers had thrown their children overboard when approached by Australian defence forces. He said this had been done 'with the intention of putting us under duress... It clearly was planned and premeditated.'

The 'children overboard' claim was then repeated by Howard and the Defence Minister. A still photograph later released to the media as evidence of the incident was actually a photo of children being rescued from a sinking ship by Australian forces. The false 'children overboard' claim was not corrected or retracted by the government prior to polling day, although doubts were known (SSCIICMI 2002).

Howard repeated newsworthy statements in agenda-setting media to keep the issue prominent. Favoured media outlets received selective briefings. On 7October, Howard invited a political reporter from the *Herald Sun* to afternoon tea at Kirribilli House. The resulting story published the next day began with a question: 'What sort of people throw their children into the water?' and a quote from Howard:

> I don't want people like that in Australia. I tell you – I don't want people like that in Australia! Genuine refugees don't do that . . . I tell you, there really is no place in Australia for people who would do that (Hamilton 2001b).

On the same day that article was published, Howard repeated the message for a Sydney audience on Alan Jones' program:

> I don't want in this country people who are prepared, if those reports are true, to throw their own children overboard . . . Genuine refugees don't throw their children overboard into the sea (2UE, 8 October 2001).

The next day, Howard repeated it again on Jon Faine's ABC program in Melbourne:

> I mean I can't imagine how a genuine refugee would ever do that . . . I certainly don't want people of that type in Australia, I really don't.

Howard employed the same technique of repetition of strong rhetoric – especially on talkback – to build up an argument that asylum-seekers were unworthy of sympathy, were 'demanding entry' and were a threat, by exploiting the classic Australian fear of foreign 'invasion' (Box 8.1). Howard repeatedly called the asylum-seekers 'illegal' – despite the fact that seeking asylum in Australia is not illegal – and if a journalist used another term, he reframed the language for them. For example, during one FM radio interview, after the host asked Howard about 'the *refugee* problem', Howard responded by talking about '*illegal asylum-seekers*' (HOFM, 2 November 2001).

Box 8.1

Examples of Howard's media rhetoric during the 2001 election

The 'flood', 'build up' and 'pipeline' of 'illegal immigrants'

Howard: 'there's a long pipeline and by taking the stand we have we have slowed the rate at which boats come to Australia' (2GB, 31 October).
Howard: '[if we] say we're going to stop doing this . . . that would be a recipe for the shores of this country to be, to be I don't want to use the word

"invaded" – it's the wrong expression – but the shores of this nation to be thick with asylum-seeker boats, thick with asylum-seeker boats (2GB, 31 October).
Howard: 'we think that the impact of our policy will certainly reduce the number of people going into the pipeline' (3AW, 1 November).
Howard: 'we believe that the measures we have taken since August have began to slow the number coming into the pipeline' (2BL, 6 November).
Howard: 'one of the reasons that we took the action we did some weeks ago, was a concern based on a large number of reports of the great build up of people in Indonesia who were wanting to come to this country' (speech and press conference, Raymond Terrace, 7 November).

Asylum-seekers 'demanding entry'

Howard: 'we decide who comes here and the circumstances in which they come' (Liberal Party campaign launch, 28 October).
Howard: 'what I'm asserting is the right of this country to decide who comes here...we cannot have a situation where people can demand entry into Australia' (*Today*, Channel Nine, 29 October).
Howard: '...people can't present themselves here and demand entry' (2GB, 31 October).
Howard: '...this country is not going to allow a situation where people can present themselves at our borders and in effect demand entry' (speech and press conference, Raymond Terrace, 7 November).

Howard's rhetoric, as well as Liberal Party campaign events and advertising, linked border protection with national security and terrorism and with the 'dangerous' and 'difficult' times ahead (Box 8.2). News stories on Afghanistan, anthrax attacks and terrorist strikes during the campaign helped reinforce the links, as did Howard's attendance at APEC in the second week (Figure 8.1). The Coalition also made maximum use of its incumbency status to make official announcements about Australia's new role in Afghanistan, 'dribbling out titbits' with each piece of information 'designed for maximum effect in a media market anxious for military news' (Charlton 2002b:118). The Liberals' advertising and picture opportunities also reinforced the 'khaki' theme with Reith filmed in a helicopter, the Deputy PM shown sighting a rifle at an army range, and Howard photographed with soldiers, visiting army barracks and farewelling departing troops (Figure 8.2).

Box 8.2

Priming: themes in Liberal Party rhetoric

The need for strength in difficult and challenging times

Liberal Party television advertisement: 'Tough decisions will have to be made. In these uncertain times, you must decide who is more likely to make those tough decisions'.

Howard: 'Clearly part of the judgement people make on Saturday is whether I'm stronger and better in these difficult times than Mr Beazley' (4QR, 6 November).

Howard: 'Undecided voters [have to decide] about the relevant capacities of myself and Mr Beazley to lead the country during these challenging economic times and also challenging security times' (2BL, 6 November).

Howard: 'There is a bigger threat to national security in its broad sense than we have probably had for a generation' (3AW, 1 November).

Howard: 'We have entered a more difficult and potentially dangerous period of our history. I don't sound undue alarm, I simply state the obvious' (Speech to the Millennium Forum, Westin Hotel, Sydney, 1 November).

Liberal Party press release: 'As the world changes, so do the threats facing Australia in the protection of its borders. To the old dangers of disease, illegal fishing and crime, have been added drug and people smuggling organised on an international scale, terrorism and sophisticated cybercrime' ('Protecting Our Borders', 23 October).

The news management was not only about agenda-setting – making certain issues prominent – but also about priming the electorate so that these issues would then become the basis for political decision-making. In the face of 'danger', 'tough decisions', the 'human flood' and 'difficult times', Howard was presented as tougher and more resolute than his opponent (Box 8.2). Some media outlets again aided the representations. In the *Herald Sun* article resulting from the afternoon tea, the headline was: 'I'll see us through, says resolute PM' and the journalist described Howard as 'very tough and uncompromising' (Hamilton 2001b). Certainly not all journalists or media outlets took the same stance as the two major tabloids. The ABC and the *Australian* were especially critical of the government's asylum-seeker policy and questioning about the 'children overboard' claims. However, the issue could not be ignored and it was prominent across different media.

Figure 8.1 Media reporting of the 2001 election
Sources: Channel Nine News broadcasts on 22 October and 7 November 2001.

The election news agenda was so dominated by Afghanistan and asylum-seekers that domestic issues occurring during the campaign were given far less attention than they would have under normal circumstances, including the collapse of Ansett, the potential sale of Telstra and new policies such as the home buyers' grant and a 'baby bonus'. Table 8.1 shows the major topics discussed on television primetime news during the campaign. Labor's campaign director Geoff Walsh (2002:130) later noted a similar pattern in other key media, saying that:

Figure 8.2 Liberal Party election advertising, 2001
Source: Liberal Party television election advertisement broadcast
October/November 2001.

[of the] last 30 page one stories from the... *Daily Telegraph*... two were
headlines on Labor's agenda, two covered the Liberal's domestic policies,
three dealt with the Melbourne Cup, two with the Kangaroos rugby league
tour... [and] 23 were devoted to the unfolding war against terror, asylum-
seekers, anthrax and jihads.

Readers of tabloid newspapers are, as we saw in Chapter 4, more likely
to be on low incomes, have minimal secondary education, earn under
$15 000 and be unemployed or in blue-collar work. They have to rely on

Table 8.1 Topics in primetime television news election stories, 2001

	Most-discussed topics (n = 248)
Week 1	Afghanistan, asylum-seekers, 'children overboard' claims
Week 2	Afghanistan, leaders' debate, Cheryl Kernot, asylum-seekers
Week 3	Asylum-seekers, APEC
Week 4	Campaign launches, asylum-seekers, Telstra
Week 5	Asylum-seekers, 'children overboard' claims
Week 6 (1 day)	Asylum-seekers, 'children overboard' claims

Source: Author.

an inadequate 'public health system, the run-down public schools [and are the ones] whose jobs are disappearing or becoming part-time' (Seccombe 2001). Yet the tabloids did not take a keen interest in poverty data, social mobility or the proportion of their readers getting into university. Especially in the Sydney and Melbourne tabloids, readers were encouraged to focus on an issue that effectively had little impact on their lives, with story after story on asylum-seekers prominent in news coverage. The Howard government's 'tough' policies were reported enthusiastically and the 'children overboard' claims, at least at first, presented as fact (Box 8.3).

Box 8.3

Headlines from the *Daily Telegraph* and *Herald Sun* during the 2001 election campaign

'Boat people throw children into ocean'
'Parents throw children off ship'
'Navy photos show children overboard'
'Proof that boat people threw children into sea'
'"13 illegal immigrants" caught at chicken factory'
'Security staff in fear of refugees'
'More boat people head for Australia'
'Death tub: 356 drown at sea'
'Muslims blame PM'
'Boat people knew the risks they were taking'
'219 boat people in navy standoff'
'Boat people hijack ferry'
'Hijack boat on the way'
'Vessel heads for Australia'
'Rift over illegals grows'

'Death boat survivors call for blood'
'Asylum-seekers drown after boat set alight'
'Boat people row rocks election'
'Two die as asylum-seekers torch boat'

On polling day, the *Daily Telegraph* used reports of a burning vessel with asylum-seekers on board as the premise to (insensitively) tell readers (twice in the one story) that asylum-seekers were '*the* burning issue' of the election (10 November: 1–2) (my italics). In the 2000s, there were three issues that Australians consistently nominated in AES surveys as being most important to them when deciding how to vote. These were health, education and taxation (Bean, Gow and McAllister 2002). In 2001, the issue of asylum-seekers was nominated fourth.

Politics and entertainment

The asylum-seeker issue animated commercial talkback radio and the tabloid press. It was a political issue about race, religion and national security, but it could also be framed in terms of crime and entertainment. Reflecting these commercial possibilities, three years later the Seven Network created the television program *Border Security*, which follows the work of Australian Customs officers as they enforce customs, quarantine and immigration laws, including preventing people from trying to illegally enter Australia. At the time of writing, six years later, this popular program was still in production. Channel Nine followed suit in 2007 creating the fictional *Sea Patrol* with a similar theme: 'young men and women battl[ing] the elements and the odds to defend Australia's borders' (Channel Nine 2010).

It is increasingly recognised that it is not only news programs that influence people's attitudes to politics. Entertainment media also play a role in the construction of political attitudes including how people view their own society, which issues they think are most important and which remedies should be applied. The audiences watching *Border Security* and *Sea Patrol* in 2007 were more likely to vote Liberal than the general population (4 per cent higher for *Border Security* and 10.3 per cent higher for *Sea Patrol*) (RMR 2007–08). This was not true of all entertainment or reality television programs. For example, it didn't apply to *Big Brother* or shows on cooking or travel, but it was true for shows based around disasters, security and crime – programs such as *The Force, Airline, Search and Rescue* and *Missing Persons Unit.*

There may be an element of self-selection involved in this (that people watching are already interested in the topic), but there may also be an agenda-setting or 'cultivation' effect. Research dating back to the 1960s and 1970s found that heavy television viewers were more likely to see the world as a violent place and to favour policies promising more police and harsher penalties for crime (see studies by Gerbner described in Ward 1995:44–5). More recent research has tended to find similar connections. Goot and Watson (2007:270 footnote) found a 'strong relationship between conservative views on law and order and dependence on commercial radio and television' in Australia. British research in the 2000s found that tabloid readers were almost twice as likely to be worried about crime as those who read broadsheets (BCS 2003). A study of American crime dramas and medical dramas found that 'both genres increase concern in viewers for the topics covered by a given program' (Holbrook 2003:2).

Popular media, both news and entertainment, directly reach a large number of people including swinging voters. An influential thesis developed in the 1940s also argued that communication from the media worked in a 'two-step flow'. It reaches 'opinion leaders' first – people who are trusted and respected in their social groups – who then filter the information to their peers and associates, including 'less [politically or media] active sections of the population' (Lazarsfeld, Berelson and Gaudet 1944:151). Bob Franklin (2004:212) recounts how a British election agent in the 1980s kept a detailed list of 'opinion leaders' in local communities 'which included vicars, teachers, doctors, keepers of the corner shop and pub landlords'. Howard reportedly believed, along these lines, that talkback listeners 'influence[d] other voters in pub bars and at dinner parties' (Suich 2004b). Tabloid readers – often older males as we saw in Chapter 4 – can also be influential in their peer groups. However, outside these direct audiences, there is also an important inter-media influence. Popular media command such large audiences and can cover stories with such intensity (even ferocity) that other media have to pay attention as a result.

Do politicians set the agenda?

The 2001 election is a striking case because the incumbent government exercised such an unusual degree of influence on the news agenda. It occurred at a time when politicians had been able to set the day's agenda with a talkback interview, and a news story would usually stay in much the same shape for about six to twelve hours (Speers 2008). By 2007, news cycles moved on faster and stretched out longer across the day. There were many of the same old agenda-setters, but some newer ones also emerged including local 24-hour television news which, as Farhi (2008b:20) has noted, has such 'intense and often immediate coverage of the day's big controversy [that it] forces [politicians] to fire back, which then compels the rest of the media to cover the response.' When 24-hour news is on all day in newsrooms, as *New York Times* political reporter Mark Leibovich (quoted in Farhi 2008b:22) has noted, this can mean that there is 'a kind of osmosis effect . . . [for journalists] it's human nature to see [a news story] on television all day and think, Maybe this is something we should follow.'

Looking at the 2007 election therefore gives a sense of news agendas towards the end of the decade, in a faster news cycle and after a period of some journalistic soul-searching following reporting of the *Tampa*. Table 8.2 charts the news agenda for the 2007 campaign and shows the most prominent stories reported on the front pages of eleven newspapers and in all five free-to-air primetime television news bulletins. These media were deliberately chosen, not only because they are the most accessed for election news, but also because they effectively illustrate how a whole day's news agenda played out. Printed newspapers start the news day and inject new stories while primetime television news sums up at the end of the news day and reflects any major shifts in the agenda across the day. Table 8.2 illustrates the striking degree of homogeneity between news outlets in deciding what topics are newsworthy. Bold text is used wherever all free-to-air television news programs or all eleven newspapers reported the same topic.

The news agenda was dominated by the two major parties' planned events – especially the leaders' policy announcements, their public statements and visuals of them out campaigning. This was supplemented by a focus on their gaffes (such as Howard forgetting the name of a Liberal candidate, Abbott showing up late for a campaign debate and Garrett's remark to Steve Price). When a policy topic was covered, this was almost invariably because one of the major parties had launched it that day or because one of their leaders had made a statement about it. Only occasionally did some other actor steal the media limelight from the major parties. These included a pensioner who abused Rudd at a seniors' event, union official Joe

Table 8.2 The election news agenda, television and newspapers, 2007

	Free-to-air television news			Newspapers	
Day	Topic(s)	Percentage of the 5 news programs that reported this issue as 1st story	Percentage that reported on it as 1st or 2nd story	Topic(s)	Percentage of 11 newspapers that reported this issue on their front page
1	Election announcement and leadership	100%		Election announcement and leadership	100%
2	Coalition tax plan	100%		Coalition tax plan	100%
3	Howard ACA gaffe	100%		Howard profile	40%
4	1 Health 2 New political ads	100% 100%		Industrial relations	50%
5	1 Gavan O'Connor on ALP 2 Howard forgetting name	80% 80%	100% 100%	Opinion polls	78%
6	ALP tax plan	100%		ALP tax plan	100%
7	1 Bennelong 2 Rudd doing hokey-pokey	100% 100%		[mixed]	
8	1 The Great Debate 2 ALP childcare policy	100% 75%		The Great Debate	100%
9	1 The Great Debate 2 Worm controversy	100% 100%		Economy Opinion polls	83% 60%
10	1 Age pensions 2 opinion polls	100% 100%		Age pensions	100%
11	Interest rates	80%	100%	Interest rates	100%
12	1 Pensioner abusing Rudd 2 Joe McDonald union official	100% 100%		1 Pensioner abusing Rudd 2 Interest rates	40% 60%
13	1 Interest rates Howard promise 2 ALP Expulsion of McDonald	80% 100%		[mixed]	
14	1 Environment (Lib Kyoto division) 2 McDonald expulsion/new Lib ad	80% 100%	100%	Environment (Lib Kyoto division)	100%
15	1 Interest rates Howard promise	60%	100%	1 Opinion polls 2 Environment 3 Interest rates/Howard promise	43% 50% 33%

Table 8.2 (*cont.*)

	Free-to-air television news			Newspapers	
Day	Topic(s)	Percentage of the 5 news programs that reported this issue as 1st story	Percentage that reported on it as 1st or 2nd story	Topic(s)	Percentage of 11 newspapers that reported this issue on their front page
16	1 Environment 2 Employment	100% 80%	100%	Education	43%
17	1 Environment 2 Costello and Swan debate	100% 80%	100%	**Environment**	100%
18	**Abbott 'bad day'**	100%		**Abbott's 'bad day'**	100%
19	1 **ALP age pensions** 2 **Coalition health policy**	100% 100%		1 Polls 2 Campaign strategy	33% 33%
20	1 Garrett gaffe – comment to Price 2 Opinion polls	60% 60%		Garrett gaffe – comment to Price	83%
21	**Garrett gaffe – comment to Price**	100%		Roads	67%
22	1 **ALP home saver account policy** 2 **Coalition roads spending plan**	80% 100%	100%	Interest rates/home buying	60%
23	**Interest rates**	100%		[mixed]	
24	**Melbourne Cup and Rudd win**	80%	100%	**Interest rates**	100%
25	**Interest rates and Howard apology**	100%		**Interest rates and Howard apology**	100%
26	**Interest rates and Howard apology**	100%		[mixed]	
27	1 **Woman knocked during mall visit** 2 Interest rates	100% 60%		1 Interest rates 2 Opinion polls	67% 67%
28	**IR *WorkChoices***	100%		**Personal lives of politicians**	100%
29	1 **ALP dental plan** 2 **Leaders on Remembrance Day**	100% 100%		Leaks about Coalition launch	86%
30	**Coalition launch**	100%		**Coalition launch**	100%
31	**Education**	100%		Education	40%
32	**ALP launch**	100%		**ALP launch**	100%
33	**ANAO report on 'pork-barrelling'**	100%		ANAO report on 'pork-barrelling'	50%

(*cont.*)

Table 8.2 (*cont.*)

	Free-to-air television news			Newspapers	
Day	Topic(s)	Percentage of the 5 news programs that reported this issue as 1st story	Percentage that reported on it as 1st or 2nd story	Topic(s)	Percentage of 11 newspapers that reported this issue on their front page
34	Security scare at Howard event	100%		1 IR 2 Strategy	40% 60%
35	Opinion polls	100%		Opinion polls	100%
36	Coalition policy on drugs and welfare	80%		Environment	44%
37	1 Environment – Lib dissent (Debnam) 2 Schoolgirl fainting at Rudd press conf	80% 100%		Howard and Costello ACA interview	57%
38	1 WorkChoices – claims of second wave 2 Coalition claims about ineligible ALP candidates	100% 80%		Coalition claims about ineligible ALP candidates	50%
39	Rudd NPC address	100%		1 Rudd NPC address 2 Lindsay pamphlet	38% 12.5%
40	Lindsay pamphlet scandal	100%		1 Lindsay pamphlet 2 Opinion polls	33% 100%
41	Opinion polls	100%		Opinion polls	100%

Note: This table examines primetime evening news and printed newspapers (the *Australian*, *Daily Telegraph*, *Herald Sun*, *Sydney Morning Herald*, *Age*, *Courier-Mail*, *Mercury*, *Advertiser*, *Canberra Times* (NT and ACT papers excluded as hard copies were not available to the author for every day of the campaign). The formal election period was from the announcement date (14 October) to polling day (24 November) but newspaper campaign coverage began on 15 October, so this table counts day one for newspapers as 15 October. For newspapers, the percentage is of those papers that had the election on their front page.

Source: Author.

McDonald, asbestos campaigner Bernie Banton and two members of the public who had the misfortune to fall over in front of the television cameras (one in a shopping centre in the wake of the media entourage and one at a Rudd press conference).

Ninety-five per cent of the time, the free-to-air news bulletins covered the same topic. Often they used the same visuals, sound bites and sometimes the same story order as well. Television camera crews are deployed selectively and sent to cover the leaders' campaign events because these are judged most likely to be newsworthy. All are drinking from the same pool of material, seeing the same thing and looking for the most television appropriate images – so a politician falling off a step or a protester dressed in a chicken suit is irresistible for television news in a way that it isn't for newspapers or radio. The homogeneity also stems from the fact that television news is designed to be quite generic, both because it has to appeal to a wide audience (and one less partisan than newspapers) and also because the same story is often used by affiliated channels in different states, so it is produced to be non-geographically specific.

Newspapers should (and did) have more variation between them for the converse reasons – most serve specific geographic markets and their audiences (and their editorial lines) are more partisan. Newspapers also have more space to report and employ more journalists so, at least in theory, they should be more able to hunt out stories beyond the parties' campaign events than television news. Given all of these factors, newspapers were perhaps not as diverse as we might expect, then. On 17 days (41 per cent of the campaign) a story was judged so newsworthy that every major media outlet covered it – all free-to-air television news programs and all 11 newspapers on their front page. These were especially stories on diary events, the signifying moments of the election narrative such as the announcement, the *Great Debate* and the parties' campaign launches. For more than three-quarters of the campaign, at least half of the newspapers were reporting the same topic on their front page. And even this does not reveal the full extent of homogeneity, because I focused on front pages and the election didn't always make it on to the front page (especially for tabloids) but was covered inside the newspaper.

Homogeneity versus independent investigation

Elections are part of an ongoing process involving many actors and issues, for which there is a multitude of information already 'out there' requiring investigation. But news reporters instead tend to view an election as a series of events – many diary-driven – that unfold over the campaign period and are best captured by following the leaders and best represented using visuals of the leaders and their verbal quotes. When elections are viewed this way, there are only so many ways the story can be told so the same topics, quotes, photos, footage and facts tend to be used.

For example, when Howard announced the 2007 election on 14 October, every free-to-air television news program that night broadcast the same two quotes from Howard's press conference ('This country does not need new leadership. It does not need old leadership. It needs the right leadership' and 'Love me or loathe me, the Australian people know where I stand'). The next day, every major newspaper had one or the other of these quotes on their front page (Figure 8.3). Howard had said over 3000 words at that press conference, but almost all news outlets reported those same 30 words. Even the visuals showed how similar news values were with the same finger-pointing photograph of Howard being used across different newspapers.

The parties have a great deal of influence on content because, despite its lamented death, 'straight reporting' still occurs with a heavy reliance on what the leaders said. Nearly half (47 per cent) of the words in front-page newspaper articles on the election announcement were direct quotes from Howard's statement at his press conference or Rudd's statement afterwards. (Both of these were not only verbal statements but were also transcribed and issued as press releases.)[1] When reporting complex policies such as tax, it was even more likely that journalists relied upon this type of party-generated information. On the day after the Coalition's tax policy launch, 45 per cent of front-page newspaper stories were derived from party PR material, including the prepared statement read out at the announcement and the accompanying media kit. Similarly, on the day after Labor's tax policy launch, 55 per cent of newspaper stories on the policy were derived from party-supplied material.

One of the methods journalists use to get to the truth behind this type of spin is to ask politicians questions. These are considered such a cornerstone of reporting that journalists complained when politicians held fewer press conferences in the 2000s. But in 2007, the Q&A sessions that were held rarely seemed to yield anything that journalists judged useful. In the three examples of newspaper reporting discussed above – the election announcement and both major parties' tax policies – only 3 to 8 per cent of the politicians' quotes in those articles were responses they gave to journalists' questions. The rest – over 90 per cent – came directly from the politicians' prepared statements or accompanying press releases – that is, what they wanted, and intended, to say.

Figure 8.3 Newspaper reporting of the election announcement, 15 October 2007
Source: Author photograph.

Table 8.3 Examples of sound bites broadcast in television primetime news, 2007 election

Date	Top sound bites	No. of news programs
19 October	Rudd [holding up laptop] 'This is the toolbox of the 21st century.'	5/5
25 October	David Vowes [to Rudd at senior citizens' club]: 'You're an ignorant bastard.'	5/5
31 October	Tony Abbott [on showing up late for a scheduled debate with Nicola Roxon]. 'I really do apologise.'	5/5
31 October	Nicola Roxon: [when Abbott had not shown up] 'I could do an impersonation if it helps' [laughter from crowd]. 'My office tells me it's quite good' [more laughter].	4/5
12 November	Costello [on Labor]: 'They'd have you believe there were never Reds under the beds just economic conservatives' [laughter].	4/5
18 November	Howard: 'This is a Rudd version of banana republicanism.'	4/5
24 November	Howard [when voting]: 'Can I change my mind?' [laughs].	4/5
24 November	Rudd: 'I'm pretty confident that I have the family's votes' [laughs and wife laughs].	4/5

Source: Author.

If journalists did not gain much from their questions it was mainly because politicians 'stayed on message'. Journalists despair of this technique but they report politicians' words nonetheless because, in the conventions of election reporting, they are so reliant on these words to tell the story. Politicians exploit this by repeating sound bites relentlessly so that even voters who only casually watched the elections of the 2000s would be familiar with the Howard phrases 'cut and run' (describing Labor's policy on Iraq in 2004), 'no ticker' (about Beazley in 1998 and 2001) and Latham's school 'hit list' (2004). Also unforgettable were Latham's 'ladder of opportunity' and his promise to 'ease the squeeze' (2004) along with Rudd's ubiquitous 'working families' (2007).

When responding to Labor's tax policy in 2007, Costello told a press conference that the ALP had copied '91.5 per cent' of the Coalition's policy. He used this statistic 11 times at the press conference to maximise the chance that it would be used as a sound bite. This worked. All television channels reported it that night and the next day's newspapers widely repeated it as well. This is not uncommon. In many cases, the sound bites chosen for evening news are reported on all channels or four out of five (Table 8.3). The news media especially like short, snappy, funny or otherwise evocative sound bites.

It is a reflection on journalistic resources as much as reporting trends that, in 2007, there was very little independent journalistic investigation beyond reacting to the major parties' campaigns. Although there were frequent claims for newspaper 'exclusives' these were most frequently opinion poll results commissioned by news outlets. In fact, polls were the main contribution by the media to driving the news agenda (Chapter 9). Other 'exclusives' were really 'drops', with details of party events or initiatives selectively leaked to newspapers. For example, on the morning of the Liberals' campaign launch, hours before it had been held, the *Australian*, the *Age* and the *Daily Telegraph* all reported specific details about what it would include. Other exclusives came from leaks, but these were leaks that had been deliberately provided to benefit the leaker. The biggest of these in 2007 was when the AFR reported a Cabinet leak that Howard government Environment Minister Malcolm Turnbull had unsuccessfully lobbied for Australia to sign the Kyoto Protocol. Although he denied it, this was widely reputed to have come from Turnbull or his allies.

It's too easy to put reporting homogeneity down to the laziness of individual journalists, as sometimes even their own editors do. Chris Mitchell (quoted in *Crikey* 16 March 2010), editor of the *Australian*, said in 2010 that 'journalists are pretty lazy. It's pretty easy to march down to the boxes in Canberra and write what Rudd's media office put out rather than chase their own ideas.' But to what extent do editors give their journalists the time, support and opportunity to 'chase their own ideas'? Will they back investigations that cost money, take time, possibly yield no major story and mean they might miss out on stories that other outlets cover?

Homogeneity has much deeper roots than journalists' 'laziness'. It is grounded in institutions and their market orientations as well as in journalism sociology. There is a strong and shared perception among journalists and news producers of what an election is about and how to report it and not much willingness to go outside this conception. Fear of market repercussions is one reason why, but other factors compound this including deadlines and the pressures inherent in campaign reporting, the 'bus' method, concentrated media ownership, centrist mass-audience-seeking media outlets and the way news media outlets influence each other.

Many of the sociological factors that Timothy Crouse (1973:7–8) noted when observing election reporting in the US in 1972 are still relevant today. As the *Boys on the Bus* author observed, the journalists:

all fed off the same pool report, the same daily handout, the same speech by the candidate; the whole pack was isolated in the same mobile village. After a while, they began to believe the same rumours, subscribe to the same theories, and write the same stories.

If there was a consensus in political reporting it was because, Crouse wrote:

> all the national political reporters lived in [the same place], saw the same people, used the same sources . . . They arrived at their answers just as independently as a class of honest seventh-graders using the same geometry text – they did not have to cheat off each other to come up with the same answer (Crouse 1973:44).

'Pack reporting' on the politics round is an old accusation and a cross-cultural one. BBC world affairs editor John Simpson – who was a political editor in the early 1980s – makes 'sheep noises to describe the herd – or flock – mentality of many political journalists' (Moss 2010). Understandably, the accusation is vehemently denied by some political reporters, who point to their competitive pursuit of scoops. Yet others do acknowledge that shared circumstances and news values lead to similar coverage. They describe how their editors scan other media outlets and berate them if they have 'missed' some story that another outlet has:

> There is this pack mentality. There is this feeling that, 'Okay, if Oakes has got it on the 6 o'clock news tonight, it is obviously right, so therefore we will all write about that tonight.' Or if Grattan is saying something, 'Grattan has been around a long time.' . . . You get a kind of sameness of commentary and a sameness of opinion . . . I do not think that we get the diversity of comment that you would see, say, in the [UK or US]. (Charlton in ASPG 2003).

Elite media: reach, issues and orthodoxies

Agenda-setting and pack reporting are not just about popular media or about topics. Interpretation is also a large part of what news media offer to audiences in the 21st century and the elite media play a special role in this. They help fashion the intellectual environment and establish dominant frameworks about what is and is not discussed, how to interpret events and issues and how to make sense of ongoing political events. Along with talk-back and tabloids, other inter-media agenda-setters nominated by journalists in 2001 were broadsheets, *AM* and Sunday morning political television programs such as *Sunday*, *Meet the Press* and *Insiders*.

By 2007, broadsheet newspapers were still vital for injecting new stories and *AM* was also still crucial because it 'top[ped] up the stories from the morning papers' (Suich 2004b:15). But the Sunday morning programs did not gain as much traction as they had in 2001, when news workers argued they 'often set the news agenda for the coming week' (ABA 2001b:110–11). Audience declines and less institutional backing for the programs on the commercial channels had played a role in making them less central but the main factor was how televised content, including interviews with politicians, was more widely available and more quickly supplanted. This included 24-hour television news on which politicians appear so regularly that they can seem like a 'home movie' channel for politicians. In this environment, there was no longer as much need for a weekly main event.

One of the only events on a Sunday morning program that did have an impact on the news agenda in 2007 was a *Sunday* interview when Oakes confronted Howard with evidence that he had personally promised in 2004 to keep interest rates at 30-year lows. This exchange featured on every free-to-air news program that evening, except rival Channel Seven, and was discussed in many newspapers the next day. Although they are not necessarily comfortable with the moniker or perceptions of their influence, the 'God correspondents' seem to be quite a distinct phenomenon in Australian political reporting and one that can drive homogeneity. In 2001, news workers had nominated Oakes as an agenda-setter in his own right. Talkback host Neil Mitchell said he was influenced by Laurie Oakes' coverage and Sky News' David Speers said: 'I think everyone stops to see what Laurie Oakes is doing' (ABA 2001b:110–1).

Like popular media, the elite media like to highlight issues that animate their audiences. The impact of this is not just on a mass public, though, but on decision-makers, so elite media are disproportionately important in how they decide to report. Putting a particular issue or interpretation on the agenda in elite media can have a wide influence on how other media understand and interpret events. An example from 2007 was the *Australian Financial Review*'s dogged focus on a theme of fiscal restraint.

From the day the election was announced, the *AFR* frequently and prominently reported warnings that 'over-spending' by the parties in their election policies could lead to inflation. The *AFR* often quoted authorities from its core readership – the business and finance community. For example, on 2 November the *AFR*'s front page carried a warning by the CEO of Westpac Bank 'that inflation is the biggest risk to the economy and the policies of both major parties are adding to the pressure on inflation and interest rates'. On 7 November, its front-page headline was: 'Poll spree at odds with RBA's inflation fight', stating again that 'Economists [were] warning on [party] spending'. On 12 November, the *AFR* pointedly warned the parties ahead of their campaign launches that 'some prominent economists are arguing it would be best if the [parties'] policy launches contained no new spending at all.'

The *AFR* was none too subtle about where its agenda lay and, like the tabloids, was playing to its readership. On the first day of the campaign, it ranked election issues for its readers based on their 'importance as vote deciders', putting 'economic management' first with a 9/10 with other issues such education ranked only 4/10 and housing 5/10.The *AFR* was not the only source of the fiscal restraint message in 2007, but it was certainly most active in highlighting it. As John Warhurst (2007) has noted, one of the ways the business community – which includes major media companies – can influence politics is to exercise 'the leverage that comes with being able to allege, or imply, that economic activity will decline . . . [if one or other of the parties] makes it unhappy.' At various times, the *AFR* quoted 'experts' from the largest banks and financial firms in Australia including HSBC, ANZ Bank, UBS, Macquarie Group and Suncorp. They were exercising that leverage and sending a warning designed to influence the parties.

The fiscal restraint theme did have an impact on how the parties' campaigns were structured and how they were viewed by the media. After the Liberal tax policy was released, it was widely represented as a 'splurge' and an 'extravagance' (*AFR* 13 November; *Age* 16 October). The *West Australian* said it 'runs risk of pushing up interest rates' (16 October). Contrary to the usual perception that the Liberals are viewed as better economic managers and are closer to business, it was Labor that was advantaged by the fiscal restraint theme because it better adapted its campaign to fit.

Labor had assiduously courted the business community in 2007 (Maiden 2007) and was determined to present itself as an acceptable alternative to the

Coalition. Rudd kept repeating that he was a 'fiscal conservative' and that the Liberals were economically irresponsible. Labor outlined less expensive policy commitments at its campaign launch (held after the Liberals' launch). The *AFR* rewarded Labor with front-page coverage about how Rudd had 'claimed the economic high ground', but all of the main newspapers framed the launch very similarly, and all within the fiscal restraint interpretation.

In the *Australian*, Paul Kelly's analysis was headed 'ALP wins the high ground on economy'. 'Mr Rudd's image of restraint' said the *Advertiser*. 'Rudd caps spending: less is the new more' argued the *Australian*. 'A smaller fistful of dollars' said the *Sydney Morning Herald*. 'A modestly priced digital revolution' said the *Age*. The *West Australian* had 'Rudd resists the urge to splurge'. The *Herald Sun* called Rudd 'frugal'. The *Daily Telegraph* described the plan as 'responsible' and Rudd as a likely 'penny-pinching prime minister'.

When commentators think about media effects and elections, they usually focus on how media reach swinging voters in marginal seats but, as Aeron Davis (2007:60) notes, 'much elite promotional activity is aimed, not at the mass of consumer-citizens but, rather, at other, rival elites.' The elite media are sites where ideas and policy proposals are tested and negotiated and where interpretations of political strategy and implications are formed. The elite media can play an agenda-setting role that is just as active – albeit often less blatant or noticeable – as tabloid and talkback media. The elite media also reach beyond their small direct audiences because they influence other media (including the popular media) and the news agenda more broadly.

Conclusion

As citizens, we can never grasp everything that is happening in the world, especially because so many events play out beyond our immediate experience. We rely on the media to search out information, sift through and prioritise it, so that we are aware of the most important matters. During an election, the news media are so broadly agreed on what these matters are that it is possible to turn on primetime television news programs and see all channels reporting the same story topic and often with the same sound bites and the same visuals.

Because this coverage is so focused upon the major parties – their events and statements – it's easy to see why journalists complain that politicians have hijacked the news agenda. But if politicians have a high degree of influence over what makes the news, this is only because the news media have fashioned the environment in which politicians' PR and spin flourish by telling the election story in a certain way – a narrow reactive focus, limited sources, reliance on major parties and their leaders, reliance on verbal statements and televisual campaign events. The news media may look as if they are dancing to the tune set by politicians but there is a mixture of resistance, frustration, capitulation and sometimes enthusiasm in following the major parties' lead. And though they stick largely within the news agenda set by the major parties, individual outlets still retain significant power to direct public attention, not only signposting what issues to think about but also, sometimes quite deliberately, how to think about them.

Chapter 9

'FROM THE CAMPAIGN TRAIL'

The framing of election news

Politics is often reported as a narrative, with a plot focused on conflict, climax and resolution. This is the case even in 'normal' periods of politics but an election campaign has an especially well-defined beginning, middle and end. The campaign proper begins with the Prime Minister driving to meet the Governor-General and asking for a dissolution of Parliament. Television crews wait patiently outside Government House to capture the drive through the gates because this is so symbolic and represents the beginning of the campaign. In the middle – sometimes called the 'rising action' in literature – are the day-to-day campaign activities, especially of the leaders. These are all building up to the climax of polling day and are usually reported in those terms: what does this mean for the likely result?

On polling day, the Labor and Coalition leaders are recorded casting their own votes in their respective electorates. This is another highly symbolic moment, shown on all of the television news bulletins that night. Some of those bulletins then morph into election night programs dedicated to reporting the vote count. Once the result is known, the winning party leader gives a victory speech and the loser a concession speech, which mark the acceptance of victory and defeat. This is the end of the main story, but some resolution also occurs in the following few days as commentators analyse the meaning of the result.

This narrative has proved a very stable formula over time, although some of the details and methods for telling the story have changed. Before television, when policy speeches were held at the start of the campaign, reporting of them used to signify the beginning. Slower vote counting in early elections meant results weren't known for days or even weeks, delaying the victory and concession speeches. However, the central points of the narrative – announcement, campaign, polling day and victory and concession speeches as culmination – have remained the same and these are staples of election reporting across different countries around the world (Strömbäck and Kaid 2008).

Within this grand narrative, there are also myriad individual plotlines and themes. Some narratives are specific to particular elections, but there are also longstanding and consistent themes around the reporting of conflict and competition. This chapter explores the main themes, but it begins with something more elementary: the limits of election coverage and how these set the boundaries for what stories can be told.

How much is reported?

The media with the most politically interested audiences devote the most attention to elections, creating a 'virtuous circle' that reinforces the activism of the already active (Norris 2000). In 2007 it was the *Australian*, with its national focus and interest in politics, that put the election on its front page every day of the campaign bar one (Table 9.1). The *SMH* had the next highest 'election newsworthiness' rating followed by the *AFR* which, although focused on business and economic news, reported the election more prominently than either the *Age* or the *Canberra Times*. Sometimes local news took precedence over the election in state-based broadsheets and sometimes stories about entertainment news did – especially in weekend editions.

Tabloids focused even more on non-election-related news, especially local interest, crime or entertainment stories. Crime stories involving children were especially prominent. Stories about drugs in playgrounds, the murder of a child, a teacher accused of rape and 'sex predators living near children' made the front page in 2007 on days when the election didn't. The *Herald Sun*, the newspaper that was least interested in the election, devoted its front page to footballer Ben Cousins' drug problems on six days of the campaign, while the Melbourne Cup horse-racing carnival took up the front page eight times. Usually this was in the form of a female model or

Table 9.1 Election newsworthiness rating for Australian newspapers, 2007

	Days during the 41-day campaign when the election did *not* make the front page	Election newsworthiness rating* (%)
Australian	1	97
Sydney Morning Herald	3	93
Australian Financial Review	4	89
Age	6	85
Canberra Times	7	83
West Australian	11	73
Courier-Mail	16	61
Daily Telegraph	17	59
Advertiser	20	51
Mercury	24	41
Herald Sun	25	39

* This is the number of days when the election campaign made the front page of the newspaper (in the form of a story about the election) expressed 'as a percentage of the maximum possible number' derived from McNair's (2000:17) 'political newsworthiness ratings'.

Source: Author.

celebrity posing with a horse and/or the Cup. According to the research on agenda-setting, these front-page choices not only signal to their audiences what is most important but also affect what they, in turn, see as important and what they know and remember.

More so than newspapers, primetime television news has very limited space. The script for an entire half-hour television news program, when typeset as newspaper copy, takes up less than one page of a broadsheet (Henningham 1988:154–5). Within these constraints, the public broadcasters devote more of their news time to elections, again reinforcing the 'virtuous circle'. The ABC and SBS provided more than twice as much time for the 2007 election than the two most-watched television news bulletins on commercial channels Seven and Nine (Table 9.2). This is not only a matter of choice and the 'virtuous circle' of catering to already politically interested audiences, but also one of different priorities and funding structures. The ABC has more time to allocate because it has no advertising and SBS (which did have advertising in 2007) had a longer one-hour bulletin.

If viewers continued watching Channel Seven or Nine after the news (watching the current affairs program on that channel and then a movie, for example), it is highly likely that they saw more political advertising that

Figure 9.1 More important than an election? Front pages in 2007

Source: Author photograph

Table 9.2 Minutes of election news coverage on primetime television news programs, 2007

	Average number of stories on the election (n = 85)	Average length of story (in minutes and seconds)	Average coverage per night (in minutes and seconds)
Channel 7	1.0	1:59	1:59
Channel 9	1.0	2:34	2:34
Channel 10	2.0	1:57	3:54
ABC	1.5	3:09	4:44
SBS	2.0	2:54	5:48

Note: average number of stories rounded to one decimal place.

Source: Author.

night than they did political news (Young 2003:140). According to Sussman (2005), this is no accident. He claims news outlets provide limited coverage of politics as an economic strategy to gain revenue from parties which then have to purchase television time to get their messages across.

To be fair, many Australian media outlets would argue that they provide more election coverage than their audiences would strictly want and that they do so as a public service and at their own commercial peril. But outlets do not merely react to the forces of general public opinion. They actively construct audiences, creating news mixes to appeal to certain tastes and encouraging (and discouraging) particular interests. It is telling, then, that on an international basis Australian coverage seems less comprehensive than in other similar countries. Despite their reputation for sound bite-style news coverage, American commercial television news stories on elections are an average of 20 seconds longer than Australian ones (Bucy and Grabe 2007:663).[1]

In the UK, front-page stories in the *Guardian* on the 2005 British general election averaged close to 820 words compared to 690 words in Australian broadsheets in 2007.[2] When the BBC reported on the 2005 British election, it devoted approximately 15 minutes to election news in both of its main half-hour bulletins every day compared to under 5 minutes on the same-length ABC news in 2007 (Bartle 2005:51). Commercial station ITV also included about 15 minutes of election-related news each day compared to the 2 minutes devoted by Australian commercial broadcasters (Deacon et al 2005:13).

This suggests something interesting about the way the news media in Australia have constructed their audiences and also about the role of media regulation (or lack thereof). In the UK, the BBC had a broadcasting monopoly from the 1920s until the 1950s and, even after commercial television broadcasters were brought in, they were required to meet standards for public service that were mandated in regulations. However, the newspaper sector in the UK was not affected by such regulations and there is far more diversity in British newspapers – at both ends of the tabloid–broadsheet spectrum. So, if the centrist nature of Australian media means that our 'quality' media are not as 'quality' as in the UK, nor are our tabloid newspapers as 'tabloid'.

During the 2005 UK election, over three-quarters of the front pages on British tabloids were about non-election issues (Bartle 2005:51) compared to an average of only 46 per cent for Australian tabloids in 2007. Australia's top-selling tabloid, the *Herald Sun*, put the election on the front page for 39 per cent of the campaign while the UK's biggest-selling tabloid, the *Sun*, made it front-page news only 21 per cent of the time (Deacon et al 2005:11). The *Sun* advertised topless page-three models to keep readers 'abreast of election swings'. Readers were told the women's bikini tops would 'come off' if their party did well or would 'stay on' if 'their parties' fortunes droop...' (the *Sun* (UK), 6 April 2005:1, 29). The *Herald Sun* drew the line at photos of (clothed) female models cuddling racehorses.

Who is newsworthy?

The election story is simplified and compressed to fit into the time and space limits explored above. Much is either abbreviated or left out. Who is shown and who gets to have a say is therefore crucial. This is not only about the outcome – that candidates who have a better chance to put their case for office to voters have a better chance of success – but is also a broader issue about how elections are understood. In Australia, despite the thousands of candidates who ran for office in the 2000s, elections were essentially represented in the news media as a contest between the rival major party leaders.

The Labor and Coalition leaders were the only actors who regularly got to have a say in their own words in most news reports. In 2007, one or other leader (usually both, for the sake of even-handedness) was quoted in 70 per cent of front-page newspaper articles. A sound bite from the leaders was included in 70 per cent of television news reports. Usually, their words shaped the news agenda but, even if they didn't get to have a say, they were usually spoken about: 95 per cent of newspaper articles and 84 per cent of television news reports included commentary about the leaders. This overwhelming focus was not just about the major party leaders' verbal statements but also about visual cues. Not only were they shown in nearly all television news stories on the election but their photos were also usually shown to signify what the election was all about – for example, graphics showing the leaders' faces were often used to introduce television news stories under headings such as 'Australia votes', 'Your call '07' or 'Decision '04'.

'Image-bites' – such as Howard's campaign morning walks in his patriotic tracksuit, a key visual in all three elections in the 2000s – are 'informationally and politically potent' (Grabe and Bucy 2009:68). People tend to have a better memory for visuals, impressions and experiences than they do for words (Grabe and Bucy 2009:55–6). But perhaps the most famous image-bite occurred the day before the 2004 election, when Mark Latham and John Howard crossed paths at a radio studio. Latham appeared to draw Howard towards him in a firm handshake and then towered over his shorter opponent in a way that was described in media coverage as 'aggressive', 'bullying' and 'intimidating'. The image made the front page of many newspapers the next day and it became folklore that this was a defining moment. Although there is no way to know its precise impact, and some have argued its impact has been overstated, according to the Liberals' campaign director this visual was so potent it crystallised voters' doubts about Latham (Gordon 2004).

The major party leaders dominate news coverage, but other major party actors are also reported – albeit far less frequently. The major party deputy leaders, Cabinet ministers and shadow ministers – especially in the more prominent portfolios such as Treasury and Health – receive some coverage. Costello appeared more often than usual for a deputy leader in 2007 when he took a more active role in the Liberal campaign. However, ministers and shadow ministers were mainly newsworthy when they made gaffes. Backbenchers and new candidates were largely absent in the most-accessed media, only likely to appear in television news clips when they were performing as a human backdrop, nodding away behind the leaders.

Female candidates were especially underrepresented in election coverage of all kinds – not just news but also current affairs, breakfast television and talkback interviews. A female politician appeared in only 20 per cent of election reports in 2001. This rose to 22 per cent in 2004 and 30 per cent in 2007 as women obtained higher leadership positions in the major parties, such as Julia Gillard as deputy leader in 2007. But, overall, female politicians were usually only *seen* in news reports, often used to add 'a bit of colour' (Norris 1997b). They were rarely ever heard until Gillard's ascension to Prime Minister in 2010. In the 930 election reports I examined for the 2001, 2004 and 2007 elections, across newspapers, television and radio, only 10 per cent included a quote from a female politician. While I had originally expected to see major differences in the representation of male and female politicians, I instead found that women were marginalised less by overtly sexist portrayals (although these were sometimes apparent) than by sheer exclusion.

Independents and candidates from minor parties were similarly excluded. During the three elections of the 2000s, only 5 per cent of newspaper articles ever quoted any minor party politician or independent, and only 4 per cent of radio clips and 6 per cent of television clips. This marginality is self-perpetuating, as the smaller parties then struggle to attract the media coverage they need to win public support. Independents and minor party politicians face the 'activist's dilemma'. In order to capture media attention, they need to do something extraordinary – such as bungee jumping to publicise a policy launch (as the Democrats leader, Andrew Bartlett, did in 2004) – but this can then undermine their authority and credibility.

In other countries, including in the US, there has been an increasing use of 'experts' in news coverage including pollsters, political insiders, business leaders, people from an NGO, lobby group or religious organisation, academics, political scientists and union leaders. But Australian election reporting went against this trend. The proportion of news reports quoting an 'expert' actually declined overall in the 2000s from 49 per cent of front-page newspaper articles in 2001 to 36 per cent in 2007 and from 35 per cent of television news stories to 26 per cent in 2007. It is difficult to know why this occurred; whether it was about cost-cutting in newsrooms – with no time or resources to seek external comments – or about broader cultural factors: perhaps a legacy of the 'culture wars' during the Howard years or the silencing of dissent from NGOs (Maddison 2007), part of a broader anti-intellectual streak, antipathy towards 'tall poppies' or a trend towards showing more 'ordinary people' in media content (Chapter 12). Perhaps it was just a greater reluctance by Australian experts to engage in media commentary?

This last explanation seems the least satisfactory because not all groups were media-shy and some were clearly more attractive sources for journalists than others. Male experts were the norm. Even in 2007, only 1 per cent of the experts quoted in newspaper reports were women, improving only marginally to 8 per cent on television. There were only two groups who were quoted more in 2007 than they were in 2001: business representatives and journalists. In 2001, business leaders constituted 15 per cent of all expert commentators quoted in newspapers, rising to 27 per cent in 2007. They were quoted nine times more often than union representatives. This discrepancy was noticeable even in 2007 when *WorkChoices* was a key issue. Was this a cause or a result of the fact that the unions turned to paid media to get their message across that year, running a very expensive anti-*WorkChoices* advertising campaign?

In election reporting, there is a very limited number and range of external sources used and this seems to be part of a broader problem in Australian journalism, not just related to the specific challenges of reporting an election. According to the APC (2006:30), newspaper articles quoting more than one source are 'relatively rare . . . [in Australia] even in longer articles', whereas one study in the US found that nearly half of all American newspaper reports (48 per cent) identified four or more sources.

How is the election story told?

Journalists not only select stories from the material that is available but also have to make those stories matter to their audiences. In election reporting, one method for achieving this is so entrenched that it is now seen as a permanent feature. Thomas Patterson (1980) observed 30 years ago in the US that the media report elections as if they are calling a horse-race with an obsessive focus on who's in front and who's behind. This seems to be common even across different countries with different political systems. The horse-race focus has been observed – to varying degrees – in election reporting in the UK, Canada, New Zealand, Brazil, France, Germany, Hungary, Israel, Japan, Mexico, Poland, South Africa and Spain (Strömbäck and Kaid 2008).

The horse-race metaphor is so dominant that it now seems quite inevitable, especially to reporters. Michelle Grattan (1993:29) argues: 'Of course, election coverage should involve a great deal more than a race call . . . But the fact remains that an election is a race, and inevitably will be treated like one.' What is interesting, however, is why it is being treated like one so much more than it was in the past. The reporting focus on who was in front increased with every election in the 2000s. By 2007, nearly half of all front-page newspaper articles (47 per cent) and three-quarters of television news reports (76 per cent) were focused on what I called 'electoral process'; that is, reporting of opinion polls and evaluation of politicians' motives, their electoral strategies, campaign tactics and likelihood of electoral success.

The news media *do* still report on policy matters – especially ones they judge to be of interest to their audiences (particularly those relevant to older Australians such as age pensions, hospitals, tax and interest rates) and the more sensational, controversial policies (such as asylum-seekers in 2001). However, as the focus on the horse-race increased, coverage of issues and policy problems and solutions (what some studies call a 'substantive focus' or an 'issue frame') declined. Stories that were mainly about policies (more than half of the news report) declined by 60 per cent between 2001 and 2007. Stories that had no, or only negligible, reference to policy rose by an almost equivalent amount of 54 per cent. These 'policy-free' stories were most common in commercial television news and tabloids.

When a policy proposal *was* reported, the focus was usually on its relevance to the horse-race rather than its finer detail or whether it would solve the problem identified (Box 9.1). This is a formula for reporting policy that focuses on cost and the policy's strategic significance (in terms of winning votes). When Labor released its aged care policy in 2001, reporting was framed in precisely the same way: 'Party leaders chase the pensioner vote', in what was then 'a $467 million pitch for the grey vote' (*Sunday Telegraph*, 14 October 2001).

Box 9.1

Putting policies in strategic terms: how the news media reported the Coalition's pension policy in 2007

A '$4 billion pitch for the grey vote' (ABC 7 pm News, 23 October).
A 'pitch for the grey vote' (Channel Nine 4.30 pm News, 23 October).
A 'multibillion dollar pitch for the pensioner vote' (Channel Nine 6 pm News, 23 October).
A '$4 billion pitch to older voters' (Channel Seven 4.30 pm News, 23 October).
A '$4 billion pitch for the grey vote' (Ten News at 5 pm, 23 October).
'Coalition offers billions in cash to win back lost elderly legions' (the *Australian*, 24 October).
A 'significant pitch by the Government for the grey vote' (the *SMH*, 24 October).
Howard 'has gone after the grey vote ... [the policy is] aimed at winning over older Australians' (the *Courier-Mail*, 24 October).

Horse-race reporting is popular with news outlets because it requires less interest and knowledge from audiences. It simplifies elections into a straight-forward concept of winning and losing, familiar from other areas of life, particularly entertainment and sports. News outlets believe it has greater appeal than a focus on 'dry' substantive issues such as policy and some academic studies that have used experiments to test audience preferences have supported this view (Iyengar, Norpoth and Hahn 2004). Adding enter-tainment and interest to their coverage has become even more important to news organisations as politics has crossed over from being a subject of news and current affairs into, as well, a topic of light entertainment, comedy and drama (Chapter 12).

Far from shying away from the horse-race metaphor, journalists unabashedly drew upon it. In news reports, the likely victor was described as 'the front runner'; stories described how one party was 'leading into the home straight' and even that, with the 'campaign half over, it looks like Labor in a canter'. The *Age* reported in 2004 that: 'As the gallopers in this two-horse race turn for home, the result is far from foregone' (*Age*, 4 October 2004). There were newspaper front pages showing the leaders on horseback racing to the finishing line. The horse-race metaphor was especially irresistible when a real horse-race made the news, as in both 2001 and 2007 when the Melbourne Cup took place during the campaign. Channel Nine News began its election coverage that day by stating: 'The latest Newspoll has the Prime Minister closing the gap [on Rudd] in their two man race.'

Aside from the horse-race, the other key metaphors used to animate an election for audiences are those relating to games and sporting contests – especially boxing but also tennis, athletics and car racing (Box 9.2). The leaders are represented as sharply polarised, described for example as being 'like prize fighters... trying to land the knockout blow' (Channel Ten 5 pm News 17 October 2007). The *Age* (24 November:1) promised its 2007 election coverage would include 'blow-by-blow analysis' of the election result.

Box 9.2

Election reporting analogies: sport

'Round one leaves Beazley bruised' (*Daily Telegraph*, 13 October 2001).
'Kim KOs tired PM' (*Herald Sun*, 15 October 2001).
'No king hit from Beazley' (*Daily Telegraph*, 15 October 2001).
'Blow for blow but no killer punch' (*SMH*, 13 September 2004).
'Challenger delivers but PM's punches tell' (*Australian*, 13 September 2004).
'Rookie cuts and scores top runs' (*Australian*, 13 September 2004).
'Gloves off' (*Illawarra Mercury*, 13 September 2004).
'They're off. The Prime Minister fired the starter's gun...' (Laurie Oakes, Channel Nine News, 29 August 2004).
'Game on' (graphic behind newsreader on day election was announced, ABC News, 14 October 2007).
'Labor leader Kevin Rudd has returned serve to John Howard's $34 billion tax plan' (the *Advertiser*, 20 October 2007).
Howard and Rudd 'traded blows for 90 minutes' (*Herald Sun*, 22 October 2007).

The other common metaphor is of politics as a form of warfare (without bloodshed). The leaders were variously described as firing the 'first shots' of the campaign, engaging in 'trench warfare', conducting a 'war of words' or an '11th hour assault' (Box 9.3). When Channel Seven promoted its coverage of the 2007 election it used an animation of Howard and Rudd sparring in a boxing ring. The *Financial Review* had a front-page image of the two leaders with pistols in hand headed: 'The Final Duel'.

Box 9.3

Election reporting analogies: war

'Leaders on the attack' (*Herald Sun*, 13 September 2004).
John Howard 'fired the first shots in a longer than usual six-week campaign' (*Herald Sun*, 30 August 2004).
'Howard has gone for the political equivalent of shock and awe on the first full day of the election campaign' (*Advertiser*, 16 October 2007).
Howard 'is staring down the barrel' (*Courier-Mail*, 25 October 2007).
Howard and Costello 'have launched a desperate rearguard action' (*West Australian*, 25 October 2007).
'The Kyoto story... has given ammunition to the Labor Party' (*Age*, 28 October 2007).
Howard and Rudd 'have fired the first shots in their duel over health policy' (*SMH*, 1 November 2007).
Howard 'will today unveil a 'shock and awe' blitz based on big-spending policy announcements' (*West Australian*, 12 November 2007).

As long as rival parties and candidates compete for office, conflict will always be a feature of election reporting but, like the horse-race, the way conflict is reported has been amplified and personalised. In the 2000s, there was an increasing trend towards the news media manufacturing drama and controversy. Bennett (2005:366) argues that news media outlets began imitating entertainment and reality television genres to 'selectively push . . . dubious plot elements into a news reality frame to create more dramatic news than the original situation would have been'.

Constructing campaign events, downplaying evidence that doesn't lend itself to simplification, casting doubt on challengers and using rumours to get a reaction from candidates were all methods for achieving this (Bennett 2005). An example in Australia of the use of rumours to get a reaction from a candidate occurred in the lead-up to the 2004 election campaign. After *Crikey* published rumours that a raunchy buck's night video featuring Mark Latham existed, the rumour was then reported in the *SMH* and News Limited papers. Latham held a press conference denying the video rumour as well as several other rumours, including a claim that he had faced charges of sexual harassment. He made an emotional appeal for the media to leave his family alone ('Cry Baby' was the resulting headline on the front page of the *Gold Coast Bulletin*). The day after Latham's press conference denying the allegations, 2UE radio host Steve Price sensationally revived the rumour by describing the supposed details of the video on *Sunrise* and claiming that he could even get a copy of it. This proved to be unfounded: Price had been duped by a hoax caller to his program.

Opinion polls

As the 'horse-race' focus became more apparent, the proportion of news stories quoting opinion poll results increased dramatically, rising by 34 per cent in newspapers and 33 per cent in television news between 2001 and 2007 (Figure 9.2). Even these quantitative figures do not capture just how much opinion polls permeated news coverage in the 2000s. Journalists tended to report each new poll 'with breathless proclamations of its importance' (Tiffen 2007:1). Even if the topic of the day was a health policy launch, reporters would often introduce their story with a summary of recent poll results. When the leaders appeared on television or radio, often the first question they were asked was about the polls. For example, a Radio 4BC host in 2001 began the interview: 'Mr Beazley, no joy for you from the polls at the moment, is there?' or, in an interview with Howard, an ABC Sydney host began by stating: 'Nice to see you here. The latest Newspoll has Labor closing the gap . . . Are you getting a bit nervous about the results?'

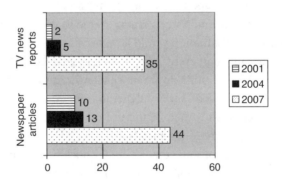

Figure 9.2 News stories quoting opinion polls, 2001–07 (percentages)

Note: For newspaper articles, n = 223 (including tabloids and broadsheets); for television news n = 238 (including public and commercial primetime television news).

Source: Author.

Peter Brent (2007:131) remarks that: 'There must be some countries more obsessed with political opinion polls than Australia, although they've yet to be found.' The fascination that the Australian media have with polls is longstanding. In 1940, Keith Murdoch sent Roy Morgan – then an employee of the Melbourne *Herald* – to the US to learn public opinion polling from George Gallup. From 1941 onwards, polls became a feature of press reporting and came to be prominent in election reporting, especially from the late 1960s. Although they were expensive, opinion polls were seen as a good investment because they could help sell newspapers. They offered something the paper could promote as an 'exclusive' – a 'scientific' reading of public opinion. They enabled newspapers to 'generate their own election stories via a new form of "pseudo event"' and their results were picked up by other media which 'generate[d] publicity for the originating papers that few other exclusives could achieve' (Goot in press).

All of these reasons still applied in the 2000s and were, in fact, magnified once politicians exerted greater control over the news agenda and journalistic resources declined. Lacking the sort of scoops that come from either journalistic investigation or the more spontaneous campaigning style of old-school politicians, polls became one of the few ways in which news outlets could initiate a story. They were especially important for horse-race reporting, as a way to keep score, but they also tapped into the greater use of commentary and analysis with reporters interpreting poll results, 'looking for meaning... pretending [they] can identify why the numbers moved over a fortnight' (Brent 2007:142).

Unlike in other countries, Australian broadcasters do not routinely commission large-scale opinion polls. Sky News did commission an exit poll in 2007 and, on the basis of its results, scored the coup of being the first to call the election result, predicting at 5.30 pm – half an hour before booths on the east coast had even closed – that Labor would gain 53 per cent of the two-party preferred vote to the Coalition's 47 per cent. This proved to be remarkably accurate (Young 2009a). SBS also commissioned a poll during the 2007 campaign but broadcasters otherwise fed off the polls commissioned by the major newspaper groups, all with their own (rival) suppliers.

Fairfax used AC Nielsen (an outlet of the American Nielsen company). News Limited used Newspoll (half-owned by News Limited) for the 2001 election and Galaxy for 2004–07, with the exception of the *Australian* which continued to use Newspoll (see Brent 2007 and Goot in press). Roy Morgan

Research carried out their own polling, not for any particular media outlet, although they did perform some specific polls for *Crikey*. During the 2007 campaign, these pollsters conducted at least 29 election polls between them, using mainly telephone polls (Nielsen, Galaxy, Newspoll, Morgan) but also some online (Nielsen) and face-to-face (Morgan) polls (Goot 2009:119–20).

Well-conducted opinion polls based on large representative samples are a valuable source of information, but a few points need to be kept in mind when interpreting their results. First, there is always an error margin because a sample of people is just that – a sample – and not the entire population. This margin of error means that, 19 times out of 20, for a survey of 1000 people that 'showed a result of 50 per cent the true figure would lie between 47 and 53 per cent' (Tiffen 2007:5). There can also be many potential errors made when collecting, tabulating, weighting and analysing data (see Brent 2007). Aside from these general factors – which apply to all opinion polls – there are also some good reasons to specifically be wary when trying to extrapolate the result of an individual poll to an election outcome (see Tiffen 2007).

In other words, a great deal of care should be taken when interpreting opinion poll results. Yet, as Tiffen (2007:5) notes, they are often reported 'with a misleading certainty about what they portend'. In Australia, the Press Council recommends that newspapers publish certain details about how a poll was conducted, but this is only a guideline – unlike in Canada where the required details are legislated – and the Press Council's guidelines are rarely adhered to in their entirety (see Box 9.4). In practice, Australian reporters have a great deal of flexibility in how they interpret and report opinion polls and, in recent years, there have been allegations of a lack of rigour in poll reporting as a result, and even of political 'bias' (see Chapters 10 and 11).

Box 9.4

What should be included in the reporting of polls

The Australian Press Council (2001) recommends that reports of polls in Australia should include:
- the exact wording of the question(s) asked
- a definition of the population from which the sample was drawn
- the sample size and method of sampling

- how and where the interviews were carried out
- when they were carried out
- who carried them out (e.g. trained interviewers, telephonists, reporters etc).

Partisan bias may be an issue in some cases (see Chapter 11), but the more widespread bias in the news media is not towards one party so much as it is towards reporting regular opinion polls to generate a sense of uncertainty and unfolding drama about the election result. Opinion polls are often used to create a narrative of a close contest between the major parties – even if there isn't – because this is far more interesting than a foregone conclusion.

In 2001, every major poll except the Morgan poll[3] was predicting a clear Coalition victory but reports in the *Age* on polling day still speculated that the result would 'be close'. Similarly, in the last week of the 2004 election, the *Herald Sun* said the result was going 'Down to the Wire' (4 October 2004) and an *AM* reporter said 'it's desperately close' (9 October 2004). Even more inexplicably, this also occurred in 2007, even though opinion polls had predicted that Labor would win for over 10 months before the election and with 'a strength and consistency that has probably never been seen before' (Tiffen 2007:1). The last polls to be reported before the election were widely reported as showing a narrowing gap and a 'close race' (Box 9.5, Figure 9.3) even though Goot (2009:131) argued: 'The idea that Labor could secure 52 per cent of the two-party preferred vote ([as predicted by] Galaxy, Newspoll), much less 53.5 per cent (Morgan), and still lose was fanciful.'

Box 9.5

The search for a 'cliffhanger': opinion polls and the 2007 election

Throughout the 2007 campaign, the *Australian*'s reporting of poll results – especially the reports of Dennis Shanahan – were derided by the online psephology community (see Chapters 10 and 11). But the *Australian* was not the only outlet searching for signs of a close race.

On the day before polling day, ABC News reported that the latest polls were suggesting 'tomorrow's federal election could be a cliffhanger' (ABC 7 pm News). SBS also reported that it 'could be a cliffhanger after all'. Channel Nine 6 pm news said Howard 'appears to be in sight of the impossible' and, in classic horse-race terms, was 'surging towards the finishing post'. Channel Ten 5 pm news reported that the latest polls showed an 'unexpected twist' and the result 'could be a lot closer than previously thought'. Channel Seven News was more cautious and read the same polls as showing that the gap had narrowed but still indicated a 'slim Labor victory'.

News Limited newspapers were more emphatic. The *Mercury* reported that 'the latest opinion polls... pointed to a cliffhanger.' The *West Australian* said they 'showed the election will be a cliffhanger and not the Labor landslide earlier polls have suggested.' The *Herald Sun* also said the latest polls 'set the scene for a cliffhanger election.' The *Daily Telegraph* described it as a 'knife-edge showdown'. The *Advertiser* more cautiously noted that the poll result 'suggests the gap is closing.' The *Courier-Mail* said the election 'will go down to the wire.'

Fairfax newspapers were also interested in signs of a closing gap but tended to explain more detail of the polls and were more tentative in their conclusions. The *Age* noted that new polls suggested the election 'was tightening'. The *SMH* reported that the Coalition was 'within striking distance of a remarkable come-from-behind victory' and 'if the Newspoll is correct, tomorrow's result is too close to call,' but also pointed out that Fairfax's Nielsen poll still suggested 'an emphatic win' for Labor.

Some political journalists do an excellent job at explaining and contextualising poll results. Others are less conscientious. But the close race narrative is not always about deliberate deception. There is no set definition of what is 'close'. Most election results at a federal level since 1949 have been close in terms of votes and almost all have been within a 5 per cent 2PP swing (exceptions were 1975 and 1969). Using a flexible and arbitrary definition of a 'close' result means the media get to tell an interesting story and, often, to have it both ways. For example, in the last week of the 2007 campaign, Morgan, Galaxy and Newspoll all predicted Labor had a 2PP vote of between 52 and 53.5 per cent and this was, as Box 9.5 shows, often reported as showing that the election result was going to be close. However, after the election, when Labor won with 52.7 per cent 'almost every commentator . . . described the result as a landslide to Labor' (Mackerras 2009:219). 'Landslide' is another flexible term.

News reports also tend to naturally emphasise change rather than stability, reporting on what has changed since the last poll – even if this is small, inconsequential or within the margin of error – rather than what has stayed the same. This was particularly obvious in 2007. But the media are encouraged by the parties – who also have a vested interest in forecasting a close race in order to prevent a backlash effect (if they're in front) or to

Figure 9.3 Newspaper reporting of opinion polls in the last days of the 2007 campaign

Source: Author photograph.

still appear a live prospect (if they're far behind). Against all the evidence, in 2001, the Liberal campaign director was telling the media 'I think this election will go right down to the wire' while, in 2004, Howard kept reiterating that 'this is going to be a very close election'. In 2007, Rudd also kept saying that the result 'will be tight'. Sometimes, the parties even leak selective bits of their internal polling to back up their claims.

That journalists might want to believe them is not only about keeping audiences interested but also about hedging their bets. A close contest is a safe prediction because, whatever the result, the commentator won't have been far wrong. This is why the hyped-up front-page headlines are, confusingly, often followed by more sober analysis on the inside pages. For example, although the *Northern Territory News* front page on election day interpreted a new poll as showing the election was 'poised to be a cliffhanger', on the inside pages it also acknowledged that the poll showed Labor was 'still well placed to reclaim power'!

Journalists in election news

It has not escaped journalists' attention that politicians exert a great deal of control over the news agenda. The way journalists report elections is at the core of this but, rather than change the conventions of reporting – for example, broaden the focus, use a wider circle of sources, conduct investigations, move from the day-to-day focus or otherwise change the main narrative – journalists have tended to take another route. Opinion polls are one way journalists have sought to regain the initiative. Another is by writing themselves into the story, giving politicians less coverage and giving themselves more.

The shrinking politician sound bite is especially well documented in the US. In the late 1960s, the average length of time a presidential candidate spoke in his or her own words on American network television during election campaigns was 43 seconds. This had shrunk to under 10 seconds by the late 1980s, then 8.4 seconds in 1992, and was down to 7.7 seconds in 2004 (Bucy and Grabe 2007:652, 653, 663, 657; Lichter 2001; see also Hallin 1992). In Australia, politicians' sound bites also reduced and by 2007 were down to 6.9 seconds, even lower than American ones. In an average television news story in 2007, reporters and other media figures (including

Table 9.3 Media speech versus politician speech in television news stories, 2007 (seconds)

	Average number of sound bites per story (n = 50)	Average sound bite (secs)
Host/anchor	1.1	15.9
Reporter	5.3	12.1
Other media figures	0.3	10.2
Total (all media)	**6.7**	**12.7**
Politicians	4.0	6.9

Source: Author.

news anchors/hosts and other journalists interviewed as part of the story) spoke for three times longer than the politicians they were reporting on (Table 9.3).

The shift to greater journalistic narration of politicians is epitomised by the practice of 'goldfishing' (or what Americans call 'lip-flap'), whereby a reporter talks over footage of a politician so that the politician's mouth is seen moving but the sound that is heard is the reporter's voice. In the 2000s, journalists became increasingly important brokers of meaning in political coverage as they paraphrased, narrated and commented on politicians' activities. This was partly about reasserting control over the news agenda but also about keeping audiences watching when politicians were seen as a 'turnoff'.

The 'interpretive turn'

The news media increasingly turned inward, not only in news reporting – where journalists were granted more space and were offering more interpretative analyses – but also in the expansion of commentary in other forms of news. Journalists appeared regularly on programs such as *Insiders* and *Meet the Press*. On radio they played a key role, sometimes as regular guests, other times as hosts of current affairs programs and talk radio. (Although not all hosts were journalists, some were self-confessed 'entertainers'.) In newspapers, the real growth in journalistic commentary was in op-ed pages, the use of regular columnists and the increase in articles by reporters headed 'Analysis'. On the internet, every major news organisation developed an online site devoted to news commentary in the 2000s – the *National Times* (Fairfax), *The Drum* (ABC) and *The Punch* (News Limited).

Some academics – but especially politicians – resent the way journalists are using their increased speaking time to interpret and to express opinions about political events. This is not a new complaint. In 1975, Liberal leader Malcolm Fraser complained: 'If I've got a criticism of the [Press] Gallery it's that there isn't enough straight reporting, too much interpreting' (Penniman 1977:199). Sometimes when politicians talk about straight reporting, what they want is verbatim reporting of their activities and statements without any pesky critical analysis, which is democratically undesirable. But 'straight' reporting was always something of a mirage.

By selecting a particular fact for discussion, we convey the opinion that it is important and then by using language (and sometimes images) to describe it, we further convey meaning about it. For example, when Labor launched its forestry policy in 2004, both of the newspapers shown in Box 9.6 reported the 'facts' of the launch on their front page in a seemingly 'straight' reporting style but, in the first line of each article, managed to convey very different impressions just by choice of words and emphasis. Some news outlets are more polemic in 'straight' news reporting than others, but even those that try hard to report in a neutral, detached manner see opinion invariably seeping into news coverage simply because it is so entwined with how we convey information. The difference really lies, then, in the extent to which journalists are up-front about which parts of their report are interpretations and about the sources and motivations behind these, and thus leave their audiences room to make their own judgements.

Box 9.6

Reporting on the 'facts' in news: one 'fact', two opinions

'Mark Latham will protect "the overwhelming majority" of Tasmania's old growth forests from logging if elected – and promises no-one in the timber industry need lose their job' (*SMH*, 5 October 2004:1).
'Mark Latham yesterday added to Tasmania's remarkable record of political payoffs by offering an $800 million bribe to the island's timber workers' (*Daily Telegraph*, 5 October 2004:1).

The rise of more overtly interpretative journalism is linked to the political and social culture of our times. (Indeed, Fraser himself has written several op-eds in newspapers in recent years.) Audiences are better educated and have greater access to information than in the past; they expect more than just a summary of what someone powerful has said. News has become so routine, so narrowly focused and narrowly sourced (as we saw in this and the previous chapter) that opinion has become one of the most interesting parts of it. There are also economic reasons behind the interpretive turn as outlets are seeking to 'value add' in an era of easily available 'breaking news', and opinion and commentary are fairly cheap ways of doing this.

However, there are also reasons beyond the economic that go to the heart of how we make sense of information in a complex world. It is unreasonable to expect journalists to only report *what* has happened. They – and their audiences – also need to consider *why*. This means dealing with perceptions as well as facts. To take an obvious example, the Coalition's *Tampa* policy in 2001: if more political reporters had been willing to consider theories about the strategies behind the policy, including 'wedge politics' and its appeal to swinging voters, their audiences would have gained a much better understanding of events than a 'straight' reporting of the facts provided (Ward 2002b). But the problem here is not that reporters never consider events in strategic terms or in terms of their design for electoral appeal. They often do. The problem is that they are erratic about when they give this sort of analysis and when they don't. Sometimes the minutiae of stage-managed events are interpreted in complex, strategic terms while other, more significant, themes and events are overlooked.

McNair described the rise of interpretive journalism as 'an intelligent journalistic adaptation to an environment which is highly competitive, information-rich and intensively manipulated by political actors'. He argues: 'We *need* the interpretative moment in journalism . . . because the world is too complex, its information flows too rapid, for us to make sense of on our own' (McNair 2000:82). The challenge is for journalists to draw on a range of sources and ideas for their analysis, to interrogate their own positions, and to be clear about which parts of their stories are interpretations and how they arrived at them. There also needs to be a balance between journalistic commentary and leaving enough time for politicians and other actors to speak, to put their case to citizens in their own words.

Meta-coverage

One of the major topics that journalists have been concerned with in their analyses is to reveal to their audiences the behind-the-scenes interactions of politics, including the 'meta-campaign' that politicians conduct for the benefit of the media. One of the most obvious examples of this self-referential 'meta-coverage' frame is the way news stories commonly show the media pack gathered around the politician (Figure 9.4). Journalists highlight how politicians try to manipulate news coverage – for example, revealing that media advisers tried to 'spin' to them before the *Great Debate* in order to lower expectations of their leader's performance or telling their readers that a barbecue staged by a leader was just a staged picture opportunity and no-one actually ate the sausages!

We know a lot more about how politics is conducted today than we did 40 years ago because of the willingness of journalists to write about it. At its best, meta-coverage gives citizens important information about how the electoral process actually works, highlighting what is going on behind the scenes and pointing out important shifts in how politics is conducted. At its worst, it can descend into simplistic representations and take a very cynical form. Matthew R. Kerbel (1999) observes that one of the main ways reporters have staged a 'fightback' against politicians' influence on the news agenda is by presenting a very sceptical view of politicians and their advisers (pointing out that they will do whatever it takes to win over voters) and by revealing politicians' information-control methods in a contemptuous manner.

Meta-coverage also helps journalists reiterate their professional role, demonstrate their distance from politicians and explain gaps in their reporting brought about by the effectiveness of political PR. For example, frustrated journalists described the 1996 election as 'one of the most sanitised, deodorised, homogenised and contrived election campaigns in living memory' due to the tight control exercised by the major parties (Crouch 1996). A similar complaint has been expressed ever since. The 1998 election was described as 'mind-numbingly boring' (Duffy 1998) while 2001 was the most 'sterile [and] closely orchestrated election campaign' ever seen in Australia (Hamilton 2001a).

In journalists' minds, there is no doubt who is to blame for making elections 'boring'. By 2007, one reporter opined that: 'By the time the parties have finished dicing and slicing the research, campaigns are reduced to a sanitised, soulless ritual performed by puppets' (Steketee 2007). A world-weary, cynical tone often creeps into coverage. For example, a newspaper graphic describing the spending promises made at a party launch was

Figure 9.4 Examples of meta-coverage in television news, 2000–07
Sources: Author compilation from various news sources.

headlined: 'Vote Buying Spree' while, commenting on the seemingly planned nature of Howard's kiss to his grandson at the Liberal campaign launch, a reporter described the moment as 'the money shot'. As Todd Gitlin has pointed out, the dominant tone of modern journalistic reporting is 'a kind of knowing "postmodern" cynicism that debunks the image and the image-maker, yet in the end seems to accept them as the only reality we have left' (quoted in Hallin 1992:23).

Journalists as political actors

While journalists have been increasingly willing to tell audiences how politicians control and disseminate information – how they court, cajole and intimidate journalists – they have been less forthcoming about their own methods, tactics and motivations.[4] Journalists are writing themselves into stories and turning the camera upon themselves, but this is rarely done with any critical scrutiny. Self-analysis often goes only as far as highlighting the importance of the role of the media but stops far short of critically interrogating it. The meta-coverage frame has therefore not reached its full potential to give audiences a full sense of how the interactions between the media and politicians work or, indeed, how those between the media and their audiences work.

It is not that the media won't report on the media. Some of the biggest stories during elections in the 2000s were, directly or indirectly, about the media – for example, in 2007, Channel Nine's use of 'the worm' during the *Great Debate* against predetermined rules; 2UE talkback host Steve Price (of the Latham bucks' night video) and his on-air revelation of a private conversation he had in an airport lounge with Labor's Peter Garrett; and Barrie Cassidy, host of *Insiders*, complaining about Rudd appearing on *Rove* rather than his show (Chapter 12). All raised interesting debates, but they were deliberate, even self-aggrandising discussions of the role of the media.

One of the few stories that was exposed rather than deliberately aired and that went deeper and raised more uncomfortable questions came when the ABC's *Media Watch* program reported an email exchange between Caroline Overington, a journalist at the *Australian*, and Danielle Ecuyer, an Independent candidate in the hotly contested seat of Wentworth.

Polls were suggesting that preferences from Ecuyer could determine the outcome in Wentworth. The email exchange gave the impression that Overington was trying to influence that outcome by lobbying Ecuyer to direct her preferences to Liberal MP Malcolm Turnbull, saying: 'Please preference Malcolm. It would be such a good front page story' (*Media Watch* 2007). Overington denied that she was trying to influence Ecuyer's preferences, said that it was an in-joke between 'a couple of girls', and argued that *Media Watch* was gaining revenge for her sledging of the show earlier in the year. But rival newspapers then published a series of flirtatious and, at turns, threatening emails that were sent to the Labor candidate for Wentworth, George Newhouse. At one point, Overington told Newhouse:

> Either you say yes to a photograph smiling and happy and out campaigning, or we stake you out at [his home address], and get you looking like a cat caught in a trap, in your PJs. Your choice (Murphy and Debelle 2007).

Overington dismissed these emails as a joke as well but, on polling day, witnesses reported that Overington confronted Newhouse at the polling booth and slapped him in the face. She later apologised for what she said was a push with an open hand.

The Overington incident raised important issues about the interactions that occur between journalists and their sources that are rarely discussed in public. It was a rare account, not of how politicians spin to journalists, but of how journalists get information and how they (deliberately or otherwise) influence political events. This raises a major issue with political reporting in the 2000s and beyond. As journalists have begun to play a more overtly (and sometimes covertly) active role, there has been no proportional increase in media accountability. We have a problem if the new reporting styles merely substitute the unscrutinised discourses of one group of political elites (politicians) for those of another (journalists, their editors, producers and managers at news organisations as well as media owners). Politicians are accountable via media scrutiny and ultimately at the ballot box but, in Australia, there is very limited media diversity and very limited media oversight in a system of self-regulation.

Conclusion

Not all media or all journalists are the same. Some try hard to avoid the worst excesses of horse-race reporting and there are many examples of first-rate journalism that provide a remarkably deep and rich analysis of events. However, a focus on the more 'entertaining' aspects of the election contest is commonly used to attract audiences who otherwise might not pay attention and to maintain the interest of audiences over a six-week campaign. Personalising information, simplifying the story, using evocative language and imagery and focusing on conflict and the horse-race are common themes that do not just occur in popular media but in public broadcasting and broadsheets as well.

A generous interpretation is that the news media use these narratives to try hard to engage audiences and that they give a remarkable degree of information, given the pressures involved in election reporting. It is difficult to tell a complex story in limited time and space, especially when it is a story that many don't want to hear about. A more critical interpretation of Australian election reporting is that the time limits and simplification merely reflect how news audiences have been constructed. Overseas experiences suggest that election reporting could be longer, more detailed and (even if worse, à la British tabloids) more varied. Australians are provided with coverage of elections that presents only a narrow spectrum of information, often repetitively. The most powerful groups have a dominant say in election news, information is sometimes presented superficially in order to maintain an interesting narrative (opinion polls are the clearest example of this), and the media do a particularly poor job at reporting on their own role.

If there is a gap in our knowledge, it is less about politicians and how they campaign and more about the media and how they operate. Reporters need to do more than just turn their cameras upon the media pack. They have to take the next step of recognising that, as powerful actors, the coverage journalists give themselves, their organisations, colleagues and the role of the media generally, should be just as probing and critical as the coverage they give to politicians.

Part III

ELECTIONS IN MEDIATED TIMES

Chapter 10

NEWS, POLITICAL REPORTING AND THE INTERNET

The internet is having an impact upon election news but also, more broadly, on news journalism and political communication. There are several dimensions to this that need to be considered. There is the impact on *citizens* and *audiences* (regarding who accesses online news, which sites they visit and what they do there), but also on *news production* and *content*: in what ways is the internet changing how news is gathered, reported and disseminated and how does this affect the *economic models* that major news organisations rely upon? Finally, there are also important questions about whether the internet has changed the nature of *public debate*, including claims that it has radically altered concepts such as 'audiences', 'news' and *journalism* in ways that will have profound implications for society and democracy.

Too often, all of these different elements are conflated in a debate that sees researchers and commentators divided starkly along cyber-enthusiast and cyber-sceptic lines. As Turner (2010:4) argues:

> To take a clear position on any of this material – . . . [but] particularly one that is sceptical about the discourse of emancipation, democratization and liberation that has become the default position for so many media and cultural studies' accounts of Web 2.0 lately – is to enter into a very testy debate.

As I plunge headlong into that debate, I should first identify myself as what the media industry calls a 'heavy internet user' – I rely almost entirely on the internet for my news. I am therefore very aware of its advantages as a news medium but, at the same time, I am also acutely aware that my experiences are not typical.

There is a type of intemperate cyber-enthusiasm that abounds in the digital industries. This is natural enough, but it can also be a trap for academics who usually have a great deal of autonomy in their working lives, a preference for detailed textual information and all-day access to broadband internet at work. None of these elements are common in the experiences of the general Australian population. As Turner (2010:5) points out: 'many of the arguments made about ordinary people's access [via the internet] . . . are made by those who are far from "ordinary" themselves: cultural, political, academic and media elites . . . '

To my mind, any claims of internet-led revolution are premature if the internet has merely allowed the same groups of people different ways to access the same sort of information they were getting before. This is one of the criteria I use in this chapter to assess the impact of the internet in terms of audience and content, but I also consider shifts in news production and economic models. At the end of the chapter, I move beyond the news industry to consider some of the broader claims that the internet is leading to a 'paradigm shift' in the definition of 'news'.

Elections online

It is not difficult to see the reasoning behind claims that the internet was a democratising force in the 2000s. The evidence seemed to be all around us. In the US, where the most detailed research was performed and where use of the internet for political purposes was comparatively advanced, the Pew Research Center found that nearly three-quarters (74 per cent) of American internet users went online during the 2008 presidential election to take part in, or get news and information about, the campaign. This was 55 per cent of the entire adult population and it was not only about passively receiving news: 13 per cent of all American adults used the internet to create their own political content and 14 per cent used social networking sites for 'political information or to take part in the some aspect of the campaign . . . ' (Smith and Rainie 2009:2, 34–5).

The role of the internet in 2008 led some American journalists to suggest that:

[it might] have been a milestone, the last election cycle in which traditional news outlets were the foremost sources of campaign information . . . [because mainstream] news accounts [by journalists] from the road . . . now seem like just one small part of the vast torrent of political information that is available on the Internet via campaign Web sites, blogs, social networking pages, Twitter feeds and crowd-sourced reporting like *Huffington Post*'s OffTheBus feature (Farhi 2008a).

The *Huffington Post* – which had transformed from a blog to a 'fully fledged online newspaper' – had involved 12 000 citizens in reporting on the election in what was hailed as 'the first open platform election coverage team' (*The Economist* 2008).

In Australia, use of the internet for political purposes was not as widespread and online developments tended to be slower. Nevertheless, much changed between the 2001 and 2010 elections. Traditional media companies transformed their offerings from little more than a 're-purposing of [their] existing news developed for other media' (Flew and Wilson 2008:134) to sites that were more immediate and interactive, with a greater emphasis on breaking news, audio and video, and visual design. Figure 10.1 shows the *Age* website in 2001; the example in Figure 10.2 shows just how much the website changed in nine years.

As with the BBC in the UK, in Australia the ABC was leading the way in online news (Figures 10.3, 10.4, 10.5). In 2007, the ABC website featured breaking news, interactive tools to follow the campaign, psephological information, maps, graphs and statistics, and ABC programs were streamed and downloadable via text, video and audio. There were blogs written by online staffers as well as an opening of the site to external bloggers and writers. There was a forum for visitors to contribute and comment.

Other news media outlets were also using blogs, videos and online polls alongside news reports and commentary pieces as well as quizzes and games, interactive maps, voting predictors and video questions. News Limited had a 'vote-a-matic' online quiz, which matched users' political views with the parties' platforms. Fairfax established a YouTube channel encouraging users to submit questions to politicians. Network Ten collaborated with MySpace

Top breaking stories: Last updated Friday 13 Jul 2001, 2:57 PM

PM vows to pursue sick Skase
The Federal Government would not stop its chase of fugitive businessman Christopher Skase because of photos showing him painfully thin and unhealthy, Prime Minister John Howard said today.

Credit cards may carry debt danger warnings
Monthly credit card statements could soon carry blunt warnings such as those on cigarette packs under NSW Government plans to curb addiction to credit card debt.

More violence pushes mid East truce to limit
In another outburst of violence on the West Bank, Israeli tanks have shelled Palestinian police posts in response to the ambush of Israeli motorists.

NSW throws gallery a $15m lifeline
NSW Premier Bob Carr today announced a government rescue for the cash-strapped Museum of Contemporary Art at The Rocks in downtown Sydney.

AFP investigates vigilante coast watchers
Federal police will scrutinise a vigilante group calling on volunteers to patrol Australia's northern waters to deter people smugglers.

Other breaking stories:

NEWS
NSW throws gallery a $15m lifeline
Fog clears but air delays continue
AFP investigates vigilante coast watchers
Fitzgerald to probe Aboriginal violence
Family frets over missing TV broker
Howard sticks to year end poll date
Credit cards may carry debt danger warnings
PM vows to pursue sick Skase
Two cut bats rensonsible: ACOSS says

NEWS
NSW throws gallery a $15m lifeline
More NEWS

WORLD
More violence pushes mid East truce to limit
More WORLD

ENTERTAINMENT
Singer Stevens still can't call the RNSS tune
More ENTERTAINMENT

SPORT
Lions fans crowned kings of big spending
More SPORT

BUSINESS
Local shares chase Wall St
More BUSINESS

Figure 10.1 The *Age* website in 2001. Courtesy of the *Age*

Source: The *Age* website, 12 July 2001: PANDORA archive, National Library of Australia. http://pandora.nla.gov.au/pan/15133/20010713-0000/www.

Figure 10.2 The *Age* website in 2010. Courtesy of the *Age*

Source: The *Age* website, 16 June 2010: screenshot by author from http://www.
theage.com.au/, accessed 1:00 pm, 16 June 2010.

for a similar project, broadcasting video questions to politicians on *Meet the Press*. Yahoo!7's election website had news footage, message boards and a 'political death match' boxing game where users could 'pit different politicians against each other'. (In 2004, Ninemsn had an online 'Election Invaders' game in which visitors could throw pies at the party leaders.)

Outside of the traditional media organisations, Google and iPrime both launched election websites. MySpace had a 'MyElection' section. *Crikey* had an 'election tracker' following the movements of the party leaders as well as providing commentary and news. Academics at Queensland University of Technology ran a citizen journalism project called You Decide (Box 10.1). *Election Tracker* hired four young people – aged under 25 – to be 'trackers' following and reporting on the campaign from a youth perspective.

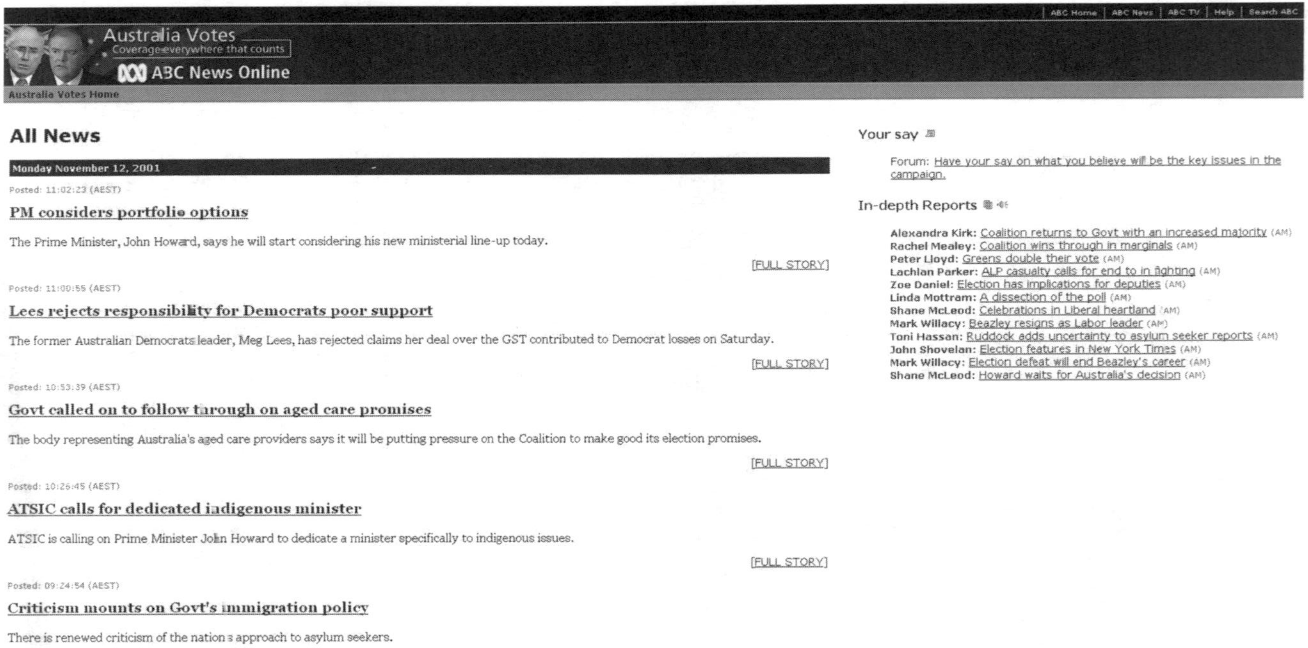

Figure 10.3 The ABC's election website, 2001

Source: ABC News online, 12 November 2001, saved by National Library of Australia, PANDORA archive.

Figure 10.4 The ABC's election website, 2004

Source: ABC *Australia Votes* 2004, 9 October 2004, saved by National Library of Australia, PANDORA archive.

There were also many political party, interest group and issue group websites. Some were satirical or critical – for example, in 2004 the john-howardlies site and in 2007 kevinruddsucks.com. Others drew upon the watchdog mantle that traditional journalism claims. The political activist group GetUp!, for example, established a site called *Promise Watch* to collect and track election promises and to hold politicians to account. Meanwhile, in a celebrated incident, independent bloggers were playing a role in holding the media to account (Box 10.2).

Figure 10.5 The ABC's election website, 2007

Source: ABC *Australia Votes* 2007, 23 November 2007, saved by National Library of Australia, PANDORA archive.

Box 10.1

Experiments in citizen journalism: *You Decide 2007*

You Decide ran for just under three months during the lead-up to the election and shortly after. It was funded by an academic grant and run by a group of academics in partnership with SBS and several other organisations. Its audience is discussed more in Box 10.3.

The project encouraged voters to interview their local candidates, conduct vox-pops with other voters and file reports on the website in text, audio and video. Overall, *You Decide* published 230 stories 'from 50 out of Australia's 156 electorates' (Flew and Wilson 2008:138). The site's most active contributor, Kevin Rennie, was from the Western Australian seat of Kalgoorlie (Bruns 2008:83). However, the most accessed news story (with 2000 hits) was an interview conducted by one of the project staffers in which the Liberal member for the Queensland seat of Herbert blamed young people for their 'financial illiteracy' and related his own story of sitting on milk crates when he couldn't afford chairs. These comments attracted both political attention and mainstream media coverage (Flew and Wilson 2008:138).

Box 10.2

Psephology bloggers and the *Australian* in 2007

In 2007, a number of blogs – especially *Possums Pollytics*, *The Poll Bludger* and *Mumble* – gave a great amount of detail and context in analysing poll results. Bruns (2008:82) argued that they offered 'their readers a virtual masterclass in psephology . . .' They also offered a damning expert critique of the way newspapers – especially the *Australian* – had been reporting opinion poll results. The *Australian's* poll result interpretations were derided for being consistently partisan (pro-Coalition) and based on inaccurate interpretations and simplistic analysis.

On 10 July the *Australian's* political editor Dennis Shanahan (2007a, 2007b) published an article (as well as a post on his blog) highlighting how a new poll showed that Howard was catching up to Rudd in terms of preferred Prime Minister. He suggested this was evidence of a turnaround in the Coalition's electoral fortunes.

Up to 250 comments – mostly critical – were posted on Shanahan's blog in response. For example: 'you are reading too much into this poll that is not supported by the actual data'; '[this is] one of the most desperate attempts to put a pro-Coalition spin on polling figures to date'; 'Dennis, the spin is getting weary, old son. These are BAD poll figures for Howard. BAD.' The critical reader postings went on until just before noon when a notice appeared on the *Australian's* site saying: 'Commenting for this article is no longer available' (Shanahan 2007b). When Shanahan posted a sarcastic response to the criticism on his blog the next day, the number of comments readers were allowed to post was suddenly limited (seemingly arbitrarily) to only 16 (Flew and Wilson 2008).

At the psephology blogs, the criticism was just as strident and obviously had an impact when, two days later, the *Australian* published an extraordinary editorial. On 12 July 2007, in an editorial reportedly written by the newspaper's editor-in-chief himself, the *Australian* attacked online sites that 'feed off the work of the *Australian*' for being a 'waste of time' and the bloggers for being 'sheltered academics and failed journalists who would not get a job on a real newspaper'. It concluded that 'unlike *Crikey* [another critic], we understand Newspoll because we own it'.

This generated further controversy when Tim Dunlop – one of the few left-of-centre bloggers writing for News Limited – posted a critique of the *Australian's* editorial. Dunlop's post was then removed from the News Limited site a few hours later, which suggested a further degree of censorship. However, an enterprising *Larvatus Prodeo* commentator had managed to copy Dunlop's article and posted it on LP so that it was still accessible.

This incident was seen as an example of the role blogs can play in opening up debate and holding the media to account, as well as evidence of the new interactivity the internet afforded and the decline of the 'journalist as hero' narrative. It also showcased the sensitivity of some traditional media and their difficulties in coming to grips with the online world.

The audience for online political news

There is no doubt that the internet has expanded the volume and sources of political communication, but has it expanded the audience? Not every Australian could get online easily in the 2000s. In 2006–07, the rate of household internet access was 64 per cent and 43 per cent of households had broadband connections (ABS 2008b). Although we are living through a 'catch up' phase in which the digital divide is narrowing, there are still stark divisions in terms of age, income, gender, education and geographical location. To take but two examples, Indigenous people are about half as likely to have broadband access compared to non-Indigenous people, and people employed in low-skill occupations are 27 per cent less likely (ABS 2006).

Of those who *did* have internet access, most were *not* going to designated news websites. For example, in 2010, less than 3 per cent of all Australian internet traffic was going to the most accessed news site – Ninemsn – and this site included email access as well as news (Hitwise 2010). In the 2000s, the internet was still a secondary news source for most Australians. Even by 2007, only 6 per cent of Australians said the internet was the medium they relied on *most* for news and information while 60 per cent nominated television (Phillips et al 2008). To put this into some perspective we can consider the ABC website, one of the most popular news sites. In 2008, the website received about a million unique visitors *a month* while a single television program – the ABC's evening news – received more viewers than that every night.

Table 10.1 shows the most popular news websites for those who had visited a news website in *the past four weeks* before they were surveyed by Roy Morgan Research. Although it casts a wide net of *monthly* access, only a core of between 5 and 10 per cent in each age group read online broadsheets or visited ABC online. With the exceptions of Google News (a news aggregator increasingly popular with younger news-seekers) and Bigpond (which was only popular with the over-50s), the top news sites were all owned by either newspaper companies (Fairfax, News Limited) or broadcasters (ABC, Ninemsn) and – demonstrating the still powerful influence of television – the most popular site for four out of the five age groups was a broadcaster (allied with an IT company in the case of Ninemsn).

Not all of these news website visitors were interested in political news. As we noted in Part I, in Australia, even though 2007 saw a heightened level

Table 10.1 Popularity of online news sites, 2007–08 (percentage of age cohort that has visited the site in the past month)

Age group	1	2	3	4	5
14–17	Ninemsn (7%)	Google News (5%)	News.com.au (3%)	SMH (2%)	Herald Sun (2%)
18–24	Ninemsn (14%)	SMH (8%)	News.com.au (7%)	Google News (7%)	Age (6%)
25–34	SMH (10%)	News.com.au (10%)	Ninemsn (9%)	Age (8%)	ABC (8%)
35–49	Ninemsn (8%)	SMH (7%)	ABC (7%)	News.com.au (6%)	Age (6%)
50+	ABC (6%)	SMH (4%)	Ninemsn (4%)	Age (3%)	Bigpond News (3%)

Source: Roy Morgan Research data supplied to the author (Single Source July 2007–June 2008, News sites visited in the last four weeks by age).

of political interest, only 5 per cent of people used it 'many times' to get election news or information. There were 55 per cent of AES respondents who had internet access in 2007 but still chose not to use it for election news – the same proportion as in 2004 (Bean, McAllister and Gow 2008). Just because political news and information become available on a new medium, this does not mean that people without previous interest in politics suddenly become interested.

Nor does the use of a different medium mean that the political news audience suddenly becomes more representative. As we noted in Chapters 3 and 4, the approximately 6 per cent of Australians who relied on the internet for their news were even more likely than general internet users to be young, highly educated and well-off and the more an online news provider focused on politics, the smaller its audience was and the more likely it was to be dominated by older, white, wealthy males. Even in the US, most of the spectacular growth in online political news access in 2008 was confined to 'the young, those with college [education], and those who live in higher-income households'. There was still not 'much growth among those over the age of 50, those with less education, or those living in relatively less well-off households' (Smith and Rainie 2009:3).

Also, while the internet greatly expanded the possibilities for news and information, there were still centralising forces. The move to faster, breaking news saw a greater reliance on a small number of wire services with news repackaged for different online outlets. It was also increasingly difficult for news organisations to have exclusive content because outlets so freely cut and pasted from each other. And online content still reflected – or even exacerbated – the reporting trends in traditional media. For example, Goot found that online news focused on the Prime Minister and the government more than traditional news media coverage and that 'Far from re-ordering old hierarchies... may have made the [2007] election a less even contest' (Goot 2008:99, 107).

Audiences for other political news sources

News online in the 2000s was not just about traditional news organisations, though. The internet lowered the barriers for entry so that anyone with a connection could in theory become a news publisher by writing content and/or linking to news providers. In practice, however, most people turned to familiar providers rather than taking advantage of the 'long tail' of the internet to get content from somewhere different. Based on his study of web traffic, Hindman (2008:135) argued that, when it came to news, media and politics sites in the 2000s, it was 'simply not true that the smallest outlets, taken together, get most of the traffic. Not even close.' Television broadcasters also dominated in the US. In 2006, the most popular news sites were CNN and ABC News and, in 2008, MSNBC and CNN (Miller 2009:78; PEJ 2008:2).

What was different was the growing role of news aggregators (especially Google and Yahoo). The main aggregators mostly linked back to established news organisations and news wires, but they did also send some traffic to magazines, blogs and primary sources of news (such as press releases). Although blogs were one of the most celebrated forms of democratisation among cyber-enthusiasts in the early 2000s, dedicated blog visitors were always the exception rather than the norm. Even in the US, in 2004 only 9 per cent of internet users said they regularly read political blogs (PRC 2005). By as late as 2008, only 24 per cent of all American adults said they read blogs (of any kind); most read only irregularly and only 9 per cent of adults had ever created one (PRC 2008c).

Working out just how many people go to political blogs or websites in Australia is no easy task. The 'unique visitor' measurement can sometimes mask more than it reveals (as discussed in Chapters 3 and 4). Server figures are even worse, as they are 'notoriously wrong' and can overstate audiences by up to 'three to four times' (Young 2010). There is much controversy within the blogging community about audience sizes. Bearing this in mind, I've headed Box 10.3 'what some online sites say...'. I've only included sites independent of the traditional media, but there were also blogs on mainstream news websites including those by Tim Blair for News Limited on the *Daily Telegraph* website and *Herald Sun* columnist Andrew Bolt (also for News Limited). Bolt (2008) reported that his blog received a 'record one million visits' in 2008 and 'as many as 13 000 comments in a week'.

Box 10.3

Online audiences: what some online sites say

Subscription email newsletters

Crikey: approximately 14 000 subscribers. 70 per cent are male, three-quarters are university educated and they are more than twice as likely as the average Australian to have a high income. Promotes itself as reaching an audience 'crammed with highly intelligent, influential decision-makers' (*Crikey* undated).

New Matilda: in 2010 had 9–10 000 subscribers. Said it had a 'loyal, discerning and affluent audience', that 80 per cent of its 'registered users are professionals who work in: media, education, health, science and political advisory roles. A further 10 per cent are in senior business or management positions' (*New Matilda* 2010).

Blogs, websites and projects

Online Opinion: 'Australia's e-journal of social and political debate' had 86 618 unique visitors a month in March 2010, according to Nielsen Net Ratings. Founder Graham Young (a former vice-president and campaign chairman of the Queensland Liberal Party) says that there is probably a core audience of about 20 000–30 000. He says the site 'struggles to get one-third female audience' and 'people under 30 years'. Seventy-three per cent of visitors have a university education (37 per cent at postgraduate level). A third earn over $100 000 per annum. A 'large proportion' of its audience are 'drawn from Academia and Government', 72 per cent are over 45 (Post Click 2010).

Larvatus Prodeo: 'an Australian group blog which discusses politics, sociology, culture, life, religion and science from a left of centre perspective', LP has about 33 718 unique visitors per month. Founder Mark Bahnisch (who has a PhD in sociology and also writes regularly for *New Matilda*, *Online Opinion* and *Crikey*) says his 'impression is that [LP's audience is] heavily skewed towards academics, students and public sector workers' but also 'widely read by political staffers and issue and party activists and journos'.

The Poll Bludger: a psephology blog run by William Bowe, a PhD student in political science. When run as an independent blog, *The Poll Bludger* received, on a typical day in March 2007, up to 510 unique visitors. The blog was hosted by *Crikey* after September 2008, increasing traffic. In 2010 the audience varied from 11 000 unique visitors per month to up to nearly 28 000 per month during March because of the South Australian and Tasmanian elections. The psephology sites see audience spikes during election campaigns. Bowe says his audience is 'male-dominated'.

Mumble: run by Peter Brent who has a PhD from ANU, *Mumble* receives about 10 000 unique visitors a month and averages about 3000 a day but, during the 2007 election, received up to 30 000. (These figures are based on server figures.) Brent says his audience is 'the political players – politicians, staffers and journalists – but extends more generally to people who are tragically interested in politics, particularly the psephological angle.' From emails and comments, he believes his readership is 'over 90 per cent male'.

You Decide: citizen journalism project run by academic researchers including Terry Flew, Jason Wilson, Axel Bruns and Barry Saunders. (The latter three also ran the group blog *Gatewatching* and *Club Bloggery*, which appeared on the ABC website in 2007.) Industry partners were also involved, including Graham Young of *Online Opinion* and SBS. The site had 2000 registered users. At its peak, it 'attracted over 12 000 readers a week'. The individual story that received the most hits got 'about 2000 overall' (Flew and Wilson 2008:138).

Box 10.4

What they do: some other Australian blogs

Club Troppo: a group blog that has existed in various guises since 2003 and takes what it calls a 'radical centrist' view of politics, economics and law. Founded by Ken Parish, an 'academic lawyer' living in Darwin.

Simon Jackman: a psephology blog run by Jackman, an Australian academic and professor of political science at Stanford University.

Possum Pollytics: originally *Possum Comitatus*, 'a group character comprising four economists', now run by Scott Steel and providing commentary on polls and politics. Has been hosted by *Crikey* since September 2008.

Catallaxy Files: calls itself 'Australia's leading libertarian and centre-right blog'. Founded by Jason Soon as a solo blog and now has eight main contributors.

Gary Sauer-Thompson: Adelaide based-academic philosopher whose website includes his *Public Opinion* blog, focusing on political commentary.

OzPolitics: a general and highly informative site on Australian politics run by Bryan Palmer. The blog is no longer online but is archived on the National Library of Australia's PANDORA website.

The Content Makers: a media and journalism blog run by Margaret Simons, freelance journalist and author. Hosted on the *Crikey* site since December 2008.

The Road to Surfdom: run by Tim Dunlop, this was one of the original Australian political blogs. Dunlop then went to News Limited to write *Blogocracy*, which was hosted on the news.com.au website and finished in September 2008. *Webdiary*: describes itself as 'independent, ethical, accountable and transparent'. Founded by journalist Margo Kingston for the *SMH* in 2000, who launched it as an independent site in 2005. The blog is now open to all contributors and moderated by a team of volunteer editors.

Pointing out that independent blogs often have small audiences is not meant to diminish the significant investments of labour, expertise and money that bloggers make. If the unique visitor figures are accurate, even the smallest of the blogs mentioned above is likely to get more people reading articles on those sites in a month than will buy this book. Obviously, I don't feel that a small audience isn't worth any effort. What I am suggesting is that we need to question some of the claims that have been made about the impact of blogs in terms of extending political news and information to new audiences. All of the online news providers in Box 10.1 have audiences that are generally older, white, male and affluent. The more formal politics-focused the outlet, the more likely this is to be true. Miller (2009:78–9) takes this point further and argues:

> The evidence suggests that blogs are closed environments – few are read by anybody at all, and of those to do with politics, only a handful are popular. The reality is that class, race, money and age delineate blogs in terms of who reads and cites them . . .

Reporting political news

Just because it was essentially the same audience who were following political news online as were following it in traditional media does not mean the internet was having no impact. On the contrary, because this is the audience that commercial news organisations rely upon for their revenue, any shifts in what it is doing – its size, where it is going for news, what type of news it accesses and how – will have major repercussions on the news industry. This, I would argue, is where the most profound changes occurred, especially for newspapers which Jürgen Habermas called 'the backbone of democratic discourse' (Jeffries 2010).

In 1950, Australians reportedly spent, on average, an hour and ten minutes each day reading a newspaper – 35 minutes for each of the morning and evening editions (Mayer 1964:228). In 2007, visitors to Ninemsn stayed an average of two minutes; visitors to the *Australian*, the *SMH* and the *Age* all stayed an average of seven minutes (Newsspace 2009a; Ricketson 2007). And these figures may not be all they seem. In the US, in May 2009, the average visitor to washingtonpost.com spent 10 minutes and 58 seconds on the site but that was for '[the] entire month. On a daily basis, this works out to just 21.2 seconds a day' (Farhi 2009). The chief economist of Google, Hal Varian (2010), told the Federal Trade Commission that time spent on online news sites is only about 70 seconds per day, compared to 25 minutes spent reading a print edition.

Online, people who go to news websites are often headline-checking and doing it from work, so they don't have time to stay long. They also have a different approach from that of the news-seekers who regularly buy a copy of their favourite newspaper. Many visitors to news websites do not go in through the homepage of the news site but are instead casual visitors who arrive from somewhere else – for example, after following a link from Google News or by doing a search. Search engines accounted for 35 to 40 per cent of 'traffic to major U.S. news sites' in 2010 (Varian 2010).

The internet has therefore transformed the economics of news audiences. Online, newspapers face competition not only from other newspapers who have migrated online but also from other media that weren't traditional competitors but now occupy the same place online. This includes television stations, radio broadcasters and newswires but also Google, Yahoo and Microsoft. Of these, newspapers find the aggregators especially troublesome, because they reproduce newspaper content in order to link to it.

Newspapers also face competition from niche providers and new players. Even if blogs only attract a small audience, four minutes spent on a psephology site is four minutes denied a traditional news provider and these are dedicated news-seekers that traditional news organisations can't afford to lose. People used to go to newspapers for a wide array of topics such as jobs, property, cars, sports, food, women's issues or finance. However, on the internet, specialists are picking off these areas of news. People can go directly to their football club's webpage, a celebrity gossip site, their favourite band's MySpace profile or the weather bureau to get a forecast. And, as the football club example shows, newspapers aren't facing competition just from other news providers but also from the subjects of their news. In the case of politics, this includes the politicians', political parties' and activists' websites.

For all of these reasons, online audiences are much harder to sell to advertisers; they are smaller, more fragmented, not loyal to a particular product, do not stay long, may come through search engines and are often not local, so are not useful for local businesses. News Limited CEO John Hartigan (2009) said 'an online reader generates about 10 per cent of the revenue we can make from a newspaper reader. So, for every reader we lose from the paper we need to pick up 10 online.' In the 2000s, this fundamentally challenged the business models that newspapers had relied on, especially broadsheets that had controlled the 'rivers of gold' of classified advertising. As Eric Beecher explained:

> an average [classifieds] page in *The Age* or *The Sydney Morning Herald* on a Saturday [brought in] $40 000 and [with] a hundred of them . . . $4 million dollars a week . . . [which paid] for all the journalists' salaries (*Media Watch*, 1 September 2008; see also Beecher 2005).

But now classified advertising works far better on the internet than it did on paper. Websites (including Ebay but also Craig's List and Monster.com in the US) have taken a large share of such ads. Even when newspapers do control a portion of online classifieds, they cannot charge advertisers the same amounts as they did for print ads when they had a monopoly or duopoly in a local market. On the internet, there is also a different kind of advertising competition with Google, Yahoo, Microsoft and non-newspaper sites like Wikipedia, Amazon and Ebay 'capturing the lion's share of traffic that can bring in ad money. And none of them has expensive newsrooms to feed' (Kuttner 2008; see also Meyer 2004).

The future of political news?

As they grappled with these trends in the 2000s, news organisations had to attract traffic to their websites in order to convince advertisers that online ads were worth paying for. Online monitoring meant they knew far more than they ever had before about which of their stories people were reading and for how long. That information showed what tabloids had always known: that the more sensational stories – especially about entertainment, crime and sex – tended to attract more attention (Box 10.5). In relation to election news, in 2007 the 'vote-a-matic' quiz was a winner for news.com.au along-side stories on aliens, Paris Hilton, television shows and the bizarre (dogs with patterns in their fur, a 'tree man'). On the *SMH* website, three election stories made the top 10 – all were published after polling day and two came from the print edition of the newspaper. However, the top-ranking election story on the *Age* website was ranked 30th, following articles on Tom Cruise, Britney Spears and Paris Hilton. The story showed a photograph of Labor MP Maxine McKew that was published on the front page of another newspaper, the camera angle directed up her skirt. It was headlined: 'Is this Maxine's "Sharon Stone" moment?' (Carey 2007).

Box 10.5

Most-read stories on online newspaper websites, 2007 (election stories highlighted)

News.com.au	SMH online	Age online
1 Paris Hilton loses inheritance	1 **Libs turn on Howard**	1 One dead, gunman at large
2 Federal Election 'Vote-a-matic'	2 Deadly shooting in crowded street	after city shooting
3 15-year-old girl jailed with 20 men	3 Welcome to the selfish city	2 Boy, 6, accused of sex abuse
4 Britney attempted rehab suicide	4 'I pretended to be dead and people got shot'	3 Hilton sues website
5 Man levitates outside the White House	5 Smile, you're on Google's candid camera	4 A climate of fear
6 Roswell aliens theory revived by deathbed confession	6 How Lori Drew became America's most reviled mother	5 Cars reduced to balls of metal in tunnel fire
7 Singing salesman makes Cowell's jaw drop	7 Naked man deepens mystery of jungle girl	6 Please remain seated for landing
8 Chihuahua puppy born with loveheart pattern in fur	8 Father orders daughter's brutal death	7 Stab victim 'continued sex act'
9 Tree man has experts baffled	9 Rudd picks new team	8 The TomKat's out of the bag
10 Spoiler: How Harry Potter ends	10 Libs implode as Costello bails out	9 High School Musical makes assault in Oz
		10 'Ismail Ax' sparks web frenzy

Note: News.com.au is the aggregate site for news from News Limited newspapers.

Sources: Hutcheon 2007; Carey 2007; staff writers 2007.

Using television meters, this is precisely the sort of information – showing which stories people select/stay for and which they turn off/ignore – that drove changes to commercial current affairs television in the 1990s. News media companies want to use it in much the same way online. As News Limited's John Hartigan (2009) said: 'We will do more research to track what people want and discard what they don't – just like television networks change their schedules if a show doesn't rate.' Following audience preferences may sound democratic but it has some worrying implications. In particular, it can become a reinforcing – rather than a challenging – of popular prejudices. Catering always to the familiar can lead to a lack of new ideas entering and can see media outlets become as risk-averse as the politicians they criticise.

Many of the visitors that are attracted to website stories are 'one-off' visitors. Catering to their tastes may boost visitor numbers in the short term but it is a dangerous long-term strategy for a news outlet trying to build a loyal audience. Also, at present, because of the digital divide, the *general* news audience that is online is heavily skewed towards younger people who usually have less interest in formal politics than older audiences. If news outlets move away from political news, what will this mean when these young (and mostly elite) audiences age? If they follow historical patterns, these younger news-seekers will become more interested in political news but, by then, will the organisations still have the resources or will to provide it? Or, perhaps, these audiences will go elsewhere for such news if outlets like Fairfax 'trash the reputation of [their] brand' by 'trawling for and writing for hits' (Bahnisch 2007). Alternatively, this audience may never acquire a high level of interest in political news because news organisations will not have encouraged them to do so.

Some may argue that none of this will matter because other politics-focused outlets will be available. The ability to cater for niche audiences is one of the internet's most central features and there are many sites – especially in the US – such as *Political Wire, Real Clear Politics, Politics1, Politico* and *Wonkette*; or *TotalPolitics, Guido Fawkes* and *Conservative Home* in the UK. Yet it is also telling that some of the most popular independent outlets began with a dedicated politics focus but then branched out to other news. The *Huffington Post*, for example, now has media, entertainment, comedy, sports, business and other news while, in Australia, *Crikey* extended from a politics-only focus to include arts, business, media, environment and culture news.

Niche news audiences aren't always appealing or, depending upon the producer's costs and their economic goals, economically viable. In the 2000s, it was difficult enough to get people to come to any 'traditional' news let alone the less popular types such as politics. Web audiences also grew accustomed to getting news free. This meant that the search for a new business model to sustain journalism was the search for a way to make money out of content that fewer people were prepared to pay for.

One business model that did seem to work for *The Economist*, the *Wall Street Journal* (which News Corp took over in 2007) and Fairfax's *Australian Financial Review* was to charge a niche and lucrative audience for access to business news (as well as charging advertisers to reach that audience). In 2009, Murdoch signalled that his company was looking at extending paywalls to other types of online news. At the time of writing there was only speculation about how this would be done; however Chris Mitchell, editor-in-chief of News Limited's only Australian broadsheet the *Australian*, said: 'We will look to charge in the next 12 to 18 months' (Tabakoff 2009b).

This meant that both of Australia's national newspapers could become subscription-based in the future, including the one with the highest amount of content focused on elections (see Chapter 9). Fairfax was also reportedly looking at a number of 'pay models' for its online news sites

> including offering readers two levels of access for sites such as the *SMH* and the *Age* – free entry for a mass audience, with a charge for 'more upmarket, high quality data' (Hyland 2009a).

No-one knows whether widescale paywalls for general news content would work – there are many who suggest they won't – but after Murdoch's announcement, Fairfax responded that it too was 'open' to charging for online news and even to forging some sort of agreement with its rival, News Limited (Zappone 2009). Given the concentration of ownership in Australia and the role that newspapers have played, this would have a major impact on Australian journalism and public debate.

Business journalism is one area newspapers have been prepared to invest in, because there is an economic model to support it online. Could something similar happen with political news? Can news organisations turn it into a commodity that a niche audience would be willing to pay for? If that succeeded, what implications would it have for democratic discourse? Or, if this is not possible and there is no economic model to sustain political reporting, will it be further downgraded in favour of more sellable topics online?

New forms of journalism?

News organisations are in flux, but they have many advantages online and in the 'real' world. They may yet figure out a model that sees them come to dominate online as they did in traditional media. All the talk of a 'crisis' in news journalism may be looked upon in the future with bemusement. Or it may be prophetic. Some of the more vulnerable companies (including those with proud histories and more philanthropic aims) may collapse. Alternatively, organisations may have to chart a third-way course and 'learn to love lower profits' (Meyer 1995). There are signs pointing in all directions and, of some signs, it is difficult to tell whether they are signs of adaptation or of resignation and retreat from news journalism.

In recent years, News Corporation's earnings have been driven more by film, DVD sales and pay TV, which subsidise the newspaper arms of the business (Tabakoff 2009a). One of the key strategies a debt-ladden Fairfax undertook was to imitate its rival by moving into entertainment as well as news and moving away from newspapers as a core business. In the 2000s, Fairfax bought up radio stations and websites. It also invested in music and other businesses. According to Fairfax Media (2008b:3): 'taken together, our growth in these key [non-newspaper] areas... [now] generate[s] 80 per cent of the company's earnings.'

If traditional news journalism organisations *do* decline, not everyone will mourn their loss. Former *New York Times* reporter Christopher Lydon, who now hosts *Open Source*, says: 'The priesthood of gatekeepers is being disbanded. It's over' (Kuttner 2007). Andrew Leonard (2008) foresees a future with 'fewer media empire dinosaurs... [but] more information, analysis, context, data and opinion... One thing there might not be a market for, however, is media moguls hoping to make obscene profits...' Some point to the way public broadcasters such as the BBC and ABC are steaming ahead amid the commercial declines and how new models of funding journalism are being explored including foundations, partnerships and non-profit models. Others still point to the role of blogs and now to citizen journalism and social networking.

It has been well documented that blogs have small audiences and even their proponents accept this, but they argue that those audiences will invariably grow and, anyway, that the impact of blogs goes far beyond their direct audiences. Blogs 'can foster open, intelligent, and productive public discussion . . . bloggers can spur journalists to produce more accurate, honest, and socially relevant reporting . . .' (Lowrey 2006:478). There are some famous examples (mostly from the US) that are frequently cited. For example, a small group of bloggers proved that a letter CBS anchor Dan Rather had relied upon to criticise George Bush's military service was a forgery by studying the font used, hastening Rather's retirement. The psephology bloggers in 2007 are another example of bloggers playing a valuable role in media critique.

These examples can suggest that there is a vast gulf, and rivalry, between bloggers and journalists in the mainstream media. The academic literature also tends to further this view, as does the discourse used by some bloggers and some news executives (some of whom have suggested bloggers are 'parasites'). However, in reality, the two groups cross over. They have much in common and many synergies.

Most blogs – especially politics blogs – have the same audiences as mainstream news media. Most feed off reporting from the traditional news media (and vice versa). Many of the topics bloggers discuss are the same. For example, the psephology blogs are tapping into a mainstream media preoccupation with polls and the horse-race. Hartigan's (2009) complaint that 'typically, less than 10 per cent of their content is original reporting' is exaggerated. There is much in the way of original analysis and commentary, but it is true that blogs do not have much in the way of resources in terms of what would be considered journalistic reporting. Most blogs also rely on mainstream media to grow their audiences and at least partly measure their success by the degree to which their content reaches across into the mainstream media. Many of the popular blogs (but certainly not all) rely on advertising, much like the conventional media.

In terms of disbanding the old 'gatekeepers', far from being ordinary citizens pitted against the elites of the old media, the blogosphere is dominated by 'small groups of white, highly educated, male, professionals who are vastly overrepresented in online opinion' (Hindman 2008:126). The bloggers who are most read are like op-ed columnists – an elite grouping even among journalists, because columnists get to have a say and their opinions matter. There are hierarchies within the blogosphere that make the more influential bloggers look very much like a 'new elite'. For example, in Australia there is a central group of bloggers who have worked across different online projects and sometimes also for the mainstream media. While many are reflective and thoughtful about their own role, for some, any challenging of that role can provoke a ferocious response. This might suggest that sometimes blogging is more about 'maintaining or seeking authority than [it is about] . . . benefiting society . . . (Lowrey 2006:478). The posturing, aggressive stance in some online domains may also help explain the lack of women.

One of the signs of adaptation in the news industry is that mainstream news organisations have tried to appropriate some of what blogs offer and have therefore made blogs look less distinctive. Traditional news providers have set up their own blogs as well as coopted some of the popular bloggers onto their sites. They have also opened up news discourse (or at least given the appearance of doing so) by allowing visitors to their sites to post comments and critiques and by using their audience members' photographs, footage and comments in news reports. The mainstream news providers no longer confine themselves to 'straight' journalism but also use, for example, comedians, lawyers, economists and industry representatives as columnists to add a more irreverent, independent voice. Their own reporters not only blog but also file video reports and go on Twitter (for example Michelle Grattan). In other words, the news media are trying to coopt and even dominate the online political discussion space that blogs operate within.

A new definition of 'news'

A growing recognition that independent blogs had not become the mass democratising movement that cyber-enthusiasts predicted meant that, by the end of the 2000s, optimists were nominating other sites – especially social networking and citizen journalism – as more likely drivers of democratisation and liberation. The problematically named 'citizen journalism' (or sometimes 'participatory journalism' or 'network journalism') is based on the principle that, because of the internet especially, journalism is no longer the domain of journalists working in news organisations (Jarvis 2006). 'The people formerly known as the audience' (Rosen 2006) are now producers as well as consumers ('produsers') and news will have to be less like a lecture to readers and more like a conversation with them (Jarvis 2006; Rosen 2006; Bruns 2008).

These principles challenged notions of traditional journalism enough for some outlets to experiment with citizen journalism projects, 'pro-am' ('professional-amateur') partnerships and 'crowd sourcing'. An example of the latter occurred in the US where *The News-Press* in Florida used a panel of retired community members, including lawyers, CEOs and accountants, working on stories with staff reporters. In the UK in 2009, during the MP expense scandals, the *Guardian* put more than 500 000 claim forms on their website and asked readers to trawl the data looking for suspicious claims and report back.

Australian news media were far less willing to experiment in this way in the 2000s, but they did open up comments fields under stories, inviting readers to converse with journalists and their audiences. (Some have done this more genuinely and less censoriously than others.) To take but one example, an article on the *Australian* website in 2007 reported: 'Late yesterday, Rudd had more than 8000 friends on [his MySpace page] while Howard had only eight.' A reader had posted a comment below that said: 'The Howard government's Myspace page is the one with 9 friends. If you check again, Howard's personal page has 12 398 friends while Rudd has only 8000 or so.'[1]

Greater interaction does change the journalist–reader and outlet–audience relationship. However, in terms of more active forms of 'citizen journalism', we have to ask how many people will want to write the sort of news reported in newspapers, given how few want to read it, and whether those who participate will be the usual suspects. One study found that, on the internet, 'only 1 per cent of consumers are [actually] enthusiastic producers of content' (Turner 2010:134). But this all depends on what is included as 'content' and this brings us to the latest cyber-enthusiast claim – that social networking is changing not just the creation and distribution of news but also the whole definition of 'news'.

On social networking sites, people *do* create content. At a minimum they have to 'post information about themselves. Most likely they will include a photograph. Normally they will soon move to sharing clips, videos, book collections and photo albums' (Simons 2008b). Proponents suggest this is about not just entertainment and personal communication but also sharing news, discussing topics, providing different accounts and views and encouraging political participation. Very little research has been performed on this, though. As with blogs and other earlier developments, much about this argument is speculative and hopeful, anecdotal and predicated on future predictions. We may find social networking is revolutionary in terms of news production and access, or we may find it can only be considered so using a definition of 'news' that has been widened so far that any (personal) communication counts.

At least in terms of audiences, though, this argument has the advantage that social networking is popular in a way that blogs never were and also is popular with women as well as men. MySpace and Facebook rank in the top most-visited websites for Australians (Hitwise 2010). People also spend far more time on these sites than on news sites. Users spent an average of 28 minutes when visiting MySpace and 21 minutes on Facebook in 2008 (Simons 2008b). This is because 'the work that goes into updating a personal presence on these sites is demanding' (Turner 2010:146). Users invest a good deal of labour, creativity and maintenance into these sites while the companies behind them (News Corp and Facebook Inc.) profit from the unpaid labour of their content-makers (Turner 2010:147–50). If this type of site is the future of news (rather than just another fad), could this mean that citizen journalism turns out to be more exploitative than liberating?

Conclusion

Optimists convincingly call for 'new thinking' on what constitutes news (Simons 2008c) and there are certainly many positive developments in political communication brought about by the internet and many opportunities in the future. Yet we also have to recognise that existing social, political and economic structures have an impact on how technology is used and the internet is no longer such a 'new' media. We have had over 20 years to assess its use. So far, much of the evidence suggests the internet has largely been 'normalised into the traditional political world' with existing inequities continued online (Ward and Vedel 2006:210). Will the future be different?

In Australia, we will see greater use of online news in the future and the digital divide will narrow further. This is partly because we are starting from a low base. In the US, about 40 per cent of internet users say they read news on the internet every day (Varian 2010). We may not necessarily see online news catch up to US levels and especially in relation to political news specifically. National contexts – including media policy but also political systems and cultural factors – have a great deal of influence over how media and technology are used. We also cannot assume that the old mass media news audience – from times when news use was a ritual and there was little entertainment media or choice – will transplant directly across to the internet. Some audience members may peel off to other activities now that they have more choice.

Another unknown is whether the audience will be large enough (or loyal and stable enough) to fund the type of newsroom journalism traditionally provided. If online news access does eventually become the norm – and we are a long way off from this point; even in the US, 70 per cent still relied on television as their main news source in 2009 (Smith and Rainie 2009) – the general internet user may access their news in segments of less than a minute's duration and be 'not much bothered who brings it to them' (Katz 2000:9). As a result, some fear that 'we are about to enter a . . . chaotic world of news [with] . . . a decidedly diminished level of first-rate journalism' (Hudson 2008:17).

For example, John Carroll (2006), former editor of the *Los Angeles Times*, argues that much of what is reported in news is traceable to newspapers and that the blogs

> noisy as they are, have virtually no reporters. They may be keen critics, or assiduous fact checkers, but do they add materially to the nation's supply of original reporting? No, they don't.

He asks: who is going to do that reporting if newspapers fade away? Others foresee a much brighter future for news based on a more open, interactive form of democratised 'journalism'. It is hard not to be attracted by their optimism, but we still do need to take into account the social, cultural, political and regulatory conditions that dictate how people (and governments and corporations) use media and technology. The internet made political news and information much more widely available in the 2000s, but involvement by the public was still selective and uneven.

Chapter 11

BIAS

In political reporting, there's no hotter issue than media bias. Politicians and their supporters regularly make allegations of political bias in news reporting. These are invariably followed by the steadfast denials of offended news workers. Bias contravenes one of the most basic assumptions about the nature of journalism – that journalists should be impartial in reporting news. Objectivity and impartiality were central to how modern journalism defined itself (Schudson 1994) and media institutions still commit themselves to those principles (Box 11.1).

When it comes to legislative requirements for impartiality, newspapers have more discretion than broadcasters because they developed from a very different environment. Limited analogue spectrum meant broadcasters had to be licensed because they were using a public resource and only a limited number could transmit at once. As part of this process, they were required to be impartial. Newspapers developed instead out of a history of 'yellow' (partisan) journalism and a tradition of press barons using their outlets to try to influence political debate. They developed from 17th-century battles over press censorship and repressive licensing that saw the notion of a 'free press' come to be seen as a cornerstone of democracy.

Advocating for a political position or party is still considered a 'property right' of owners. The Australian Press Council says a newspaper 'has a right to take sides on any issue' (APC 1977). In its election guidelines it also 'upholds the right of a newspaper ... to favour the election of one party and to oppose the election of another', but it still expects that news reports

Box 11.1

Impartiality: legislative requirements, guidelines and codes

ABC: The ABC is legally required to ensure that its news and information programs are 'accurate and impartial according to the recognised standards of objective journalism' (*The ABC Act 1983*). The ABC has a formal *Charter of Editorial Practice* and *Editorial Policies*. In 2007, the *Editorial Policy* directed journalists: 'Do not unduly favour one perspective over others' and 'Be balanced...As far as possible present principal relevant views on matters of importance' (ABC 2007b: 32).

SBS: The SBS is also governed by its own Act. Its *Codes of Practice* state: 'The commitment to balance and impartiality requires SBS to present – over time and across the schedule of programs broadcast on the relevant service . . . a wide range of significant views, not misrepresenting them or unduly favouring one over another . . .' (SBS 2007).

Commercial TV and radio: Television channels in Australia are bound by the *Broadcasting Services Act (1992)* to 'give reasonable opportunities for the broadcasting of election matter to all political parties contesting the election, being parties which were represented in either House of the Parliament for which the election is to be held at the time of its last meeting before the election period'.

Professional codes: The Media Alliance (part of the MEAA (union)) has a *Code of Ethics* that applies to all of its members. It states that journalists should 'Report and interpret honestly, striving for accuracy, fairness and disclosure of all essential facts...Do not allow personal interest, or any belief, commitment, payment, gift or benefit, to undermine your accuracy, fairness or independence' (Alliance Online 2009).

---

should be fair and balanced, and that fact and opinion be made clearly distinguishable (APC 2009a). These different aims can be difficult to reconcile and Australians, recognising that newspapers play more of an advocacy role, tend to believe that newspaper journalists are the most biased (RMR 2007).

What is 'bias'?

To be biased is to have an inclination, leaning or predisposition. In political terms, this is usually towards a political party, a policy or an ideology.

Sometimes bias is explicit, such as when a newspaper editorial openly advocates a vote for a particular party. At other times, a media outlet may make a case for a party or policy without explicitly stating that it is doing so. For example:

> [when] stories about high-living students or social security fraud or asylum-seekers are reported as news, but in such a way as to make a particular point (about welfare 'scrounging' or immigrants 'swamping' a country) (Street 2001:20–1).

Bias is sometimes volitional and wilful, but at other times it is 'unwitting'. For example, the ingrained routines of news production that see a reliance on official sources produce a particular world view. There can also be unintended 'ideological bias' that can only be detected 'in a close reading of the text [that reveals] . . . the hidden assumptions and value judgements' contained within it (Street 2001:21). This can include assumptions about class, race, gender and sexuality.

Bias is easy to allege but difficult to 'prove'. Some commentators seem to think that anything which opposes their world view is biased while others make serious attempts to study and document bias using a range of methods, including content analysis and stopwatch counts of time allocated to different parties. It's not uncommon to see the more mathematically inclined academic studies using complicated formulas such as:

$$P_{ijt} = \sum_{j=0}^{J} I_{jt} \qquad \text{(Gans and Leigh 2009)}.$$

Most of us don't use formulas but probably still think we can identify bias in news and examples where a journalist or news outlet seems to be pushing an agenda. It is much harder to identify exactly how we've come to that conclusion or to separate our analysis from our own world view. (The same applies to studies of bias.) And sometimes we might get it wrong; imagining that there is a motive behind a particular story when there isn't one. People are usually quicker to see bias against what they believe in than to see it where someone is in agreement with their own beliefs. In other words, we ourselves are biased.

Putting all of this aside, even if we can identify bias, there is still the issue of whether it matters. Some think bias is avoidable and should be avoided because it has no place in either good journalism or free and fair elections. (Journalists and politicians tend towards this view.) Others think bias is unavoidable because we are all subjective. The concepts of bias, balance, objectivity and impartiality are highly contested.

There is also the more pragmatic question of whether bias matters in terms of election results. What is the effect, for example, if a newspaper owner promotes a particular candidate or party through the newspaper's outlets? Given that many newspaper readers have their own strong views already, perhaps this doesn't matter a great deal (see Chapter 5). However, the concentration of news media outlets in Australia, the close results of elections, and the way news is communicated between outlets and between people, mean bias may make a very big difference. Politicians certainly seem to believe this.

Journalistic cultures and media markets as drivers or restraints on bias

What counts as bias and what significance is attached to it vary between different journalistic cultures. In some countries, journalists tend to take an adversarial position to reporting politicians. In others, it ranges from a forthright 'advocacy type' of reporting to 'a more detached style' or, as in some European countries, journalists taking 'a more supportive and mediating position . . .' (Strömbäck and Kaid 2008:10). In Britain, the press is famously partisan. The most popular tabloid, Murdoch's *Sun*, makes overt political endorsements, including on its front page ('*The Sun* backs Blair' (1997); 'Labour's lost it . . . Now it's lost *The Sun*'s support too' (2009)).

In comparison, Australian newspapers are much more temperate and centrist (blandly so, according to some critics). A small media market has meant reduced opportunities for overt partisan bias because it would be commercially unsound to risk alienating so many potential consumers, especially when support for the major parties tends to divide quite evenly. Television stations are even more inclined to strive for a neutral (if brief and horse-race focused) presentation of news. According to Australian news producers, slanting the news on television 'would create great controversy – the broadcasting law could be breached and, worse, ratings might suffer' (Suich 2004c).

This all helps explain why serious studies of Australian media outlets have tended to find no systematic bias. A study of newspapers concluded that 'Australian media are quite centrist, with very few outlets being statistically distinguishable from the middle of Australian politics' (Gans and Leigh 2009:1). A study by other academics using a different methodology also did not 'find any evidence of systematic bias towards one political party' (APC 2008:38). The ABC was the subject of many studies – both internal and external – using different methodologies in the 2000s. None found any evidence of systematic partisan bias. For example, one study comparing Channel Nine and ABC news coverage found that 'both . . . operated in an extremely professional manner' with very few stories that could be classified as unbalanced (Turner 2005:105).

Such findings did not persuade the ABC's staunchest critics, who continued to voice allegations of left-wing bias (Box 11.6). Bias generates a lot of passion among journalists, politicians and media critics, but it tends not to be such a big concern for the general public. Less than a quarter of Australians thought that the media were biased in 2007. Those who did tended to divide fairly evenly in terms of whether they thought the media were biased to the Left or the Right (RMR 2007). This again suggests that the Australian media tend to be fairly centrist but, even if this is true, it doesn't mean there have been no allegations of bias. On the contrary, any deviations stand out and are much remarked upon.

The accusations: who/what is biased?

'The media' and journalists in general

In the US, conservatives were very effective at publicising their complaints of a 'liberal media' in the 1990s and 2000s. In Australia, this accusation was also made. For example, John Howard referred to 'dominant left-liberal elements in the media' and, on another occasion, spoke of an 'intense' 'left liberal grip' on 'large, though not all, sections of the media' (Howard 2008; see also Costello 2009). This has the proverbial grain of truth to it, because journalists do tend to identify themselves as being liberal or left-of-centre in their views. This has been found in many countries.

In Australia, Henningham (1998b:99) found a 'major ideological gulf between Australian journalists and the general public . . . journalists are significantly more liberal than the public is.' Only 9 per cent of journalists surveyed in 2004 identified themselves as conservative or right-wing, while 55 per cent described themselves as liberal or left-wing (36 per cent put themselves in the centre) (RMR 2004). For conservative critics, this is strong evidence that journalists' liberal/left views influence their perceptions and thus their reporting.

But the first point to note about such findings is that being 'liberal' does not equate to being 'left-wing'. Journalists do tend to be 'liberal' – to support free speech, freedom of information and tolerance, for example – but they also tend to be anti-collective action and anti-bureaucracy. The second point to note is that it is not clear just how much journalists' own political preferences translate into the news they report. There a number of factors that dilute and constrain this.

For a start, there still exists a strong sense of professional ethics. Columnists and polemic commentators aside, professional journalists who want to maintain long careers and the respect of their colleagues and readers avoid presenting political news in a way that is unfair, inaccurate or partisan. They try to insulate their coverage from accusations of bias by giving time to all major sides of a story. There are also checking procedures designed to ensure political balance. If a reporter loses perspective, editors and producers are there to correct them. To assume bias, we have to assume these procedures either don't work or are part of some conspiracy to let bias through.

There are also the basic daily realities of newsmaking, especially during elections. As we saw in Chapters 8 and 9, the news of the day is heavily influenced by the news management strategies of newsmakers including politicians, governments and corporations. On television, for example, what the leaders say and do sets the tone for the evening news and, in the current news formula, there is little room to deviate from this to push a blatant partisan agenda or leap into a political monologue.

Journalists answer to supervisors and, in the commercial media, to owners. This exerts a certain type of pressure and might suggest, if not a conspiracy, at least an inducement to let some biases through. In 2004, 73 per cent of Australian journalists agreed that media proprietors 'use their outlets to push their own business and/or political interests to influence the national debate' (RMR 2004). Another survey found that 32 per cent said they felt obliged to take into account the political views of their proprietor when writing stories (RMR 2006).

Even where owners do not have strong political views or insist upon a predetermined editorial line (and this was much less common in the 2000s than in the past), they still play an important role. Owners and managers set the strategic goals for their company including developing the news formula their outlets use. This news formula – designed to attract a loyal, predictable audience – determines how news will be selected and written up. Journalists share a vested interest in using the formula to create sellable news. If their personal views go against the grain of this or of any set editorial line, they are very likely to be suppressed.

To conduct their everyday newsgathering, journalists are also anchored, as we saw in Chapter 6, to the institutions they are supposed to be most critical and inquiring about (politicians, parties). The journalists who get promoted tend to be those who get on best with these institutions and the news which is most sellable is that which looks like the rest of the news. These are all conservatising and centralising tendencies.

The Press Gallery

Given these tendencies, the Press Gallery can tend to operate like a 'pack' (Chapters 8 and 9) and has sometimes been accused of bias as a group. Interestingly, these accusations have often been about political leaders rather than parties. Personality – charisma, power and accessibility – seem to play a role. Haupt and Grattan (1983:43) suggest there might be some psychology involved:

> The Press Gallery falls for strength and flattery. Its two great love affairs since World War II were with Menzies and Whitlam . . . the archetype wise old man who was so often missing in the childhood of the upwardly-mobile, neurotic people whom journalism seems to select for duty in Canberra.

There can be a degree of self-interest as well. In the mid-to-late 1980s, the Press Gallery was said to 'love' Bob Hawke because he was 'a feast' on television and was 'useful to [the Press Gallery; he] made it easier to get better film, better quotes, better images' (Haupt and Grattan 1983:42; see also Parker 1990). The Gallery also had a relationship with Keating that was characterised by affection in the early 1990s but, towards the end of his term, by mutual resentment (Watson 2002; Williams 1997:184–7). By contrast, no-one seems to have ever accused the Gallery of loving

Howard. Howard reportedly believed the Gallery was irredeemably pro-ALP and never accepted his political mandate. Former Labor speechwriter Dennis Glover (2005:205) said: 'It's true many Gallery members loathe[d] Howard . . .', although he noted 'many also loathed or had no respect for [Labor leaders] Beazley, Crean and Latham.'

Individuals

It is problematic to generalise the views of 'the media' or the Press Gallery as a whole, but some critics have been more specific and have identified individuals, especially columnists and talkback hosts (discussed in Chapter 12), but also Press Gallery reporters. Reflecting some of the criticisms, *Crikey* ranked Gallery reporters on a 'bias-o-meter' but, significantly, began by acknowledging that 'the vast majority of [Press Gallery] members are level-headed, conscientious types... [and] it's hard to ascribe bias to them.' *Crikey* ranked Michelle Grattan dead-centre neutral, calling her 'the consummate pro... [with a] trademark impartiality' who set the standard for all. Oakes was rated as slightly to the Left but as one of 'the game's great pros, a reporter first... Imperiously above the fray' (Kerr 2007a). Some of those ranked to the right received more criticism, including Dennis Shanahan (see Chapter 10) and Glenn Milne of the *Australian*.

Of course, where you stand politically affects how you define 'Left' and 'Right' and how you determine bias in others. For example, *Crikey* ranked Paul Bongiorno of Channel Ten as slightly to the Right, but Coalition supporters complained in 2007 that Bongiorno and Ten News were biased against the Coalition (Savva 2010:267–8). Despite the fact that conservative politicians have generally praised Oakes' fairness, contributors to an Andrew Bolt blog characterised Oakes as 'far left', 'part of the privileged, upper-middle class pinkoes who almost totally dominate the mass media' ('Pieman' 2010). And, of course, *Crikey* itself has been accused of left-wing bias by conservatives.

Outlets, companies and owners

For some analysts, journalists are merely small cogs in large, powerful organisations and owners are the real source of bias. Some commentators overstate this – journalists are not the mere mouthpieces through which powerful moguls speak. But it's also naive to think that owners have no influence. Some of the most infamous examples happened in the 1960s and 1970s.

In 1972, disillusioned with the McMahon Coalition government, Rupert Murdoch and his papers played an active role in Labor's election campaign, offering both editorial and material support. By 1975, Murdoch had fallen out with the Whitlam government and his papers took such an unrelentingly anti-Labor stance that News Limited journalists went on strike to protest against proprietor interference (Griffen-Foley 2003:228–34). Rupert's father Keith Murdoch was also known to intervene directly to influence news content (Griffen-Foley 2003:8–34). Frank Packer 'used his newspapers as platforms for political and personal vendettas' (Windschuttle 1988:264; Griffen-Foley 2003; Suich 2004c). Sometimes owners campaigned for a particular party or individual. Other times, editorial interference was more about commercial interests than directly political ones. In 1961 Warwick Fairfax Senior advocated a vote for Labor because the Menzies government's misapplied credit squeeze had shrunk Fairfax advertising revenue.

These were times when newspaper proprietors had 'absolute authority, often wielded' (Suich 2004c). By the 2000s, some outlets were still ruled by dynastical structures and hands-on proprietors. Others were more corporatised with 'boards and diffuse lines of command and shareholders' that made it harder for there to be one consistent line in the organisation and also meant that moguls couldn't promise things (Carney 2005). Influence in the 2000s seemed to be less about blunt editorial interference than about organisational culture, with news producers reporting that ownership was 'a subconscious pressure, which led to self-censorship' (ABA 2001a).

Explicit partisanship: editorial endorsements

Editorials are where the 'official' company line on political matters is expressed. These are probably not well read by general readers, but they send strong messages to journalists at the company as well as to political elites and there is usually a degree of fit between the editorial endorsement of an outlet and the balance of its reporting and commentary.

Table 11.1 Newspaper editorial alignments, 2001–07 elections

State	Newspaper	Company	Endorsement 2001	2004	2007
National	Australian	News Ltd	Coalition	Coalition	ALP
	Australian Financial Review	Fairfax	Coalition	Coalition	Coalition
NSW	Sydney Morning Herald	Fairfax	Coalition	None	ALP
	Daily Telegraph	News Ltd	Coalition	Coalition	ALP
Vic	Age	Fairfax	ALP	Coalition	None
	Herald Sun	News Ltd	Coalition	Coalition	Coalition
Qld	Courier-Mail	News Ltd	Coalition	Coalition	ALP
WA	West Australian	West Australian Newspapers Ltd	Coalition	Coalition	Coalition
SA	Advertiser	News Ltd	Coalition	Coalition	Coalition
Tas (Hobart)	Mercury	News Ltd	Coalition	Coalition	ALP
ACT	Canberra Times	Rural Press Ltd (2001–07) Fairfax (May 2007–)	None	ALP	ALP
NT	NT News	News Ltd	None	None	ALP

Source: Author (from election-eve newspapers 2001–07).

In Australian editorials, there is a long history of consistent support for conservative parties.

Fairfax's endorsement of Labor in the *SMH* in 1961 was the first time the paper had advocated a vote for the ALP since its founding in 1831. When the *Australian* endorsed Whitlam in 1972, this was the only time Murdoch papers had editorialised for Labor (Windschuttle 1988:308). In 1988, Windschuttle also noted that no publications of 'the Packer family's Consolidated Press [had] ever supported Labor in a federal election'. When the Herald and Weekly Times editorialised for Bob Hawke in the *Herald* in 1983 'this was the first time the paper had supported Labor in over one hundred years' (Economou 2008). Windschuttle (1988:263) claimed that newspapers prior to the 1980s generally exhibited a 'strong anti-Labor bias in political reporting... not just in their editorial commentaries but in the selection, layout and angles of their basic news stories.'

In the 2000s, there was a similar pattern of general conservative preference allied with a pragmatic shift to the ALP in 2007 when it looked to be the likely victor. The 12 newspapers in Table 11.1 combined had 36 opportunities to recommend a vote to their readers. On four occasions a newspaper declined to offer an endorsement, 22 times newspapers advocated a vote for the Coalition and on nine occasions newspapers recommended a vote for the

ALP. Seven of these nine occasions were in 2007 and for some papers that was still a novel experience. The *Courier-Mail* noted this was the first time in 72 years that the paper had supported Labor federally (Economou 2008). The *Australian* hadn't endorsed Labor since 1972. The *SMH* hadn't since 1987 and still sounded reluctant, saying: 'It is a matter of the greatest regret that [Howard] . . . mishandled his chance to choose a time to step down' (23 November 2007:16).

For conservatives, the newspapers' history of support for Coalition parties merely reflects the inadequacies of the Labor Party but, for some analysts, the conservative leanings of commercial media organisations are entirely predictable. McChesney (2003) says large media businesses around the world are

> politically conservative, because [they] are significant beneficiaries of the
> current social structure . . . and any upheaval in property or social relations –
> particularly to the extent that it reduces the power of business – is not in their
> interest.

(See also GUMG 1976; Herman and Chomsky 1988). Scepticism about the impact of corporate interests is not merely the domain of left-wing academics. The 2001 ABA survey found that 'Australian audiences believe that the business interests of media organisations are the greatest source of influence on what they read, hear or see in news and current affairs' (ABA 2001b). What were those interests in the 2000s?

Commercial interests and bias in the 2000s

As businesses, media organisations have an underlying interest in a *stable economy* and *economic growth*. These factors were mentioned repeatedly in editorials supporting the Coalition, even in the newspapers that conservative critics see as left-wing: the *Age* and the *SMH*. The *SMH* acknowledged in 2004 that it editorialised for Labor only three times in 173 years 'mainly because the party's economic policies were unsuitable'.

One economic issue that News Limited papers cared about in the 2000s was *lower taxation*. In 2004, the *Australian* ran a campaign it called 'Too Much Tax' with a focus on income-earners paying the top tax rate. The

Australian said it wanted lower taxes to 'encourage ordinary Australians to work harder and earn more'. Other News Limited papers echoed this. The *Daily Telegraph* said: 'Australians [were being] penalised for their effort and achievement', which was interesting, given that more of its readers were on low incomes (under $15 000) than in the top tax bracket ($50 000 plus) (Table 4.1).

Media companies are large employers, so *industrial relations* was a major issue. The *Australian* acknowledged in 2007: 'We have always supported the [Howard] Government's IR policy [*WorkChoices*].' The *Herald Sun* argued that IR reform was a considerable achievement of the Howard government and the *Daily Telegraph* said: 'People are better off now.' This was not just a News Limited view. At Fairfax, an *SMH* editorial argued: 'we believe Work Choices was the right policy, a necessary reform.' More predictably, the *AFR* with its business audience was also supportive and called Labor's 2007 plans to abolish *WorkChoices* 'regressive'.

In *The Latham Diaries*, Latham (2005:270) recounted a dinner he had with News Limited's Lachlan Murdoch and John Hartigan before the 2004 election. According to Latham, 'Two main political issues' were discussed: 'AWAs and Foxtel'. AWAs (Australian Workplace Agreements), made possible under *WorkChoices*, were individual contracts negotiated between employers and employees without unions. At the time, only about 2.4 per cent of the Australian workforce was on AWAs (ABS 2004). Latham noted that News Limited had the 'highest number of AWAs in the country; all their journalists are on individual contracts'. Latham (2005:270) said: 'Hartigan pressed hard for me to drop [Labor's] policy dedicated to their abolition, but I told him there was no chance of that.'

Media policy

An even more important issue for media organisations – that affected their fates (and fortunes) very directly in the 2000s – was media policy. Under the Hawke and Keating governments, changes to media policy benefited the existing main players – especially Murdoch and Packer (owner of PBL) (Barry 2007:348). Hawke considered himself a 'mate' of Kerry Packer's, but Keating and Packer fell out very publicly, reportedly over pay TV policy (Savva 2010:117; Watson 2002; Williams 1997:185). While television owners can't use editorials, and their news programs have to comply with broadcasting law, this didn't prevent Packer from making his views known.

A year before the 1996 election, Kerry Packer was interviewed on his television network by Ray Martin on *A Current Affair*. During the interview, he endorsed John Howard as the prime-minister-in-waiting, saying: 'I think he'd do a good job' and 'I think he's an honest man.' This was a significant political intervention. An enraged Keating – who knew that Howard and Packer had recently met – told journalists that the endorsement meant a deal had been done, that 'Howard had given Packer "the nod"'. . . [because] a Howard government would change the cross-media rules enabling Packer ownership of both Channel 9 and Fairfax' (Watson 2002:551).

Once in office, the Howard government did try to lift restrictions on owning only one newspaper, radio or television station in the same city, but this stalled in 1997. There was dissent from within the Coalition over the impact on regional areas; media owners wanted changes but had different aims; and the Howard government was in no hurry to alienate any of the main players when there was little political capital to be gained from the issue.

At the next election (1998), Kerry Packer again publicly endorsed Howard. Eleven days before the election, he attended a Liberal Party luncheon. Asked by the media afterwards whether Howard's government deserved another term, Packer replied: 'Of course it does.' He said Labor needed 'another few years in the wilderness' before it was returned to office. The following year, the Howard government decided (against the advice of the Productivity Commission) to give existing television networks a monopoly over the introduction of digital television. This was widely seen to favour Packer and his Nine Network. In August 2001 – just as the *Tampa* issue was going on – the Howard government announced that it planned to repeal cross-media ownership rules if re-elected. To some observers the announcement's timing suggested it was an inducement to favourable reporting at a critical moment (Marr and Wilkinson 2003:253).

The Howard government's second attempt to deregulate media ownership failed in 2003 when Labor and the minor parties joined forces to prevent a watering down of the rules. By the time the laws were finally changed in 2006–07, media businesses had also changed. Packer, tired of waiting for change, had sold his stake in Fairfax in 2001. After his death in 2005, PBL was more focused on gambling and the internet. Nevertheless, the major players – News Limited, PBL, Fairfax and Kerry Stokes – all benefited from the law changes (including a $4.5 billion windfall for PBL). For some analysts, this meant the commercial media organisations had a vested interest in seeing a Coalition government re-elected, especially in 2001 and 2004. Some of the major allegations of anti-Labor bias in the 2000s stemmed from this view. Others rejected the associations between media policy and news reporting as a baseless conspiracy theory and identified pro-Labor bias in public broadcasting as the major issue of the decade.

We should note before examining some of these accusations that it is not only owners who bully politicians. Keating was said to have initiated policies that destroyed the HWT company and disadvantaged Fairfax in 1986, reportedly as payback for perceived anti-ALP bias (Chadwick 1989:20). In the UK, there were reports from media insiders that, before Murdoch backed Blair in 1997,

> Blair privately made it clear to Murdoch that how a future Labour government would treat his multifarious media interests in Britain depended on how Murdoch's papers treated Blair and the Labour Party during the campaign (Neil quoted in McNair 2000:153).

It has also been argued that media owners' power may exist more in their ability to make politicians believe that they can shape public views than in any such actual power. Nonetheless, bluff or not, Australian politicians have always taken the power of media owners very seriously and some outlets have been particularly associated with political interventions.

News Limited

News Limited arouses strong feelings among journalists and commentators alike. In 2004, 40 per cent of surveyed journalists identified News Limited as 'the most politically biased media organisation in Australia' (RMR 2004). Rupert Murdoch is a controversial figure around the world whose news

outlets have displayed 'an intellectual orthodoxy and an ideological uniformity' (McKnight 2005:54). One of his former editors said:

> Rupert expects his papers to stand broadly for what he believes: a combi-
> nation of right-wing Republicanism from America mixed with undiluted
> Thatcherism from Britain... [including] free market economics... [and a
> conservative] social agenda (Neil quoted in McKnight 2005:72).

In the 2000s, News Limited's reporting on two stories was particularly
controversial and seen to influence election results – the Iraq War and the
Tampa incident. Murdoch publicly supported the Iraq War and an analysis
of his more than 175 newspapers around the world found that all but
one were pro-war (Greenslade 2003). This included Murdoch's Australian
outlets, including the *Mercury*, which had originally displayed a contrary
editorial stance but was reportedly directed to change its position (Manne
2005:76).

Robert Manne (who has himself been accused of being left-wing by
conservative News Limited columnists) – argues that, between 2002 and
2004, Labor's policy on Iraq was reported with 'contempt' and 'persistent,
harsh and frequently shrill criticism' in Murdoch papers (Manne 2005:96).
While the fraudulent 'weapons of mass destruction' justification for Iraq
and the mismanagement of the post-invasion seriously damaged Labour
and Tony Blair in the UK, in Australia, during the 2004 election, 'Iraq was
barely discussed.' Manne (2005:97) suggests that one plausible explanation
was Murdoch's domination of 'the metropolitan press'.

In 2001, News Limited tabloids reported the *Tampa* incident in a manner
that was not only about agenda-setting but also exhibited a strong editorial position supporting the Howard government's stance (see Chapter 8).
Unlike the Iraq War, though, support was not unanimous across all News
Limited papers. The *Australian* in particular opposed Howard's policy on
asylum-seekers, which shows not only that newspapers have to take account
of their different audiences, but also that Murdoch's papers are not always
editorially aligned. What made the *Australian*'s condemnation especially
significant was that it had been the subject of allegations of pro-Coalition
bias (Box 11.2). Its editor said the paper's news pages were 'rigorously
straight' while its op-ed pages were 'centre-right' (ABC 2006). Others saw it
as more partisan. Rob Chalmers (2009), the longest-serving member of the

Press Gallery, said that during the Howard years the *Australian* was 'overtly biased towards Howard' despite 'as good a staff of journalists as any paper in the country, many of whom were critical of many aspects of the Howard government'.

Box 11.2

Critical descriptions of the *Australian*, 2004–07

A 'long history of being a mouthpiece for Howard' (Murray 2007).
The 'leading organ of John Howard's culture wars' and a bastion of 'eleven years of right-wing dogmatism' (Hamilton 2006b).
The '*Government Gazette* . . . where the idea of balanced political coverage consists of having supporters of both John Howard and Peter Costello on staff' (MacCormack 2007).
In 2004, Labor adviser Dennis Glover said he felt that the *Australian* was 'out to get us' (Glover 2005:204).

The op-ed pages at the *Australian* played an important role in the 'culture wars' during the Howard years. These were ongoing debates about various issues including multiculturalism, the teaching of history, the treatment of refugees, Aboriginal reconciliation, a republic and a general rallying against elites – especially in universities – and against 'political correctness' (McKnight 2005; Scalmer and Goot 2004). The *Australian* had a mix of columnists but its conservative columnists outnumbered, and were more prominent than, those considered left-wing and, when external contributors were used, a pattern of dominance of 'conservative-sourced' articles was evident (McKnight 2005:56–7).

Bias might be about political ideology but it might also be about stirring up debate, selling newspapers and the commercial value attached to being close to a government. It is difficult to pinpoint where factors begin and end. During the Howard years, the *Australian* was widely said to be 'on the drip' (Suich 2004c). It was 'favoured with a steady flow of leaks from Howard's office while the Fairfax papers got nothing' (Chalmers 2009). This access provided the paper with exclusives that were especially important for the *Australian*. For many readers it is their second paper, so the *Australian* has always had to convince readers they are getting something 'better or different from the standard fare' in order to get them to 'switch from their usual broadsheet or buy two papers' (Tiffen 2009).

It is also important to stress that media organisations are neither mono-lithic nor static. In its election eve editorial in 2007, the *Australian* sup-ported Rudd. Some put this down to the usual desire to back a winner, others suggested that personal connections in the small world of Australian politics and media played a role.[1] But the *Australian* also included some prominent voices from the Left in the 2000s and pursued several stories that were damaging to the Howard government including the AWB scandal and the government's weak case against terror suspect Mohammed Haneef. It was a vocal critic of the *Tampa* policy and played an important role in exposing the 'children overboard' claims. The government's response to this was rather telling though. Reportedly, 'a senior prime ministerial adviser called [the] *Australian*'s Canberra bureau and asked if Rupert (Murdoch) had gone over to Labor' (Such 2004c).

If Labor supporters thought News Limited coverage was sometimes directed against them, they were not the only party to complain. In 2004, the *Herald Sun* ran what can only be described as an extraordinary campaign against the Greens (Box 11.3). In the lead-up to the election, the Greens' support had been increasing and there was speculation that Green pref-erences could decide who would win government or that they could hold the balance of power in the Senate, thus preventing planned reforms by a fourth-term Howard government including media ownership law changes and *WorkChoices*. As the *Herald Sun* pointed out, the Greens 'have voted with the government just 2.5 per cent of the time over the past three years' (McManus 2004b).

Box 11.3

The *Herald Sun* and the Greens, 2004

Two days after the 2004 election was called, the *Herald Sun* published an article that was printed in full or excerpted in Murdoch papers around the country. The full headline was 'Greens back illegal drugs' with two subheadings 'Open door plan for all refugees' and 'Family home tax, gay marriage nod'.

The article stated that 'Ecstasy and other illegal drugs would be supplied over the counter to young users in a radical policy framed by Senator Bob Brown's Greens.' The article claimed that 'Greens policies' included 'laws to force people to ride bicycles more often and eat less meat. Driving farmers from their land. Medicare funding for sex-change operations. Capital gains tax on the most expensive family homes' and [to] 'train our soldiers, sailors and airmen in the art of "non-violent resistance"' (McManus 2004a).

Bob Brown made a complaint to the Australian Press Council. In an unusually strident finding, the APC upheld the complaint, calling the article 'irresponsible journalism'. It said *Herald Sun* readers 'were seriously misled' and 'in the context of an approaching election, the potential damage was considerable' (APC 2005). Bob Brown argued that the article was 'unbelievably damaging to the Greens. In my calculations it cost us hundreds of thousands of votes . . .' Others speculated it cost the Greens at least one Senate seat if not more.

The story was not an isolated incident. The *Herald Sun* consistently lambasted and ridiculed the Greens during the election campaign, describing them as 'radicals', 'extremists' and 'tree-huggers' (McManus 2004a). In an article titled 'Greens means mad', Andrew Bolt said the Greens had 'policies which could kill the weak and most vulnerable of us.'

Channel Nine (PBL)

Kerry Packer's son James took a more active role in PBL in the early 2000s and after his father's death in 2005. While Kerry's politics were generally characterised as opportunistic and pragmatic, James had more formal party connections and reportedly joined the Liberal Party in 2003. Just before the 2004 election, as PBL's executive chairman, he endorsed the Howard government in a speech. As with his father's public endorsements in 1995 and 1998, this renewed speculation that the Packers expected media ownership changes in return for their support.

This became even more pertinent after Latham indicated in 2004 that, if Labor won office, it would permit a fourth free-to-air television network. The Packers had strongly campaigned against new competitors. To add insult to injury, Labor also planned to ban junk food advertising during children's television programs. When Channel Nine broadcast a damaging – if overhyped – profile on Latham two months before the election campaign, there were suggestions that PBL was actively campaigning against the ALP (Box 11.4; Figure 11.1).

The Nine Network also included some softer profiles of Latham on other programs (such as *60 Minutes* and *Burke's Backyard*) but the unusual nature of the *Sunday* report and other examples from Nine and the *Bulletin* were enough to fuel theories about whether 'Kerry Packer and Rupert Murdoch

Box 11.4

PBL, the ALP and Latham in 2004

In July 2004, ads promoting the *Sunday* program promised an 'unauthorised' and 'explosive' profile on Latham was going to reveal 'a violent incident in Latham's past'. The man responsible for initiating the 40-minute profile was *Sunday*'s executive producer, John Lyons, who had been the author of a *Bulletin* piece on Paul Keating in 2005 that was described as a 'hatchet job' and part of 'the Packers'... vendetta against Paul Keating' (MacCormack 2008).

The 'violent incident' turned out to be a minor skirmish that Latham had with a Liverpool resident 15 years before, when he was a councillor, which had been reported in the *Age* four months earlier (on 13 March). The man claimed Latham had tried to punch him, but Latham implied the man was drunk and said he had merely taken hold of him to get him out of the room. The profile was 'a marketing triumph for the Nine Network'; it attracted '30 per cent more viewers than usual' (Price 2004). It also encouraged greater speculation about, and reporting on, Latham's past.

Figure 11.1 The *Bulletin* and Mark Latham, 2004–05

Source: Author photograph of, from left to right: the *Bulletin*, 5 October 2004; 27 September 2005; 7 September 2004.

[were] waging a campaign against [Latham] through their television stations and newspapers' (Marriner 2004). As far away as Malaysia, there were suggestions of a plot to 'stop Latham', which involved not only Murdoch and Packer but also Seven Network owner Kerry Stokes 'who makes no secret of his close association with Howard' (Boey 2004).

When there have been claims of bias on television and radio, they have often been in relation to current affairs programs rather than news bulletins. Laurie Oakes (2006) has said that 'contrary to the claims of various politicians and commentators – [Kerry Packer] did not attempt to exercise political power through the news bulletins of the television network he controlled.' He also said that Kerry Packer 'knew he couldn't tell me what to say' (Elliott 2010). Savva (2010:118) outlines what she says is apparently the 'one and only time' he tried, over a story on Keating. Peter Meakin, who was in charge of the Nine Network's news and current affairs from 1993 until 2003, also said: 'In all the time I worked for Kerry Packer I never received riding instructions. Nothing like News Limited – though I don't know what Kerry was doing behind the scenes' (Suich 2004c). Others have suggested there was no need to issue instructions because there was 'a climate of self-censorship and second-guessing' at PBL and Packer 'terrified people' (Barry 2007:444).

Fairfax

Fairfax also advocated for the Coalition's media ownership law changes and benefited from them. Yet the allegations of bias directed at it in the 2000s – especially from News Limited columnists – were usually claims of pro-Labor bias. The *Australian's* Janet Albrechtsen called Fairfax 'the safest Labor seat in the country' while Piers Akerman called Fairfax 'the ALP's print arm' and Bolt called the *Age* 'the Spencer Street Soviet'.

As with other outlets, there is evidence both for and against claims of bias. In a bias study by Gans and Leigh (2009), the *Age* was the only one of 27 outlets that was 'significantly distinguishable from the centre'. It was the only newspaper to be 'significantly slanted' and 'pro-Labor'. Like all outlets, the *Age* and *SMH* write for their audiences and their readers are more educated, left-leaning (see Chapter 5) and interested in post-materialist concerns. The *Age* has a high proportion of Green voters among its readers and its agenda

during the 2007 election included a heavy focus on environmental issues
and an emphasis on global warming as a scientific fact (Box 11.5).

Box 11.5

Age article headlines during the 2007 election campaign

'How serious are we about Global Warming?'
'Warming linked to mass plant, animal extinctions'
'Global warming sizzling at a red-hot pace'
'Imperative for a coherent, global climate policy'
'Poll spotlight on climate'
'Warming puts heat on political leaders'
'Rift on Kyoto exposes depth of leadership failure'
'Earth losing race against rising carbon emissions'
'Climate change "serious threat" to coastal towns'
'World warming much faster than we thought'
'The greenhouse effect'
'Australia scores badly on global emissions growth report'
'Australia is not a climate change leader: Here are the facts'

However, there are also many cases of Fairfax displeasing Labor. For example, Keating had a well-known and long-running 'fight' with the *SMH*
(Williams 1997:184). The *SMH* pursued investigations into Latham's past
that appalled him. Fairfax's commercial interests and its management structure are also difficult to reconcile with left-wing bias claims. For example, in
2002 former Liberal Party Treasurer Ron Walker (who was Liberal Treasurer
for 15 years) was appointed as a Fairfax board member and became chairman of the board (2005–09). Between 2001 and 2004, the *SMH* and the *Age*
only endorsed Labor in one of three possible election-eve editorials. The *Age*
supported Australia's involvement in the war in Iraq and in 2004 advocated
a vote for the Coalition mainly on the basis of its economic record, hardly
the behaviour of a socialist newspaper (8 October 2004:16).

The ABC

The ABC was the subject of some of the most virulent complaints of bias in
the 2000s, which was ironic given that it had the most prescribed, monitored

and evaluated political coverage of any media organisation in Australia. Unlike the commercial broadcasters, it had detailed editorial policies which were publicly available and an Election Review Committee which monitored broadcasts for balance. It also had an extensive and complex procedure for dealing with complaints and regularly published details of complaints received. Nonetheless, during the 2000s, conservative commentators and politicians consistently alleged pro-Labor bias at the ABC (e.g. Akerman 2006; Alston 2003; Flint 2005; Switzer 2007) (Box 11.6).

Box 11.6

The ABC and the Howard government

On 28 May 2003, Communications Minister Richard Alston – the Minister responsible for public broadcasting – made a complaint to the ABC. Included was a 68-point document listing examples of what Alston saw as an anti-US and anti-Coalition stance in the AM program's reporting of the Iraq War. He made this complaint public by outlining his allegations in the Age.

An internal inquiry at the ABC acknowledged two of the 68 instances, saying the language used on AM had 'lacked objectivity' and been sarcastic or 'excessive', but otherwise cleared the program of systematic bias.

Alston's complaint was then referred the ABC's Independent Complaints Review Panel (ICRP), which upheld 17 of the 68 complaints but 'taken as a whole' found 'no evidence overall, of biased and anti-Coalition [of the Willing] coverage as alleged by [Alston]' (ABC 2003:8).

Unsatisfied with these two inquiries, Alston then took his complaint to the ABA. The ABA added an additional four breaches of the ABC *Code of Practice* to the 17 breaches of editorial standards, but still found no systematic evidence of bias, saying that 'AM's coverage of the Iraq War was of a high standard overall' and 'balanced overall' (ABA 2005:13 and 15).

ABC (2007b:31) guidelines state the need to be impartial, but they also tell reporters to 'Be questioning. Serve the public interest by investigating issues affecting society and individuals.' This mission naturally brings the broadcaster into conflict with political actors. During the first Gulf War, Hawke was also a vocal critic of ABC reporting. Defenders of the ABC argue that its critics often confuse journalistic scepticism and critical enquiry with bias. Some argued the Minister's bias allegations in 2003 were an attempt to apply political pressure to the ABC and part of ongoing attempts by the

Howard government to intimidate the broadcaster through funding cuts and politically motivated board appointments (e.g. see *Media Watch* 2004). A more self-conscious stance after the bias allegations saw the ABC in 2004 hire an external auditor to count 'the seconds each party gets on air' and whether the time was 'favourable, neutral or unfavourable' (*Media Watch* 2004). The media-monitoring agency Rehame found no major difference in share of voice allocated to the two major parties (Green 2004). In 2006, the ABC introduced even stricter anti-bias rules and an internal watch-dog to review programs to ensure they were fair and balanced. In 2007, the ABC commissioned media-monitors to perform another external share-of-voices count. This found that the Coalition actually received a greater proportion of election coverage on television, radio and the internet (Chadwick 2008).

Share of voice

It is quite remarkable how much attention was focused on the ABC in the 2000s while commercial television was largely ignored, even though that was where most Australians got their news from. Using the same measure of balance that the ABC used in its balance tests (share-of-voices), I analysed the time given to speakers from the two major parties in election news stories (Table 11.2). Across the three elections, the Coalition received more air-time in every instance except in Channel Seven News in 2004. Is this evidence that all television stations (including the ABC) were biased towards the Coalition?

While the Coalition did receive a high proportion of time (68 per cent) on Nine News in 2004 – the year Nine was accused of running a campaign against Latham – it received even more time on SBS in 2001 because of the *Tampa* and its international implications. More time doesn't necessarily mean positive coverage. What the table reflects is not so much systematic bias towards conservatives, but that incumbency confers a major news-generating advantage. A government is paid greater attention, has more resources, has a record to defend and is called upon during the campaign to comment on domestic and international matters.[2]

For newspapers, I applied a similar share-of-voice test by comparing the number of words quoted from Labor and Coalition spokespeople. In

Table 11.2 Equal time? Speaking time provided to the two major parties on television news bulletins, 2001–07 (percentages)

Year	Channel	Program	Stories (n =)	ALP	Coalition
2001	SBS	World News	10	27.2	72.8
2001	ABC	7 pm News	12	40.4	59.6
2001	10	5 pm News	28	41.3	58.7
2001	9	6 pm News	20	46.5	53.5
2001	7	6 pm News	17	48.5	51.5
2004	9	6 pm News	8	32.0	68.0
2004	ABC	7 pm News	17	41.0	59.0
2004	10	5 pm News	18	42.0	58.0
2004	SBS	World News	7	43.0	57.0
2004	7	6 pm News	8	53.6	46.4
2007	ABC	7 pm News	13	37.8	62.2
2007	7	6 pm News	14	41.0	59.0
2007	SBS	World News	17	44.6	55.4
2007	9	6 pm News	14	46.5	53.4
2007	10	5 pm News	18	46.8	53.2

Source: Author.

2004 and 2007, both parties were allocated almost the same number of words in front-page stories. This is the natural outcome of an 'impartial' news formula that demands quotes from 'both sides' of politics. It was only in 2001 that Coalition politicians were quoted significantly more than Labor ones and this was true in both News Limited and Fairfax papers, which again confirms how effective the asylum-seeker issue was in terms of agenda-setting. It also confirms that share-of-voice counts by themselves tell us nothing about the *context* in which party spokespeople are reported.

We have to look at content to arrive at a view about whether the attention was critical scrutiny or partisan promotion. But we also need to be aware that not everything is discernible even in content. As Haupt and Grattan (1983:39) point out:

the [media] have the power to help [politicians] or harm [them]. It is not [always] a question of bias in what is reported or left unreported, or in the way it is reported – it is whether they help you with advice, or a tip-off, or a soft question that allows the candidate to look good.

Conclusion

News is never a straightforward reflection of reality. Selecting topics invariably means privileging one account of what has happened and what it means over many other possible interpretations. At the same time, politics is always about contradictory information and emotionally charged value clashes. This guarantees that the news media's version of reality will never satisfy everyone and will especially disappoint those with strong views.

When it comes to partisan bias, most of the time journalists and news outlets are assiduous in their pursuit of impartiality and try hard to be balanced – at least in terms of the two major parties – to explore different issues and have a mix of views. Accusations of bias offend journalists because they are not just about content but also about motivation; they imply that the journalist has a motive. Many – perhaps most – times this isn't the case, however, there are occasions when owners, outlets or individuals deliberately shape the presentation or content of news to advance the cause of a particular leader, party or policy.

We can't know how audiences view these incursions. Some may ignore them, some may be persuaded and some will reject them, but the fact that organisations try is an important matter. Sometimes their advocacy is overt, but at other times it is without acknowledgement and, for newspapers, in contravention of the principle that a 'paper's editorial viewpoints and its advocacy of them must be kept separate from its news columns' (APC 2009a). Worst of all is when bias is part of a quid pro quo and when bias is accompanied by hypocrisy, with outlets failing to declare their interests and casting themselves in the protective cloak of 'impartiality'.

When it comes to bias, what matters is not just the presence or absence of views. There are degrees of bias. For example, News Limited was accused of bias during recent election campaigns but not at the level seen in 1975. During the 2000s, bias rarely became a major public concern and this is partly because, even where an outlet was running a political agenda, it still provided space for alternative and oppositional views – perhaps not enough to dilute its overall presentation of an ideological or partisan case, but enough to prevent characterisation of it as a one-sided propaganda machine.

When it comes to political views, media outlets send out mixed, contradictory and confusing messages. This is why, for every perceived example of bias, there is usually another indicator pointing the other way. Glover (2005:205) optimistically suggests that Australian news reporting tends to have 'its own self-correcting ethical codes. And bias on one side is usually counterbalanced by bias on the other.'

So long as it is overt and there is ideological diversity, partisanship can add vibrancy to a debate and engage audiences who can weigh the evidence for themselves. Rigid adherence to outdated modes of presentation sometimes hides more than it reveals – for example, when two candidates are given equal space for the sake of balance, even though the journalist knows that one is lying, or when a stopwatch attempt at mathematical balance leads to coverage that is timid and dull. But there needs to be a full spectrum of bias, including space for viewpoints that are unpopular or eccentric. In Australia, it is in this sense that the media are most biased. They tend to construct accounts of politics structured by already dominant values and interests. There is a narrowness about news which is focused upon incumbents, authority, the major parties and 'official' (especially male) sources. There has also been a conservative bias and a bias towards corporate interests but, perhaps again in a self-correcting and counter-balancing force, there is a push-pull between individual journalists' views and the organisational cultures they work in that tempers this.

Because there will always be perceptions of bias, the airing of those claims is healthy for a democracy. What is unhealthy is when politicians are satisfied with media coverage because they have so much power that journalistic critique and enquiry are stifled. Or when media owners have so much power that politicians and their supporters are afraid to voice concerns about what they see as unfair treatment. While we probably won't ever settle precisely what bias is or validate it with hard data, we still need to retain the concept as a valuable analytical tool. When they report news, outlets present us with a particular version of reality. Thinking about bias is an important way to critique and analyse what is presented. The fact that there will always be others who disagree with our analysis only makes the notion of bias more interesting, not less valuable.

Chapter 12

NEWS, THE PUBLIC AND DEMOCRACY

Democracy is for, and about, citizens. So too, at least in theory, is political journalism, and especially during elections. That there is a 'public', however conceived (and this is not always made explicit), made up of citizens in need of information is the underlying basis for all of the promises that news outlets make and the high expectations we have about what journalism can provide. This chapter concludes the book by summarising the major trends in election reporting in the 2000s, considering them in light of two major questions about 'the public': what do people want from political news and what does democracy need? Finally, what happens when these two principles clash?

The public and the media

The first part of this book was devoted to political news audiences, but media audiences and 'the public' are not the same thing – even if they do overlap at some points. Audiences develop in relation to particular media forms. They consist of individuals who consume those media – often in private – for a range of reasons including entertainment and relaxation. A 'public', on the other hand, is 'people engaged in activities (and spaces) that are in some ways socially visible, that is, not private'. So while the media can construct audiences, those audiences become 'real publics only through the processes of engagement with issues and discursive interactions among themselves' (Dahlgren 2009:73–4).

This notion derives from the concept of a 'public sphere' outlined by German philosopher Jürgen Habermas (1989) in *The Structural Transformation of the Public Sphere*. In Habermas' theory (1974:49), what the media ideally contribute to democracy is a space where 'something approaching public opinion might be formed'. They mediate between society and the State and provide a public forum for citizens to collectively reflect on issues of communal importance, especially issues 'connected to the activity of the State'. In the public sphere, information is disseminated and rational debate – including the expression of different views – is facilitated. For Habermas, the dialogue facilitated by the press and in the coffee houses and salons of roughly the mid 17th century to the 18th century was 'the nearest historical approximation we have ever had of the ideal of the public sphere' (Craig 2004:50).

But in another, and perhaps more important, sense, the public sphere designated an ideal of how public opinion *ought* to be formed through a sphere that is open to all citizens, where information is unrestricted, and where free, critical and self-critical discussion goes on and leads to consensus. Such a sphere is public in a special way because it is where the opinions of private individuals lose their private character as they are subjected to rational debate and criticism. To the extent that they are informed by this process and survive it, they cease to be merely private and become matters of public opinion.

For Habermas, the story of the public sphere after the 18th century was one of decline. As the press became an industrialised and commercialised mass medium, this effectively eliminated the public sphere because the media came to see their audience not as citizens in need of information but as consumers who could be sold goods and services and who, themselves, could be packaged and sold to advertisers. Under these circumstances, 'what was once . . . [a forum for] rational-critical debate became just another domain of cultural consumption, and the . . . public sphere collapsed into a sham world of image creation and opinion management' (Thompson 1993: 178).

There have been many critiques of Habermas' theory since its 1962 publication and its English translation in 1989 (for example, Fraser 1992) and he also made revisions to it in his own later work. It is now more broadly accepted that there is no unitary public sphere but multiple 'publics' organ-ised around different needs and interests. There were criticisms that the original theory – based as it was on early media effects research – mischar-acterised audiences as passive consumers who were easily manipulated by media techniques. There were also critiques from a feminist perspective, which examined the notion of where women fit in notions of the public and the private. There were postmodernist critiques of the notion of 'rationality' and Marxist critiques suggesting that those elite men in the coffee houses were not embodying universal principles of reason and truth but were, instead, characteristically attempting to put forward their own interests and ways of life as constituting what was best for a society as a whole. Many pointed out that, far from being an ideal public sphere, the coffee house public sphere was an exclusive domain of men with education, property and leisure. It excluded women and most men in society.

Nevertheless, despite all the criticisms, Habermas' notion of a public sphere has been enormously influential and particularly as a normative ideal of the role of the media in a democracy. There are many commentators whose ideas about what the news media can contribute to democracy stem from this framework.

What the public needs?

The public sphere ideal depends upon citizens who are willing to reflect on political issues, to obtain information from the media and elsewhere and to participate in rational debate with other citizens in order to have their views challenged or strengthened. It is an active form of citizenship. Here, for many commentators, is the essence of the problem and this was illustrated in the first part of this book. The sociological reality is that most citizens are only semi-attentive to politics and choose not to avail themselves of the more detailed political media. As Zaller (1992:47) observes, most politics 'is notoriously low key and uninvolving. The stakes are theoretically high, but people find it hard to stay interested.'

Given the sort of political news habits outlined in Part I, Dahlgren (2009:13) has noted: 'Clearly there is not much chance that a vast major-ity of people of a Western liberal democracy will become "active citizens", or even well-informed citizens.' This has led to very different views about how we should judge political news and evaluate its democratic role. Many media and politics scholars continue to advocate the importance of the news media acting as a public sphere, but other theorists argue we need to revise our expectations – both of the news media and of citizens. McNair (2000:12) argues that the 'ideal public sphere...has never existed – and may never exist outside of the intellectual imagination.'

In the best-known repudiation of the 'active citizen' model, journalism scholar Michael Schudson (1998:9) said that we 'require a citizenship fit for our own day' and this means there 'must be some distribution across people and across issues of the cognitive demands of self-government.' Zaller (2003:119) notes that Schudson recognises '[m]ore than most public intellectuals' that citizens are 'entitled to multidimensional lives' and that there are other things – 'virtuous things' – that citizens want to do with their time besides engaging in politics including time with nature, music, friends and family (see also Schudson 1998:312).

The best way to understand Schudson's position is to consider it in his own words. Schudson argues that we should expect citizens to be 'monitorial' rather than informed:

> A monitorial citizen scans (rather than reads) the informational environment in a way so that he or she may be alerted on a very wide variety of issues for a very wide variety of ends and may be mobilized around those issues in a large variety of ways (Schudson 1998:310–11).

He also says:

> [the] monitorial citizen engages in environmental surveillance more than information-gathering. Picture parents watching small children at the community pool. They are not gathering information; they are keeping an eye on the scene. They look inactive, but they are poised for action if action is required. The monitorial citizen is not an absentee citizen but watchful, even while he or she is doing something else.

Applying this notion to news content, Zaller agreed that 'much criticism of news is based on an ideal of citizenship and a standard of quality that are neither realistic nor necessary for the functioning of democracy'. He argued that 'it does little good to urge a standard of news quality that requires more of citizens than they are able or willing to give'. For Zaller, the news media don't need to give every citizen a 'Full News' diet but need instead to provide enough information for citizens to scan the environment for events that require a response, acting as '"burglar alarms" about acute problems' and calling 'attention to matters requiring urgent attention . . . [in an] excited and noisy tone' (Zaller 2003: 109, 110, 122).

What the public wants?

The disjuncture between these two schools of thought was not only a matter of academic theory but was also being played out in practice in news journalism in the 2000s. It is the contradictions between the public sphere ideal (still very strong in scholarship and journalism) versus the sociological reality of news audiences (and the economic and market realities facing media organisations as they tried to capture those audiences) that help explain many of the trends identified in news coverage in this book. While traditional journalism continued to draw heavily upon the ideals of the public sphere role, this was acting in concert with much looser (Schudson and others of like mind would say more 'realistic') standards of news aimed not at creating 'informed citizens' but at capturing the attention of citizens who had multifaceted interests – some public, some private, some about public affairs, some about entertainment.

This has led to one of the key trends in election reporting: a reduction in the space provided for political news in traditional media forms. In 2007, the most-watched commercial television news bulletins averaged two minutes of federal election news a night (Table 9.2). Nearly 30 years before, during the 1980 election, they had provided double this – an average of four-and-a-half minutes. This was not just a commercial media trend; the ABC also reduced its election news from eight minutes per bulletin in 1980 to four-and-a-half minutes in 2007 (Goot 1983:174; Table 9.2).

As one major broadcaster noted in the UK: 'Political news must be interesting before it is done. It doesn't have an automatic place in the news agenda any more.' In public sphere terms, this reduction is obviously a great loss – how can citizens learn about politics and discuss it if it is not covered? But for others it actually reflects a democratic development because it means 'the media [are] increasingly responsive to popular definitions of what is important' (McNair 2000:177).

At the heart of this responsiveness were commercial factors. The traditional news business in the 2000s was neither as predictable nor as profitable as it once had been. There were no longer the stable, loyal mass audiences of bygone eras waiting for the thud of their morning newspaper or to switch on television news at the same time every day after work. Nor were there advertisers who could be charged exorbitant rates in the absence of competition. As that model broke down there was more emphasis placed on commercial criteria in the selection and presentation of news.

This wasn't just an issue for 'old' media like newspapers or television (which faced similar audience/advertiser problems) but also an issue for new media trying to make money from news. 'God bless Tiger [Woods, following his sex scandals],' Yahoo chief executive Carol Bartz was quoted as saying in 2009, revealing that all of the main Yahoo news sections got a 'huge uplift' from the story. 'It is better than Michael Jackson dying; it is kind of hard to put an ad next to a funeral.' Nor were shifts in audiences an issue only for commercial media. Even public broadcasting needed, if not popularity, popular support and large enough audiences to justify its state subsidy.

Previously, there had been a paternalism about news – that politics was of general interest to citizens and, if it wasn't of interest to them, that it should be – as well as a need to capture a large mass audience. As the mass media, one-size-fits-all approach taken in newspapers and television news bulletins became increasingly unsatisfying for the hard-core politics-news junkies, especially the younger ones, in an era of greater choice, the elite audience started deserting traditional mass media products and taking to more specialist fare. As this occurred, formerly elite media products were having to seek broader audiences and were invariably talking to audiences that were less interested in politics. This shifted the way politics was reported and communicated.

Changes in news formulas designed to have more popular appeal saw a blurring of the old lines between conventional politics and popular culture; between 'politics' and 'entertainment' and between 'news' and 'entertainment'. This was especially evident in the growth in 'soft news' presentations of politics.

Figure 12.1 Channel Seven advertising its polling night broadcast, 2007
Source: Channel Seven advertisement, circa November 2007. Reproduced with permission of Channel Seven.

Soft news

In election reporting there was a greater focus on the horse-race aspects and increasing attempts to make politics more 'fun' and less 'boring'. In 2007, when Channel Seven advertised its election night coverage, it branded its opponents who represented traditional journalism approaches – including the ABC's Kerry O'Brien and Nine's Laurie Oakes – 'boring' (Figure 12.1). On election night, Seven used animations to report election results including cartoons of the leaders jumping for joy when they won seats, a duck (from sports coverage of cricket) to mark a loss and a 'tower of power' showing the breakdown of seats (Figure 12.2). Trying to compete in similarly entertaining terms, Channel Nine promoted its election coverage as a circus, asking viewers to 'roll up' for Nine's 'election extravaganza' with all 'the thrills and all the spills' (Figure 12.3). On election night, Nine also used animation, including images of putting photos through a shredder to signal the Coalition's defeat.

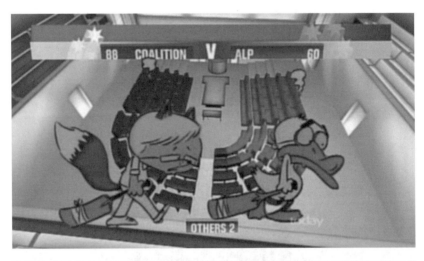

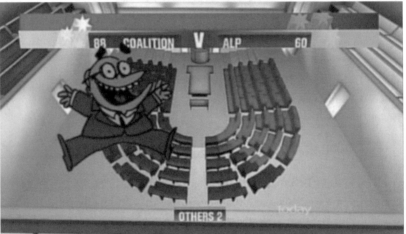

Figure 12.2 Channel Seven animations used in polling night broadcast, 2007
Source: *Today Tonight* 23 November 2007 story promoting Seven's election night coverage. Reproduced with permission of Channel Seven.

In public sphere terms, these devices are simplistic and trivialising, distracting citizens from more significant issues such as public policy and lessening their ability to participate in political life. However, those drawing on different views of what citizenship requires see these devices as symbolic of the media using more inclusive news values, making politics accessible

Figure 12.2 (*cont.*)

and taking account of different audience needs. In other words, one person's example of 'dumbing down' in soft news is another's example of journalists working hard to try to make complicated and difficult stories more understandable to more people. Even the broadcasters seemed to straddle these different views. Despite all their focus on fun and entertainment, they still highlighted their journalistic authority, with Seven promising 'the team you can trust' and Nine promising the 'most accurate results' and the 'most experienced team'.

Figure 12.3 Channel Nine advertising *The Great Debate*, 2007
Source: Channel Nine advertisement, 22 November 2007.

The way in which election news was presented in media with high proportions of female audience members such as breakfast programs, talkback
radio and commercial current affairs also highlighted the crossovers between
traditional journalistic authority and entertainment and a commercial
agenda. For example, in 2007 *Sunrise* mixed debates between rival politicians over 'serious' issues such as the environment with pop-psychology

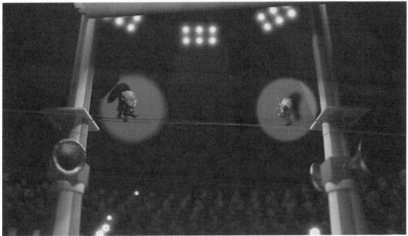

Figure 12.3 (*cont.*)

analysis of the leaders' personalities. On *Mornings with Kerri-Anne* butchers were asked to contribute their thoughts on the election and give a rating on a 'Lamb Chop Index' – a neat fusion of the voice of 'ordinary people' with the commercial promotion of a meat industry campaign.

Political news was no longer the domain of news and current affairs alone but was also conveyed through satire and comedy. In the US, some researchers have found that watching comedy programs imparts valuable political information, especially for viewers who would otherwise not be exposed to political news (Baum 2003), while others have found either no evidence or inconclusive evidence of this (Prior 2003). There was no Australian equivalent to US programs *The Daily Show* and the *Colbert Report* in the 2000s but there were programs providing specifically politics- or election-focused humour (such as *The Chaser*, ABC), others critiquing news reporting (*Newstopia*, SBS) and some that were more broadly based around topical discussion, comedy sketches and interviews (including *The Panel*, Ten and *The Glasshouse*, ABC). There were also FM radio appearances with comedy sketches or political interviews and satire and comedy on the internet, especially in 2007 with mash-ups, parodies and YouTube clips on elections.

In 2007, Rudd made a much-discussed appearance on the Channel Ten comedy program *Rove Live*, which had a young audience, the kind that it is difficult to reach through conventional news and current affairs. His appearance highlighted the tensions between the two schools of thought on citizenship when ABC *Insiders* host, journalist Barrie Cassidy, complained to Julia Gillard that Rudd wouldn't come on *Insiders* – a panel program with political commentators and journalists – but was going to appear on *Rove*. Other journalists also expressed concern that soft news asks soft questions, doesn't interrogate politicians properly and is 'vaudeville' rather than the 'serious' analysis that a democracy needs. However, journalist Christian Kerr noted that *Rove*'s audience was over 1.3 million while *Insiders* was 214 000. He made a strong case for the democratic value of soft news:

> No-one is more self righteous than the self consciously quality media when they are feeling spurned... Cassidy's behaviour was precious – precious and profoundly anti-democratic... Politicians are supposed to come to the people, not the other way. More engaged voters are better informed. All the studies show that they make up their minds how to vote long before elections. Why should Rudd waste his time talking to the *Insiders*' audience? Cassidy does realise what his show is called, doesn't he? It's not just Rudd's job as Labor leader to talk to voters who don't obsess over politics. Arguably, it's his democratic duty (Kerr 2007b).

As Kerr noted, the ABC program's name inadvertently reflected what many people in the 2000s were finding 'troubling' – a sense that both journalists and politicians were part of the same 'charmed circle' that 'has access to insider information and the levers of decision-making' (Blumler and Coleman 2010:151). Traditional outlets, aware of this perception, increasingly sought to include 'ordinary people' in their content. *Insiders*, for example, began a 'Your Shout' segment, promoting it as a chance for 'people anywhere in Australia to air a grievance or just sound off about issues that concern them'. As we saw in Chapter 10, other programs – like *Meet the Press* – used the internet with viewer questions via YouTube while online newspapers experimented with user comments under stories.

'Ordinary people' in news

For a form that is created for 'the public', 'ordinary people' have often been surprisingly absent from news content. This tends to reflect how journalists have been traditionally conceived in terms of speaking *to* citizens – presenting them with information – rather than speaking *with* them. In the 2000s, there was a noticeable trend that Turner described as 'the increasing visibility of the "ordinary person" in the media'. This included in reality television, talkback radio and people posting images and material on the internet, including social networking sites and blogs.[1]

As Turner (2010:1) notes, the 'widening of access [doesn't] necessarily carr[y] with it a democratic politics.' Just because we see 'ordinary people' more in media content – and even producing more of it themselves – this does not necessarily mean that it has an empowering effect. Reality television, for example, has been criticised for being exploitative as well as empowering, while online contributions (on social networking for example) can be both celebrated for their inclusive properties and critiqued as a form of 'unpaid' labour benefiting media companies.

In election reporting, television news especially relies upon 'ordinary' citizens for visuals that capture the colour and movement of the campaign. This is also a synergy television shares with politicians who structure their campaigns around events that will show the leader interacting with citizens, for example, at school and factory visits. In both 2001 and 2007, 98 per cent of television news clips showed members of the public, mostly in crowd scenes. Members of the public also got to speak more in news clips over the decade, rising from 29 per cent of reports in 2001 to 38 per cent in 2007. This was less about *vox pops* (which had gone out of style since the 1970s and 1980s) and more about showing exchanges between politicians and voters. Citizens tended to be cast as bit players surrounding the leaders as the central actors. What television news liked especially was when 'ordinary people' jeered and heckled politicians: part of the old public meeting-style expressions of dissent that serve as an important reminder that elections are about the public and politicians are accountable to citizens.

There were quite a few examples in the 2000s of politician-heckling, but especially in 2007 and particularly directed at Howard on his morning walks (possibly reflecting anger over *WorkChoices*). Rudd also encountered a Tasmanian pensioner who abused him for interrupting a music recital. However, perhaps the most vivid democratic image was one broadcast in news bulletins on polling day. After Howard arrived at his local polling station, he started shaking hands as he moved forward along the queue of people waiting to vote. One man who was waiting in the queue yelled out: 'Queue jumper! Get back in the queue like everyone else!' (Channel Ten, 5 pm News). The lack of deference shown to the then prime minister and the fact that Howard obediently stood in line waiting for 25 minutes, and was thus rendered an 'ordinary citizen' himself, did suggest something rather poignant about Australian politics.

Talkback has often been considered one of the most democratic news forms because 'ordinary people' get to call in and put their views directly to politicians and the host. There is a great deal of variation in the talk-back market from ABC programs to commercial ones, with hosts who are former journalists and take journalism ethics seriously and others who are entertainers rather than journalists. At some programs, the callers who get through are heavily screened by producers and, sometimes, there is a con-trived selection towards those who agree with the host (Adams and Burton 1997). However, the call-in process has also been heavily manipulated by the political parties.

The parties engage staffers and volunteers to call in pretending they are 'ordinary listeners' – especially during elections. These callers tend to use formal, polite, even sycophantic tones and make partisan comments, sometimes filled with statistics and figures, that sound as if they are reading from a script. The examples in Box 12.1 come from 2001 and all suggest a plant by the Liberal Party, but Labor used the technique as well. The stacking became so obvious that, by 2007, caller questions to politicians were used much less frequently. Talkback tended to have more standard interviews between the host and politicians, lessening its claim to be a uniquely democratic medium.

Box 12.1

Stacking talkback calls, 2001

Caller: 'Yes, good morning Prime Minister. Prime Minister, one of the things that concerns me is that health and education are primarily administrative financial responsibilities of the States and I note your GST funding will in fact give them discretionary expenditure. What I find difficult to understand is why Labor is putting so much stress on health and education without establishing standards of any sort whatsoever and in fact knowing very well that those decisions are going to be made at the State level. It almost seems to me as though they are trying to buy the votes of their trade unionists that are so dominant in those sectors.'

Howard: Well Bill, you have got a very good point...' (6 November 2001, interview on Radio 4QR Brisbane).

Caller (Doris): 'Good morning Prime Minister. I'd like to say a very special thank you for the $25 000 that was awarded to the wives of the prisoners of war who passed away; it's allowed me to do desperate repairs to my home, thank you. I thank you also for my pension and I thank you for services that we get with a discount; it really makes a lot of difference. I congratulate you on your firm stand with our illegal immigrants and I would also like to say that I'm very proud of your leadership and you get my 100 per cent support' (25 October 2001, interview with Ben Knight, ABC regional radio, Victoria).

Caller (Natasha): 'Oh good morning Paul, good morning Prime Minister. Look, I've just got a bit of a comment actually and it's a thank you really because I got a letter from Bank West on Friday and our interest rate payments have come down about $36 a month in the last fortnight and with the new family and a new baby that really, really helps so just a thanks very much' (23 October 2001, Radio 6PR, interview with Paul Murray).

Opinion polls were not only about the horse-race or score checks but were also another way that news organisations tried to present their coverage as reflecting citizens' interests and their input. However, ever since opinion polls have been used, there have been concerns that they are less about reflecting public opinion than about manipulating it – through the questions asked and creative interpretations of the results. Aside from the focus on polls conducted by polling firms, in the 2000s there was also a trend towards self-selecting polls of audience members. Newspapers, radio and television broadcasters advertised telephone and online polls where audience members could call, SMS or click to vote 'yes' or 'no' to some proposition ('Have the

Garrett remarks harmed Labor's election campaign?' was one from Sky News in 2007.) Because these polls used a self-selecting sample, they were worthless as a measure of general public opinion and were generally treated as such, barely remarked upon by even the outlets who conducted them. In 2010, the *Age* even added a disclaimer to its online polls that 'These polls are not scientific and reflect the opinion only of visitors who have chosen to participate.'

One of the most famous 'voice of the people' devices in Australian election reporting is the 'worm' used for *Great Debates* by Channel Nine (Box 12.2). The 'worm' represents not only high-minded democratic ideals about 'the

Box 12.2

The 'worm'

Members of Channel Nine's studio audience for the *Great Debate* twist a dial or punch in numbers to indicate their support for what the leaders are saying and this is collated and broadcast as a line on the screen. First used in 1993, in 2001 and 2004 Nine only showed the worm after the debates – once the leaders had finished speaking. This was part of an agreement with the parties, who have sometimes argued that the worm distracts viewers from what the leaders are saying.

In 2007, Sky News hosted the debate and Channel Nine and the ABC broadcast it live as well. When Nine used the worm – in defiance of conditions that been set reportedly at the urging of the Coalition – its direct feed of the *Debate* was cut 25 minutes into the broadcast. It switched to a back-up feed from the ABC and continued with the worm. Ten minutes later that back-up was pulled. Nine then switched to the Sky feed and kept the worm going.

This prompted a mini-debate about freedom of the press, with Nine claiming it had never agreed to the conditions and that it was disappointed the ABC and the National Press Club had conspired with the Liberals to repress journalistic freedom. Nine has also been on the receiving end of criticisms with concerns about Nine's methodology and claims its studio audience for the worm is unrepresentative and probably not as 'undecided' as the network promotes. The worm appeared to be especially critical of Howard and awarded the debate to his opponent for all three debates in the 2000s.

will of the people' but also about entertainment. In 2004, after the leaders had spent over an hour debating their policies and credentials in the actual *Debate*, the Channel Nine host introduced the 'worm' in classic horse-race fashion by saying: 'Now for the fun. Who won and who lost.' But is this type of simplification outweighed by the fact that such events can attract people who might not otherwise tune in to politics? (see Chapter 2).

In the US, Holbrook found that the gap in political knowledge between the least and most educated American voters shrinks immediately after televised presidential candidate debates. This sounds promising although we should note that, in the US, debates operate very differently. Unlike in Australia, the format and rules for American presidential debates are worked out by a non-profit, non-partisan committee (although it has links to the two major parties). The debates are 'covered uninterrupted by all major networks' at primetime (Holbrook 2002:449). There are more debates (three in 2008, for example) and more open formats. Some of the debates have predetermined themes and, in the days beforehand, news outlets run pre-debate stories outlining the differences between the candidates on those issues. This reminds us that context affects how political news is produced and the extent to which it might encourage political interest or further political knowledge.

Hard and soft interviews

Interviews with politicians are a key part of political reporting and one that also underwent significant change in the 2000s. There continued to be 'hard' interviews in the manner of authoritative journalists interrogating politicians, as epitomised by those on ABC radio and television (including Kerry O'Brien and Tony Jones) and Laurie Oakes on Channel Nine. But there were also growing instances of politicians conducting interviews with non-journalists such as talkback hosts or comedians and FM radio hosts. This again raises tensions between traditional journalistic values of informed questioning about public policy issues versus the entertainment values and merging of popular culture with formal politics.

While some argued that 'soft' interviews were an inadequate means of political scrutiny, others claimed that they were actually more challenging for politicians because the questions were, unlike 'hard news' journalism, sometimes unconventional. The adversarial style of traditional interviews was also, some said, too 'aggressive' and turned some people off whereas soft news interviews took politics to a broader audience. Yet others observed that, no matter who the interviewer was, or how sharp their questions, it was hard for any to get a response that wasn't scripted in an era of politicians staying on message, meaning there was sometimes little to differentiate responses to 'hard' and 'soft' questions (Boxes 12.3 and 12.4; Young 2008).

Box 12.3

Howard answering questions on plans to sell Telstra, 2001

Journalist: 'Mr Howard... do you stand for the full privatisation of Telstra?'

Howard: 'I stand for fixing things in the bush before there is any further movement on that front. That's what I stand for' (31 October, doorstop, Brisbane).

Journalist: 'You seem to retreating from your long-held commitment to the full privatisation of Telstra.'

Howard: 'I am repeating the policy, Michelle.'

Journalist: 'Which is for full privatisation.'

Howard: 'I am repeating, the policy is that we don't sell another share till we've fixed things in the bush.'

Journalist: 'And then you sell.'

Howard: 'Michelle, you can say anything you like, I've answered your question, I'm not adding anything to it' (31 October, doorstop, Brisbane).

Mitchell: 'With respect I think it is a simple and direct question. Is it your intention to sell Telstra?'

Howard: 'It is our intention to fix things in the bush and we will sell no more shares in Telstra until that occurs and it is my intention not to speculate beyond that' (1 November, interview with Neil Mitchell, 3AW).

Clarke: 'Mr Howard... are you going to sell Telstra? Yes or no?'

Howard: 'We're not going to sell any more shares in Telstra unless and until things in the bush are up to scratch.'

Clarke: 'So once they've improved yes?'

Howard: 'Well the time to, you asked me that question, for you to ask me that question is when I'm satisfied, I'm not now so it's an academic question.'

Clarke: 'When might you be satisfied?'

Howard: 'I can't say.' (31 October, interview with Phillip Clarke, 2GB).

Liebmann: 'Telstra, are you or are you not going to sell off what's left of Telstra?'

Howard: 'We are not going to sell any more of Telstra until we are completely satisfied, completely satisfied that services in the bush are adequate' (29 October, interview with Steve Liebmann, *Today*, Channel Nine).

Box 12.4

Rudd answering allegations that he had too many ex-union officials on his team, 15 October 2007

On *Sunrise* (Seven), Rudd: '...my front bench, I've got people there who are barristers, solicitors, school teachers, economists, people who have worked

in small business, former local mayors, I have a rock star, Peter Garrett, and myself, an unemployed diplomat, there you go...'
On *Today* (Nine), Rudd: 'On my front bench now I have barristers, solicitors, school teachers, I have people who are economists, university lecturers, I have a former rock star, Peter Garrett, and of course, I'm an unemployed diplomat who speaks Chinese. There you go.'
On *The 7:30 Report* (ABC), Rudd: '...we have people in Labor's front bench who have worked as barristers, solicitors, teachers, economists, mayors of municipalities, we have former rock stars, underemployed diplomats who speak Chinese...'

Opinion and partiality

If there was growing discontent with politicians who were repetitive and 'boring', there was also concern that the 'impartial' presentation of news was having a similar effect because it requires such a formulaic presentation. Print journalism tries to balance viewpoints within specific stories by including quotes from both major parties, while television uses a 'follow the leader' presentation of daily events that ensures both major parties are covered. This is what leads to the high degree of similarity in news reports. In the 2000s, news outlets kept to these formats but were also increasingly willing to give up the ideal of objectivity in other forms because there was a market for partiality. As Glover pointed out, there are media sites where 'bias isn't just tolerated but is the whole point' (Glover 2005:192) including talkback radio and newspaper columns.

In newspapers, some of the most prominent columnists in the 2000s were conservatives such as Andrew Bolt (*Herald Sun*), Piers Akerman (*Daily Telegraph*), Miranda Devine (*SMH*), Gerard Henderson (*SMH*), Janet Albrechtsen, Christopher Pearson and Greg Sheridan (all from the *Australian*). On the other side of the ideological divide were columnists such as Phillip Adams (the *Australian*), David Marr (*SMH*), Robert Manne (various), Adele Horin (*SMH*) and, online, Guy Rundle (*Crikey*).

Even 20 years before, there were no columnists like these in newspapers but some came to exercise significant interpretative power in the 2000s. For example, Andrew Bolt not only had a large column in the top-selling newspaper in the country but also ran what he called 'the most-read political blog in Australia', was 'a regular commentator on Channel 9's *Today* show and ABC TV's *Insiders*' as well as, from 2010, a host on the breakfast show of a new Melbourne radio station (Bolt 2010). Speaking across newspapers, television, radio and online made Bolt's claim that conservative voices like his were marginalised in a liberal media establishment increasingly difficult to accept.

Opinion was a way to appeal to audiences who had more choice of media for entertainment and leisure activities if they weren't satisfied with the formulaic presentation of traditional objective journalism. Opinion allowed newspapers to morph into a form that looked more like a magazine as a response to television, with a greater emphasis on personalities, colour and movement. It also offered the chance for new voices to be heard – including non-journalists and others independent of the media and politics even if, in practice, it sometimes seemed to lead to a new 'interpretative elite' (McNair 2000:82).

When breaking news was everywhere, outlets also had to have something distinctive to offer that was original and worth paying for. Columns had a commercial value because they tended to be read quite well and could build up a following. They also had other advantages because a newspaper could still claim to be impartial by including columnists from different sides of the debate but, at the same time, reserve their 'property right' to 'take sides' by promoting certain topics, views or columnists above others, by giving them more space or by having more – or more powerful – representatives from one side of the debate than the other. When talking about the value of op-eds in newspapers, Chris Mitchell, the editor-in-chief of the *Australian*, said in 2003 that 'Devoted readers like to have their prejudices reinforced by both the editorials and the op-eds' (Jackson and Doman 2003).

In the 2000s, the power of columnists and talkback hosts stemmed from the way they could sit between the ideals of objectivity and the use of polemic as a form of entertainment. They styled themselves differently from the traditional style of 'objective' journalism, using emotive, attention-grabbing, provocative language designed to grab readers' attention and provoke feelings and responses. But they also drew upon (and benefited from) the accoutrements of the news media with its 'fourth estate' role. Those generated some expectation of fairness. Yet the talkback hosts and columnists made no claim to being dispassionate and were sometimes patently unfair by the standards of impartial journalism.

One of the more controversial hosts, Alan Jones, was a former Liberal staffer and unsuccessful Liberal candidate (Masters 2006). He never bothered to hide his partiality or follow the usual method of journalistic enquiry in questioning politicians, as Jones' first interview with Howard after he won office in 1996 illustrates (Box 12.5). According to a Rehame study of the 1998 election, between 31 August-30 September, Jones 'did not say one positive thing about the ALP, its policies, or leadership' (McCabe and Farr 2001).

Box 12.5

Alan Jones interview with Howard after he won the 1996 election

Jones: 'Prime Minister, good morning.'
Howard: 'Good morning, Alan.'
Jones: 'Thank God for you, thank God for you, well done.'
Howard: 'Thank you.'
Jones: 'Well done' (quoted in Coorey 2001).

At the same time as there was a growth in partiality and opinion in news, some outlets were also trying to reassert their independence and shifting the way they addressed audiences. For example, in 2004, the *SMH* refused to give an election endorsement, saying: 'expressing a preference for one party in an election will taint us in the eyes of some readers... they will think that if we are partisan at election time, then we will be partisan at other times.' In 2007, on the front page of the *Daily Telegraph* the day after Howard announced the election, it repudiated the election editorial in even stronger terms, saying it 'has long been one of the least democratic features of our democracy. It's not a transparent decision-making process – if anything it's remote and elitist.' The *Daily Telegraph* said, 'We want to hear from you first, with an Editor's blog seeking reader views.'

These were interesting acknowledgements of the disconnection between partisan endorsements and claims to journalistic impartiality. We shouldn't read too much into them – after all, the *SMH* went back to endorsing a party in 2007 and the *Daily Telegraph*'s desire for more 'transparent decision-making' only went so far. But they did seem to be symbolic of a growing recognition that the outlets were addressing better-educated audiences and needed to build different relationships with them. The *Daily Telegraph*, for example, saw its university-educated readership double between 1997 and 2007 (Scalmer and Goot 2004:143; Table 3.1; Table 4.1).[2] More educated audiences are more resistant to claims that don't stand up to their level of scrutiny and more likely to expect a different relationship than occurred in the top-down media paternalism of the past.

News, media use and the future

At the end of the 2000s it was increasingly difficult to characterise media, let alone predict their future. Even the very notion of separate media was declining as people were watching television on computers, listening to radio through pay TV and reading newspapers on mobile devices. In terms of news media and politics and elections, some commentators characterised the changes as largely positive with a more chaotic, less predictable and less controlled (by media moguls and political elites) media that was more diverse, more interactive and responsive than in the past. An optimistic view was especially evident among those who believe the internet had transferred power to 'the people' and who foresaw a world of networked citizen journalism and a new era of communication. By contrast, others argued that the internet was generating fairly conventional rather than innovative news, and that the optimists were overstating the pace of change and romanticising the contributions of gifted amateurs – many of whom came from privileged backgrounds themselves.

Some argued that we were witnessing not a 'brave new world' of journalism but a journalism crisis – especially in newspapers. They pointed to news organisations with less money, reduced quality and fewer audience members. However, it might be a step too far to equate a crisis in journalism to a crisis of democracy, given that journalism doesn't always equate with the public interest. There were still many examples of media self-interest and attempts to manipulate public opinion in the 2000s.

For some critics, this is why a radical shake-up in media was precisely what was needed, rather than lamenting the decline of something that either never existed or was already dead. Alan Kohler (2009) expressed a variant of this argument when he said that:

Most of what is called quality journalism [in Australia] is not quality at all – it is leaks planted by vested interest, to journalists who need to stay onside with those interests (politicians . . . etc), or it is plain bias – either from the journalists or the proprietors.

The fundamental problem, in democratic terms, with 'quality journalism' – no matter which media form distributes it – has always been that it was taken up only by a small proportion of people. In the past, there were suggestions that a more educated society would see more people consuming 'serious' news. The educated population grew from 3 per cent of Australians with a university degree in 1962 to 21 per cent with a bachelor degree or higher in 2007 (ABS 2007a; Mayer 1964:268). However, as we saw in Part I, the proportion of those who are highly interested in politics and access 'quality' media remains small and does not seem to have grown much over time (see Sparks 2000:33).

Media outlets that *do* seek to broaden their appeal to other groups change their content to do so and then become more apolitical in the process. For example, the *Age* achieved a comparatively high proportion of female readers and white-collar workers for a broadsheet. It had introduced more supplements on fashion, food and travel as well as a 'lifestyle' magazine with columns on beauty, homes, travel and entertainment. Fairfax's online newspaper sites attracted a younger audience than their printed copies (Table 3.1) but their content was 'much more celebrity and entertainment focused' (Gawenda 2008).

The ABC is a particularly interesting case study. In a multichannel environment, as audiences fragment, spending on production becomes more constrained. But, as with the BBC in the UK, the ABC has been somewhat shielded from this and both public broadcasters have been playing a more central role in recent years. Traditionally, one of the great strengths of the public broadcasters is their ability to raise issues that are socially important but not commercially profitable. For Australian journalists, the ABC still plays an important role as an example of 'best practice' in journalism. Despite all the allegations of bias in the 2000s, it retained a high degree of public confidence as well (ABC 2002; 2007a:35).

However, the ABC has not been unaffected by the trends in news forms. It has reduced election news in TV bulletins and has its own opinion elements (e.g. *Q&A*, *Unleashed*) and formats that blur politics and entertainment

(*The Chaser*). Also, as its audience broadened in the 2000s, an increasing number of its viewers complained that the broadcaster provided *too much* coverage of federal politics – up from 27 per cent the previous year to 35 per cent in 2007 – suggesting even greater pressure to lessen traditional politics coverage (ABC 2007a:39).

Conclusion

Most of the significant trends in election reporting of the 2000s are not substantially in dispute and have been broadly observed in political reporting in other mature, liberal democracies as well. What is heavily contested is the meaning of these changes because different models of citizenship, news and democracy are being employed to judge them. Did the changes reflect what the public wanted (and needed) or what media organisations wanted? Who benefited from the changes and did they enhance the prospects for a well-functioning democracy or diminish them? These questions *are* in substantial dispute.

There is no doubt that there were many positive developments in the 2000s for media audiences, including a greater degree of choice and control in media content. At the beginning of the decade, many Australians could not access the internet either at home or at work. By 2010, the media world had changed profoundly. As Mark Scott (2009b) has noted:

> In years to come, young people will be amazed when you tell them that it was virtually impossible to read a copy of *The New York Times* in Melbourne, or, that if you got home at ten past seven you had no hope of watching the news that night; that you couldn't view catch-up TV from your phone on a bus; that you would have to wait days to see footage of a major world event . . .

Media audiences gained a great deal in the 2000s but 'publics' may have been less well served. There were more monitorial citizens and fewer conforming to the Habermasian ideal of active well-informed citizenship. When it came to getting political news, there were two different public spheres in operation. There were also large inequalities in news access and political participation, a gap between 'informed elites' and 'entertained majorities' (Dahlgren (2009:44) or between 'those who know' and 'those who accept'

(Keane 1999). 'Hard news' use was still linked with political interest, political knowledge and participation, and with education, wealth and social position. Conversely, those who relied upon popular or soft news were still disproportionately poorer, less educated and politically alienated.

This seemed to indicate that news formats might not only be matters of 'taste' but also that there might also be a level of *benefit* in accessing the more detailed and informative sources. This still needs enquiry. We cannot presume that soft news or news showing ordinary people (or any other type of political news) is necessarily empowering; we have to look at the *outcomes* associated with its use. Similarly, as more political information is made available to citizens, we still need to find out what people actually do with that information and whether it benefits them or society more broadly.

This brings us closer to the essence of the debate about news journalism, for it is a verdict on the state of democracy itself. Those who dispute that the news media need to provide serious, detailed, public affairs/politics-focused information in order for democracy *to function well*, advocate a division of intellectual labour that already exists. So if you believe that democracy is functioning well despite those divisions, this is an entirely reasonable view. For others, the inequalities behind those divisions – because they align with broader political, social and economic inequalities – mean that democracy still has a long way to go, and so does news journalism.

Ultimately, making assessments about media performance – in this case about election reporting – requires drawing on some normative standard of citizenship and democracy. If we judge the Australian media by the highest standards of the public sphere, they fell far short in the 2000s. If we judge outlets by their own promises this is also the case, because those promises were based upon the same public sphere ideals. However, if we judge them based on the actual past, on the election reporting of say the 1950s or 1960s, what was available in the 2000s was far less controlled, less deferential, more diverse, insightful and inclusive.

It is therefore possible to accept that changes in news values in the 2000s were not necessarily bad at the same time as questioning whether the commercial pressures that fostered them did not also lead to some negative outcomes such as decreases in journalism resources, investigative journalism and political reporting aimed at general audiences. In comparison with journalism in more recent eras – say the 1970s to 1990s – there did seem to be some losses in these areas. So even if we are willing to accept a less active standard of citizenship than the Habermasian ideal requires, we still need to be confident that the media retain their ability to sound alarms. And while political participation will always be less than the full involvement of all citizens, we can still aim for a better, and more inclusive, democracy than we have now. Indeed, this has always been the driving force behind the struggle for democracy.

Appendix

RESEARCH METHOD

For this study, over 10 000 media texts on the 2001, 2004 and 2007 elections were collected from television, newspapers, radio and the internet. I used a combination of methods to analyse segments of this material. Quantitative *content analysis* is one of the few ways of systematically classifying and describing media content and I used this method on a sample of 965 election reports (Tables i and ii). I also used *qualitative analysis* for specific samples, paying particular attention to discourse – words, text and talk – as well as to the visual dimension of television clips, newspaper, magazine and website photographs and graphics. The other main method was a process I called '*media mapping*' to trace the subject and sources of media reports across each day of the 2007 election campaign. This allowed me to analyse processes of agenda-setting, news cycles and news flows (mostly outlined in Chapter 8).

Space limits prevent me from describing the methodology in its entirety but, given the quantitative basis for some of the claims I make, it is important that I outline the sample used for the content analysis. To narrow down the sample to a reasonable size appropriate for content analysis, I used a systematic sampling method often known as the 'nth' method or 'constructed week'. This approach involves selecting every nth unit from the total population available. In their study of models for sampling news content, Riffe et al (1993) found this method of sampling to be more reliable than random or consecutive day sampling and found that one constructed week was a very suitable measure of a whole year's media content (let alone a six-week election campaign); precision increased only slightly by using two or three constructed weeks.

In this case, every sixth day of the election campaign was chosen. This meant that six days were included for each election including every day of the week except Saturday (because the three elections were six-week

Table i Summary of the content analysis sample by medium and year

	Television	Radio	Newspapers	Total
2007	399	30	77	**506**
2004	117	37	79	**233**
2001	89	33	67	**189**
Pre-2001*	37	0	0	**37**
Total	*642*	*100*	*223*	**965**

Note: TV includes 7 cinema clips from 1929–54.
* Pre-2001 = seven from 1998, ten from 1993, two from 1984, six from 1983, four from 1980, one from 1966, two from 1963 and one each from 1961, 1954, 1951, 1937 and 1929.

Table ii Summary of the content analysis sample by program type/genre

Television		Radio		Newspapers (front page)	
News	366	News	30	News story	221
Current affairs	135	Talkback	42	Feature article	1
Breakfast	104	Current Affairs	21	Opinion	1
Comedy	17	Comedy	4		
Other	20	Other	3		
Total	*642*	*Total*	*100*	*Total*	*223*

campaigns). In the case of the 2004 and 2007 elections, the sixth-day method meant that the last date was polling day, but the content was judged to be too unrepresentative on that day to be included in a sample seeking an overview of reporting of the whole campaign. The sample included a mix of routine campaigning days plus policy announcements and party campaign launches. The vast majority of the television sample was recorded in Melbourne; however, there were also 100 clips from Brisbane, Perth and Sydney. Contrasting these clips with the Melbourne ones confirmed that affiliated channels in different states frequently used precisely the same reports, just with a different host introducing them. For newspapers, the constructed week method was also used, but only front-page stories from the 12 metropolitan newspapers were analysed. If more than one election story appeared on the front page, only the most prominent (highest-placed and largest story) was included in the sample.

A coding sheet with 126 questions about each media text was developed using some categories or questions adapted from previous studies and some new questions (for example, when analysing which issues were discussed in reports, the lists of issues came from the relevant AES; the categories used for the variable 'type of story' mirrored those used in another study (Semetko et al 1991: 27; see also e.g. Denemark et al 2007; Esser and D'Angelo 2003, 2006; Hallin 1992; Lichter 2001; Semetko 1996). The sheet was pilot-tested and adapted twice before the final version. (A copy of the coding sheet is available on request from the author.)

The coding sheet was then used by a team of six trained postgraduate researchers under my supervision to systematically code 965 media reports (Tables i and ii). This included using a stopwatch to time the length of every sound bite in television and radio clips, as well as counting words and quotes in newspaper articles. The analysis took the coding team over eight months and, in all, they coded over 120 000 individual variables. The data was entered into SPSS 16.0 for analysis.

The content analysis sample was unusually large and diverse, as it focused on newspapers, radio and television and used over 100 variables for each media text. Most content analyses of election reports have focused on only one medium and used smaller samples or fewer variables. For example, some of the better-known studies used fewer than 200 television clips (e.g. Coleman and Banning 2006 and Grabe and Bucy 2009), while one of the largest single-medium studies, by Lichter (2001), analysed over 2000 television news clips but using only four main variables.

NOTES

Chapter 2

1   All figures are rounded. In order to ascertain the adult population, the 15–65 plus age groups were used from the population of Australia in 2007. This equalled 14.2 million of working age plus 2.8 million over 65 (17 million in total) (ABS 2008a).

2   Or broadsheet-style paper in the case of the *Australian Financial Review* (*AFR*).

3   In this map, I have not added up all of the broadsheets separately because it is likely that the audiences cross over as research shows that many news junkie broadsheet readers in Australia buy both a national and a state version – e.g. the *Australian* and the *SMH* or the *AFR* and the *Age*. For radio, the total radio listening population of the five capital cities in 2007 was 11 338 000. The figure for ABC local radio is then an average of the five major cities' ratings in period 1, 2008. TV ratings are five city aggregates of the five most populous cities in Australia. Sources: APC 2008b: 12–15; ASTRA (2008); *Crikey* 2008; CRA 2007, 2008, 2009; MPA (2008); NMRA (2007a, b, 2008); OzTAM statistics provided to the author; OzTAM (2008a, b).

Chapter 3

1   The *Canberra Times* was owned by Fairfax only after May 2007 following a merger between Fairfax and Rural Press Ltd.

2   The Roy Morgan data are for Australians over 14 years, so percentages relate to Australians 14 years and over.

3   This may seem confusing given that Table 3.1 and 3.2 show that Australians over 50 years make up 38% of the population, but this is because the Roy Morgan percentages are based on Australians over 14 years whereas the OzTAM data include those under 14.

4   Others were time-shifting their viewing and changes to ratings measurements from 2010 mean this can now be taken into account.

5   It is both an emailed newsletter to subscribers and a website. While Chapter 2 focused on *Crikey* subscriber numbers, the data in Table 3.1 relate to visitors to the website.

Chapter 4

1   There is a politically interested working-class audience that uses non-elite media to follow political news. It is harder to identify as such today, but historically was especially apparent when there were union news publications and radio stations

operated by trades and labour councils (such as 2KY radio station, originally owned by the Labour Council of New South Wales) (Goot 1977).

2   Due to the data available, it again focuses on metropolitan areas. It doesn't include, for example, regional newspapers or television. Due to space limitations, it also doesn't show local newspapers, free commuter newspapers (*mX*) or magazines.

3   Which it had acquired in 2007.

4   Table 4.1 shows the audiences for the three major talkback radio stations – this shows all of the program audiences for these stations averaged.

5   The blue-collar group is taken here to be the OzTAM groups for labourers, farm hands, factory hands, tradespeople, drivers and police, as this is how the occupations are grouped in OzTAM data.

6   This excluded specials, such as those on 9/11 and the elections in 2001 and 2007. In most cases, the top 10 programs remained consistent between 2001 and 2007.

Chapter 5

1   Thanks to Rodney Tiffen for pointing this out to me.

2   We need to note about this evidence that, if the survey sample is compared to the first preference votes that were actually cast for the House of Representatives nationally in 2007, Labor voter numbers in the sample were 4.4 per cent higher than actually voted for Labor, whereas Coalition voter numbers in the survey were 8.2 per cent lower. This could represent sampling biases or that some respondents shifted their vote between the survey and polling day, but it's also noteworthy that, in the surveys, 8.0 per cent of respondents did not give a response and these might have been intending, or later became, Coalition voters.

3   Whereas for news junkies wanting a 24-hour news radio station, the only option is News Radio, which helps explain the similar results in the Sydney and Melbourne markets.

Chapter 6

1   I could find no formal documents on this. I contacted MEAA in December 2009 to ask how many times members had been sanctioned for breaking the code of ethics over the past 10 years and whether this information was publicly available. I did not receive a response.

2   Removal came via the *Broadcasting and Television Amendment (Election Blackout) Act 1983* but a blackout on paid political advertising in electronic media remained (not in newspapers or the internet; only applying to those who hold broadcasting licences – that is, television and radio licence holders) from midnight on the Wednesday before polling day.

Chapter 7

1   Although radio tended to be different.

Chapter 8

1   I obtained these results by comparing the newspaper coverage of these events with all the material the parties put out to promote that event – including press releases, speeches, announcements, their statements in press conferences, doorstop interviews and media interviews. I then added up how many sentences in those

newspaper articles came from direct quotes (whether attributed or not) from the parties' PR material.

Chapter 9

1 In the US, the average length of a primetime television news story on the 2004 presidential election was 2 minutes. In Australia, for the federal election held in the same year, the average for the three commercial free-to-air television news programs was only 1 minute 37 seconds.
2 Based on analysis of front-page election stories between 5 April 2005 and 5 May 2005.
3 Which deviated widely from the rest and was, later, roundly criticised for its inaccuracy.
4 There were exceptions including books and articles by Margo Kingston, Margaret Simons and Niki Savva. It's interesting that these main contributions were from women and journalists who went on to work outside mainstream journalism.

Chapter 10

1 Interestingly, when I checked this article again in 2010, all of the comments below had disappeared.

Chapter 11

1 Rudd was the godfather of editor-in-chief Chris Mitchell's son (Murray 2007; see also *Australian Conservative* 2008)
2 To really test this, though, we would need to consider a sample when the ALP is in government. If the Coalition still routinely receives greater opportunity to speak, this would suggest other factors are in play.

Chapter 12

1 See Griffen-Foley 2004 for historical antecedents.
2 This includes those 'now' at university and those who 'have diploma or degree'.

REFERENCES

AAP [Australian Associated Press] (2005) 'Fed: I know how Brogden feels, says Kernot', 11 September.

ABA [Australian Broadcasting Authority] (2000) *Commercial Radio Inquiry: Final Report*, http://www.acma.gov.au/webwr/_assets/main/lib100654/commradinq_fin.pdf.

—— (2001a) *How News is Made in Australia*, Sydney, ABA.

—— (2001b) *Sources of News and Current Affairs*, Sydney, ABA.

—— (2005) *Investigation Report 19362*, http://www.acma.gov.au/webwr/aba/newspubs/radio_tv/investigations/broadcast_operations/documents/radio/2005/1362.pdf.

ABC [Australian Broadcasting Corporation] (1998) *Four Corners* episode 'The uncertain eye', 2 February.

—— (2002) 'ABC valued by 91% of Australians – Newspoll', Ultimo, NSW: ABC.

—— (2003) 'Report of the independent complaints review panel', Ultimo, NSW: ABC.

—— (2005) 'ABC news and current affairs – accuracy and impartiality', *ABC Fact Sheet*, Ultimo, NSW: ABC.

—— (2006) *The Media Report*, 9 March, http://www.abc.net.au/rn/mediareport/stories/2006/1586075.htm.

—— (2007a) *Annual Report 2006–07*, Ultimo, NSW: ABC.

—— (2007b) *Editorial Policies: March 2007*, Ultimo, NSW: ABC.

—— (2008) 'What is ABC News Radio?', *ABC*, http://www.abc.net.au/newsradio/about/history.htm.

—— (2009) *ABC Charter 1983*, http://www.abc.net.au/corp/pubs/ABCcharter.htm.

ABS [Australian Bureau of Statistics] (1997) '4172.0 - Cultural trends: a statistical overview', Canberra, ABS.

—— (1999) 'Strong growth in home use of information technology: media release 63/99', Canberra, ABS.

—— (2003) '4102.0 - Australian social trends, 2003–Paid work: longer working hours', Canberra, ABS.

—— (2004) 'Employee earnings and hours, May 2004', Canberra, ABS.

—— (2006) '8146.0.55.001 - Patterns of internet access in Australia, 2006', Canberra, ABS.

—— (2007a) '6227.0 - Education and work, Australia, May 2007', Canberra, ABS.

—— (2007b) '8146.0.55.001 - Patterns of internet access in Australia, 2006', Canberra, ABS.

—— (2008a) '3235.0 - Population by age and sex, regions of Australia, 2007', Canberra, ABS.

—— (2008b) '4102.0 - Australian social trends, 2008', Canberra, ABS.

ACE [Administration and Costs of Elections Project] (2009) 'Overview of media and elections', http://aceproject.org/ace-en/topics/me/me10.

ACMA [Australian Communication and Media Authority] (2007) *Digital Television in Australian Homes, 2007*, report prepared by Eureka Strategic Research, Sydney, ACMA.

Adams, Phillip and Burton, Lee (1997) *Talkback*, Sydney, Allen & Unwin.

Administration and Costs of Elections Project *see* ACE.

AEC [Australian Electoral Commission] (2007a) 'House of Representatives – two party preferred results 1949–present', http://www.aec.gov.au/Elections/Australian_Electoral_History/House_of_Representative_1949_Present.htm.

—— (2007b) 'House of Representatives – first preferences by party', http://results.aec.gov.au/13745/Website/HouseResultsMenu-13745.htm.

—— (2009) 'Voter turnout 1901 – present (national summary)', http://www.aec.gov.au/Elections/Australian_Electoral_History/Voter_Turnout.htm.

AFC [Australian Film Commission] (2005) *Pay TV*, Canberra, AFC.

—— (2009) 'Trends in audience share', *Get the Picture*, http://www.afc.gov.au/gtp/wftv-ratingstrends.html.

AFR [*Australian Financial Review*] (2009) *Media Kit*, Fairfax Media AdCentre, http://www.adcentre.com.au/the-australian-financial-review.aspx.

Akerman, Piers (2006) 'Battling ABC bias', *Daily Telegraph*, 16 October.

Albright, Jeremy J. (2009) 'Does political knowledge erode party attachments? a review of the cognitive mobilization thesis', *Electoral Studies* 28(2): 248–60.

Alliance Online (2009) 'Code of ethics' *MEAA*, http://www.alliance.org.au/code-of-ethics.html.

ALP [Australian Labor Party] (1987) *Campaign Manual*, Canberra, National Library of Australia, (Manuscripts, MS4985, Box 468, folder 84/5/20).

Alston, Richard (2003) 'Contradiction and exaggeration: Our ABC's spin on war in Iraq', *Age*, 29 May: 17.

Ang, Ien (1995) 'The nature of the audience' in John Downing, Ali Mohammadi and Annabelle Sreberny-Mohammadi (eds), *Questioning the Media* (2nd edn), London, Sage, pp. 207–20.

APC [Australian Press Council] (1977) 'Reporting guidelines: accusations of bias', http://www.presscouncil.org.au/pcsite/activities/guides/gpr15.html.

—— (1999) 'Reporting national politics', *Press Council News*, 11(1), http://www.presscouncil.org.au/pcsite/apcnews/feb99/canberra.html.

—— (2001) 'Reporting guidelines: general press release no.246 (iv): opinion polls', http://www.presscouncil.org.au/pcsite/activities/guides/gpr246_4.html.

—— (2005) 'Adjudication No. 1270', http://www.presscouncil.org.au/pcsite/adj/1270.html.

—— (2006), *State of the News Print Media in Australia 2006*, Sydney, APC.

—— (2008), *State of the News Print Media in Australia 2007*, Sydney, APC.

—— (2009a) 'Reporting elections', http://www.presscouncil.org.au/pcsite/activities/guides/elections.html.

—— (2009b) 'Complaints Statistics 2008–2009', http://www.presscouncil.org.au/pcsite/complaints/statistics/stats09.html.

ARTKC [Australia's Right to Know Coalition] (2007) 'Background: the state of free speech in Australia', 10 May 2007.

ASPG [Australasian Study of Parliament Group] (2003) 'On being a political reporter', transcript of meeting 17 March, Parliament House, Brisbane http://www.parliament.qld.gov.au/aspg/papers/030317.pdf.

ASTRA [Australian Subscription Television and Radio Association] (2008) 'Subscription TV', http://www.astra.org.au/article.asp?section=2&option=1&content=1.

Australasian Study of Parliament Group *see* ASPG.

Australian Associated Press *see* AAP.

Australian Broadcasting Authority *see* ABA.

Australian Broadcasting Commission *see* ABC.

Australian Bureau of Statistics *see* ABS.

Australian Communication and Media Authority *see* ACMA.

Australian Conservative (2008) 'Tide of opinion turning at the *Australian*', http://australianconservative.com/2008/06/tide-of-opinion-turning-at-the-australian-2/

Australian Electoral Commission *see* AEC.

Australian Film Commission *see* AFC.

Australian Financial Review *see* AFR.

Australian Press Council *see* APC.

Australian Subscription Television and Radio Association *see* ASTRA.

Australia's Right to Know Coalition *see* ARTKC.

Bahnisch, Mark (2007) 'The state of political blogging', *Larvatus Prodeo*, 30 September http://larvatusprodeo.net/2007/09/30/the-state-of-political-blogging/

Baird, Julia (2004) *Media Tarts*, North Carlton, Scribe Publications.

Banducci, Susan A. and Karp, Jeffrey A. (2003) 'How elections change the way citizens view the political system', *British Journal of Political Science*, 33: 443–67.

BARB [Broadcasters' Audience Research Board [UK]] (2009) 'Weekly top 30 programs, week ending 12 April 2009', http://www.barb.co.uk/report/weeklyTopProgrammes Overview/?report=weeklyterrestrial&requesttimeout=500&flag=viewing summary.

Barnes, Allan (1972) '"Image" that's the thing now', *Age*, 10 November: 9.

Barnhurst, Kevin (1998) 'Politics in the fine mesh', *Media, Culture & Society*, 20(2): 201–18.

Barry, Paul (2007) *The Rise and Rise of Kerry Packer Uncut*, Sydney, Bantam.

Bartle, John (2005) 'The press, television and the internet', *Parliamentary Affairs*, 58(1): 43–55.

Baum, Matthew A. (2003) 'Soft news and political knowledge: evidence of absence or absence of evidence?' *Political Communication*, 20: 173–90.

BCS [British Crime Survey] (2003) Home Office, UK.

Bean, Clive (2005) 'How the political audiences of Australian public and commercial television channels differ', *Australian Journal of Communication*, 32(2): 41–55.

—— Gow, David and McAllister, Ian (1998) *Australian Election Study 1998 [computer file]*, Canberra, Australian Social Science Data Archive, Australian National University.

—— Gow, David and McAllister, Ian (2002) *Australian Election Study, 2001: User's Guide for the Machine-readable Data File*, SSDA Study No. 1048, Canberra, Australian National University.

—— McAllister, Ian, Gibson, Rachel and Gow, David (2005) *Australian Election Study 2004 [computer file]*, Canberra, Australian Social Science Data Archive, Australian National University.

—— McAllister, Ian and Gow, David (2008) *Australian Election Study 2007 [computer file]*, Canberra, Australian Social Science Data Archive, Australian National University.

Beecher, Eric (2005) 'The decline of the quality press?' in Robert Manne (ed), *Do Not Disturb*, Melbourne, Black Inc, pp. 7–27.

Bennett, Scott (1996) *Winning and Losing: Australian National Elections*, Melbourne, Melbourne University Press.

Bennett, W. Lance (2005) 'Beyond pseudoevents: election news and reality TV', *American Behavioral Scientist* 49(3): 364–78.

Blair, Tony (2007) 'Speech to the Reuter's Institute', 12 June, http://news.bbc.co.uk/1/hi/uk_politics/6744581.stm.

Blumler, Jay G. (1987) 'Election communication and the democratic political system' in David L. Paletz (ed), *Political Communication Research*, New York, Ablex Publishing, pp. 167–75.

—— and Coleman, Stephen (2010) 'Political communication in freefall: the British case and others?', *The International Journal of Press/Politics* 15: 139–54.

—— and Gurevitch, Michael (1981) 'Politicians and the press: an essay on role relationships', in D.D. Nimmo and K.R. Saunders (eds), *Handbook of Political Communication*, London, Sage, pp. 468–96.

Boey, K.C. (2004) 'Australian media under scrutiny amid political rumour mill', *New Sunday Times* (Malaysia), 11 July: 5.

Bolt, Andrew (2008) 'A million blogging warnings to a lazy media', http://blogs.news.com.au/heraldsun/andrewbolt/index.php/heraldsun/comments/column_a_million_blogging_warnings_to_a_lazy_media/.

—— (2010) 'Profile', *Andrew Bolt* blog, *Herald Sun* online http://blogs.news.com.au/heraldsun/andrewbolt/.

Bolton, Geoffrey (2001) 'Sir Edmund Barton' in Michelle Grattan (ed), *Australian Prime Ministers*, Sydney, New Holland, pp. 22–35.

Braithwaite, Alyssa (2007) 'Seven wins television ratings year', *Australian*, 2 December.

Brent, Peter (2004) 'Howard's battlers: the electoral evidence?', paper presented to the *Australasian Political Studies Association Conference*, University of Adelaide, 29 September–1 October 2004.

—— (2007) 'Poll position: making sense of opinion polls' in Kerr, Christian (ed), *The Crikey Guide to the 2007 Federal Election*, Camberwell, Vic., Penguin, pp. 131–47.

British Crime Survey *see* BCS.

Broadcasters' Audience Research Board *see* BARB.

Bruns, Axel (2008) 'Citizen journalism in the 2007 Australian federal election', *eJournalist*, 8(1), pp. 75–89.

Bucy, Erik P. and Grabe, Maria Elizabeth (2007) 'Taking television seriously: a sound and image bite analysis of presidential campaign coverage', 1992–2004, *Journal of Communication* 57:652–75.

Burton, Lee (2000) 'The options generation: a discussion of young Australians' media use', *Australian Screen Education* 22, Autumn: 54–63.

Butler, Barbara Ann (1998) 'Information subsidies, journalism routines and the Australian Media', *Prometheus*, 16(1): 27–46.

—— (1999) 'Source strategies, subsidies and subterfuge: building the prime-time campaign news agenda during the 1998 federal election', *Australian Journal of Communication* 26(3): 111–26.

Cappella, Joseph and Hall Jamieson, Katherine (1996) 'News frames, political cynicism and media cynicism', *The Annals of the American Academy of Political and Social Science* 546: 71–85.

Carbonne, Suzanne (2001) 'And now voters, it's time to take your seats', *Age*, 9 October.

Carey, Adam (2007) 'The click of the crop', *Age*, 20 December, http://www.theage.com. au/articles/2007/12/20/1198175314652.html.

Carney, Shaun (2005) 'The last bully baron', *Age*, 31 December.

Carroll, John S. (2006) 'What will become of newspapers?' http://www.mediadb.eu/ fileadmin/bilder/reports/john_s._carroll_-_what_will_become_of_newspapers.pdf.

Casimir, Jon (1998) 'The big turn-off', *Sydney Morning Herald*, 22 June, The Guide: 4.

Chadwick, Paul (1989) *Media Mates*, Macmillan, South Melbourne, Vic.

—— (2008) 'Report of the chairman ECRC', *ABC Online*, http://www.abc.net.au/corp/ pubs/documents/ABC_Coverage_of_the_2007_Federal_Election.pdf.

Chaffee, Steven and Frank, Stacey (1996) 'How Americans get political information: print versus broadcast news', *The Annals of the American Academy* 546, July: 48–58.

Chalmers, Rob (2009) 'Rudd versus News Ltd', *Inside Story*, 9 July.

Channel Nine (2010) 'Seapatrol Website', Ninemsn Online, http://channelnine.ninemsn. com.au/seapatrol/.

Charlton, Peter (2002a) '*Tampa*: the triumph of politics' in Solomon, David (ed), *Howard's Race*, Sydney, HarperCollins, pp. 79–107.

—— (2002b) 'The terror campaign' in Solomon, David (ed), *Howard's Race*, Sydney, HarperCollins, pp. 108–30.

Cincotta, Katie (2007) 'Talkback radio enjoys its 40th birthday', *B&T Weekly*, 13 April, p. 16.

CMH [Consolidated Media Holdings] (2004) 'Television ratings', http://www.pbl.com. au/australian_television_ratings_week_36.htm.

Cohen, Barry (1980) 'A winning campaign', Canberra, Australian Labor Party, National Library manuscripts (MS 4985, Box 468, folder 84/5/20).

Colebatch, Tim (2000) 'And in news just to hand, Australians back the media', *Age*, 20 March:1.

Coleman, Stephen and Banning, Renita (2006) 'Network TV news' affective framing of the presidential candidates', *Journalism and Mass Communication Quarterly* 83(2): 313–28.

Commercial Radio Australia *see* CRA.

Consolidated Media Holdings *see* CMH.

Converse, Philip (1966) 'Information flow and the stability of partisan attitudes' in Angus Campbell et al., *Elections and the Political Order*, Wiley, New York.

Coorey, Phillip (2001) 'Jockeys who give PM easy ride', *Advertiser*, 3 December: 19.

Costello, Peter (2009) 'Opinions count for much more in modern politics', *Age*, 15 April.

CRA [Commercial Radio Australia] (2007) 'Commercial radio: a snapshot', *CRA Online*, December, http://www.commercialradio.com.au/files/uploaded/file/Advertising% 20on%20Radio/Snapshots%202007_forweb_amended.pdf.

—— (2008) 'Radio facts', *CRA Online*, http://www.commercialradio.com.au/index.cfm? page_id=1007.

—— (2009) 'Why advertise on radio?', *CRA Online*, http://www.commercialradio.com. au/index.cfm?page_id=1023.

Craig, Geoffrey (2004) *The Media, Politics and Public Life*, Sydney, Allen & Unwin.

Craig, John (1993) *Australian Politics*, Sydney, Harcourt Brace.

Crikey (undated) 'About Crikey', *Crikey Online*, http://www.crikey.com.au/About.html.

Crisp, L.F. (1965) *Australian National Government*, Croydon, Vic., Longman.

Crouch, Brad (1993) 'Wild scenes as protesters pelt Hewson with fruit', *Herald Sun*, 21 February: 4.

—— (1996) 'On the campaign trail', *Sunday Telegraph*, 18 February.

Crouse, Timothy (1973) *The Boys on the Bus*, New York, Random House.

—— (1998) 'Newspaper and the press' in Adam Briggs and Paul Cobley (eds), *The Media: An Introduction* Essex, UK: Longman, pp. 81–96.

—— Iyengar, Shanto, Lund, Anker Brink and Salovaara-Moring, Inka (2009) 'Media system, public knowledge and democracy', *European Journal of Communication* 24(1): 5–26.

Dahlgren, Peter (2009) *Media and Political Engagement*, London, Cambridge University Press.

Dale, David (2008) 'Kids muck up ABC ratings as SBS soars', *Sydney Morning Herald*, 1 December.

Dalton, Russell J. (1996) *Citizen Politics* (2nd edn), Chatham NJ, Chatham House.

Davis, Aeron (2007) *The Mediation of Power*, London, Routledge.

Deacon, David, Wring, Dominic, Billig, Michael, Downey, John, Golding, Peter and Davidson, Scott (2005) *Reporting the 2005 UK General Election*, Communication Research Centre, Loughborough University.

Delli Carpini, Michael and Keeter, Scott (1996) *What Americans Know About Politics and Why It Matters*, New Haven, Yale University Press.

Denemark, David (2005) 'Mass media and media power in Australia' in Shaun Wilson, Gabrielle Meagher, Rachel Gibson, David Denemark and Mark Western (eds), *Australian Social Attitudes*, Sydney, UNSW Press, pp. 220–49.

—— Ward, Ian and Bean, Clive (2007) 'Election campaigns and television news coverage', *Australian Journal of Political Science* 42(1): 89–109.

Druckman, James N. (2005) 'Media matter: how newspapers and television news cover campaigns and influence voters', *Political Communication* 22 (October–December): 463–81.

Dudley-Nicholson, Jennifer (2009) 'Australians spend much more time online', *Australian*, 5 March.

Duffy, Michael (1998) 'Only one deserves to lose, honest', *Daily Telegraph*, 3 October.

Dyer, Glenn (2008) 'Alan Jones – yesterday's parrot?', *Crikey*, 18 June, http://www.crikey. com.au/2008/06/18/alan-jones-yesterdays-parrot/.

—— (2008b) interview with the author, 3 November.

Economist, The (2008) 'On the brink', 3 May.

Economou, Nick (2008) 'Leading or following? editorials, alignments, elections and the 2007 federal election', *Communication, Politics & Culture* 41(2): 30–46.

Edgecliffe-Johnson, Andrew (2007) 'News channel set to be chief loser in clash over access', *Financial Times*, 14 March: 3.

Elections Canada (2000) 'Rules for the Publication of Opinion Polls', 23 October http://www.elections.ca/content.asp?section=med&document=oct2300a&dir= pre&lang=e&textonly=false.

Electoral Matters Committee *see* EMC.

Elliott, Geoff (2010) 'TV networks slam Tony Abbott over licence fee bribe claim', *Australian*, 17 February.

Ellis, Bob (2002) 'What dark secrets motivate our political reporters?', *Canberra Times*, 10 July: 13.

EMC [Electoral Matters Committee] (2009) 'Inquiry into Voter Participation and Informal Voting', Melbourne, Parliament of Victoria.

Entman, Robert M. (2002) 'Framing: towards clarification of a fractured paradigm', in Dennis McQuail (ed), *McQuail's Reader in Mass Communication Theory*, London, Sage, pp. 391–7.

Esser, Frank and d'Angelo, Paul (2003) 'Framing the press and the publicity process: a content analysis of meta-coverage in campaign 2000 network news', *American Behavioural Scientist* 46(5): 617–41.

——— and d'Angelo, Paul (2006) 'Framing the press and publicity process in US, British, and German general election campaigns: A comparative study of metacoverage', *Press/Politics* 11(3): 44–66.

——— Reinemann, Carsten and Fan, David (2001) 'Spin doctors in the United States, Great Britain and Germany: metacommunication about media manipulation', *Harvard International Journal of Press/Politics* 6: 16–45.

Evans, Gareth (1998) 'Politics and the media circus: sideshow alley', *Australian Quarterly*, March–April, pp. 16–18.

Eveland, William P., Marton, Krisztina and Seo, Mihye (2004) 'Moving beyond "just the facts": the influence of online news on the content and structure of public affairs knowledge', *Communication Research* 31(1): 82–108.

Faine, Jon (2005) 'Talk radio and democracy' in Robert Manne (ed), *Do Not Disturb*, Melbourne, Black Inc, pp. 169–88.

Fairfax (2003) 'Only the taxman . . . advertisement', *AdNews*, 24 October: 39.

Fairfax Media (2008a) 'Fairfax Publications: Fairfax Digital Network', *Fairfax Media*, http://www.adcentre.com.au/fairfax-digital-network.aspx?s_rid=www:footer.

——— (2008b) *Annual Report*, http://www.fxj.com.au/announcements/sep08/FXJ_Annual_Report_FINAL_v3.pdf.

——— (2009) 'Advertise with 3AW', http://www.3aw.com.au/advertise-with-3aw/20081119-6b83.html.

Farhi, Paul (2008a) 'Off the bus', *American Journalism Review* 30(6): 28–33.

——— (2008b) 'Cable's clout', *American Journalism Review* 30(4), pp. 18–24.

——— (2009) 'Build that paywall high', *American Journalism Review*, June–July http://www.ajr.org/Article.asp?id=4800.

Farr, Malcolm (2002) 'Howard's Campaign' in Solomon, David (ed), (2002) *Howard's Race*, Sydney, HarperCollins, pp. 131–43.

Farrell, David and Schmitt-Beck, Rüdiger (eds) (2002) *Do Political Campaigns Matter?* London, Routledge.

Fiske, John (1992) 'Popularity and the politics of information' in Peter Dahlgren and Colin Sparks (eds), *Journalism and Popular Culture*, London, Sage, pp. 45–63.

Fitzgerald, Julian (2008) *Inside the Parliamentary Press Gallery*, Mawson, ACT, Clareville Press.

Flew, Terry and Wilson, Jason (2008) 'Journalism as social networking: the Australian *youdecide* project and the 2007 federal election', *Journalism* 11(2): 131–47.

Flint, David (2005) 'The left-wing bias of Australia's media', *Online Opinion*, http://www.onlineopinion.com.au/view.asp?article=3274.

Franklin, Bob (2004) *Packaging Politics*, New York, Arnold.

Fraser, Nancy (1992) 'Rethinking the public sphere: a contribution to the critique of actually existing democracy' in Craig Calhoun (ed), *Habermas and the Public Sphere*, MA, MIT Press, pp. 109–42.

Free TV Australia *see* FTA.

Freudenberg, Graham (2000) Recorded interview with Graham Freudenberg AM, interviewer: John Farquharson, Oral History Section, Canberra, National Library of Australia (CTRC 3994).

FTA [Free TV Australia] (2007) 'Free TV ratings' http://www.thinktv.com.au/Content_Common/pg-2007-Ratings.seo.

—— (2008) '2008 Ratings Review', http://www.freetv.com.au/media/News-Media_Release/2008_Summer_Release.pdf.

Gaber, Ivor (2000) 'Government by spin: An analysis of the process', *Media, Culture and Society*, 22: 507–518.

Gans, Joshua S. and Leigh, Andrew (2009) 'How partisan is the press?', http://people.anu.edu.au/andrew.leigh/pdf/MediaSlant.pdf.

Gardiner-Garden, John and Chowns, Jonathan (2006) *E-Brief – Media Ownership Regulation in Australia*, Parliamentary Library, Parliament of Australia, Canberra.

Gawenda, Michael (2008) 'Do newspapers have a future? And how long is that future?', *AN Smith Lecture in Journalism*, University of Melbourne, 7 October, http://www.unimelb.edu.au/speeches/Docs/AN%20Smith%20Lecture%20by%20Michael%20Gawenda.pdf.

Gilbert, Sheldon, Eyal, Chaim, McCombs, Maxwell E. and Nicholas, David (1980) 'The State of the Union Address and press agendas', *Journalism Quarterly* 57(4): 584–8.

Gitlin, Todd (1983) *Inside Primetime*, New York, Pantheon.

Glasgow University Media Group *see* GUMG.

Glover, Dennis (2005) 'Is the media pro-Labor?' in Robert Manne (ed), *Do Not Disturb*, Melbourne, Black Inc, pp. 191–215.

Golan, G. (2006) 'Inter-media agenda setting and global news coverage', *Journalism Studies* 7(2): 323–34.

Goot, Murray (1977) 'Radio Lang' in Heather Radi and Peter Spearritt (eds), *Jack Lang*, Sydney, Hale and Ironmonger, pp. 121–3.

—— (1983) 'The media and the campaign', in Howard R. Penniman (ed), *Australia at the Polls: The National Elections of 1980 and 1983*, Sydney, Allen & Unwin, pp. 140–215.

—— (2000) 'More "relaxed and comfortable": public opinion on immigration under Howard', *People and Place* 8(3): 46–60.

—— (2002) 'Distrustful, disenchanted and disengaged?' in David Burchell and Andrew Leigh (eds), *The Prince's News Clothes*, Sydney, UNSW Press, pp. 9–46.

—— (2008) 'Is the news on the internet different? Leaders, frontbenchers and other candidates in the 2007 Australian election', *Australian Journal of Political Science* 43(1): 99–110.

—— (2009) 'Getting it wrong while getting it right: the polls, the press and the 2007 Australian election', *Australian Cultural History* 27(2): 115–33.

—— (in press) 'The commodification of public opinion' in Robert Crawford, Kim Humphrey and Judith Smart (eds), *Consumer Australia: Historical and Contemporary Perspectives*, Newcastle UK, Cambridge Scholars Publishing.

—— and Watson, Ian (2007) 'Explaining Howard's success: social structure, issue agendas and party support, 1993–2004', *Australian Journal of Political Science* 42(2): 253–76.

Gordon, Michael (2004) 'Threatening? Me? Fair shake, protests Latham', *Age*, 30 October.

Grabe, Maria Elizabeth and Bucy, Erik Page (2009) *Image Bite Politics*, New York, Oxford.

Graber, Doris A. (2006) *Mass Media and American Politics* (7th edn), Washington DC, Congressional Quarterly Press.

Graf, Joseph (2006) *The Audience for Political Blogs*, Institute for Politics, Democracy and the Internet, George Washington University, www.ipdi.org.

Grattan, Michelle (1993) 'The rocky road of election reporting', *The Sydney Papers*, 5(4): 29–33.

—— (1998) 'The politics of spin', *Australian Studies in Journalism* 7: 32–45.

—— (2005) 'Watching the watchdogs', *Deakin Lecture*, University of Melbourne, 2 May.

Green, Joshua (2001) 'More than TV: Channel Ten and diversity in free-to-air broadcasting', *Media International Australia, Incorporating Culture & Policy* 100: 49–63.

Green, Murray (2004) 'ABC coverage of the 2004 federal election', *ABC Online*, 1 December, http://www.abc.net.au/corp/pubs/documents/ABC_coverage_of_the_2004_Federal_Election.pdf.

Greenslade, Roy (2003) 'Their master's voice', the *Guardian*, 17 February.

Griffen-Foley, Bridget (2003) *Party Games*, Melbourne, Text Publishing.

—— (2004) 'From tit-bits to Big Brother: a century of audience participation in the media', *Media, Culture & Society* 26(4): 533–48.

Grubel, James and Cole, Malcolm (2002) 'Lib chief in attack on media', *Courier-Mail*, 13 April: 6.

GUMG [Glasgow University Media Group] (1976) *Bad News*, London, Routledge.

Habermas, Jürgen (1974) 'The public sphere: an encyclopaedia article (1964)', *New German Critique* 3: 49–55.

—— (1989) *The Structural Transformation of the Public Sphere* (trans. Burger, T. with the assistance of Lawrence, F.), Cambridge, MA, MIT Press.

Hall, Stuart, Critcher, Charles, Jefferson, Tony, Clarke John and Roberts, Brian (1978) *Policing the Crisis*, London, Macmillan.

Hallin, Daniel C. (1992) 'Sound bite news: television coverage of elections, 1968–1988', *Journal of Communication* 42(2): 5–24.

Hamilton, Clive (2006a) 'Who listens to Alan Jones? Webpaper June 2006', Manuka, ACT, Australia Institute.

—— (2006b) 'The *Australian*', 18 February, *Crikey* http://www.crikey.com.au/2008/02/18/the-australian-we-didnt-mean-it-really/.

Hamilton, John (2001a) 'Out of touch with people', *Herald Sun*: Election Guide 2.

—— (2001b) 'I'll see us through, says resolute PM', *Herald Sun*, 8 October 2001: 7.

Harley, Judith (1990) 'Campaigning in the old-fashioned way', *Age*, 21 March: Tempo 3.

Hartigan, John (2009) Speech to the National Press Club, 1 July, Canberra, http://www. news.com.au/heraldsun/story/0,21985,25718006–661,00.html.

Hartley, John (1999) *Uses of Television*, London, Routledge.

Haswell, Sandra (2001) 'Attention please! This political campaign is for you', *Australian Journalism Review* 23(2): 129–47.

Haupt, Robert and Grattan, Michelle (1983) *31 Days to Power: Hawke's Victory*, Sydney, Allen and Unwin.

Hay, Colin (2007) *Why We Hate Politics*, Cambridge, Polity.

Henderson, Anne (2001) 'Joseph Aloysius Lyons' in Michelle Grattan (ed), *Australian Prime Ministers*, Sydney: New Holland, pp. 152–67.

Henderson, Gerard (2002) 'The Gallery gurus don't know best', *Age*, 9 July.

Henningham, John (1988) *Looking at Television News*, Melbourne, Longman Cheshire.

—— (1995) 'Political journalists' political and professional values', *Australian Journal of Political Science* 30: 321–34.

—— (1996) 'The shape of daily news', *Media International Australia* 79: 22–34.

—— (1998a) 'The Australian journalist' in Myles Breen (ed), *Journalism: Theory and Practice*, Sydney, Macleay Press, pp. 333–42.

—— (1998b) 'Ideological differences between Australian journalists and their public', *Press/Politics* 3(1): 92–101.

Herman, Edward and Chomsky, Noam (1988) *Manufacturing Consent*, New York, Pantheon.

Hewson, John (2006) 'Tame media is bad news', *Australian Financial Review*, 31 March: 94.

Hilmer, Fred (2002) 'Why the cross-media laws should go – for all our sakes', *Age*, 5 June: 15.

Hindman, Matthew (2008) *The Myth of Digital Democracy*, Princeton University Press.

Hitwise (2010) 'Top Websites and Search Engine Analysis, for the week ending 24/04/2010', http://www.hitwise.com/au/datacentre/main/dashboard-1706.html.

Holbrook, R. Andrew (2003) 'Agenda-setting and priming in the prime-time hour', paper presented at the *Midwest Political Science Association Conference*, April 3–6, Chicago, Illinois (later version at http://www.infoamerica.org/documentos_pdf/setting01.pdf).

Holbrook, Thomas M. (2002) 'Presidential campaigns and the knowledge gap', *Political Communication* 19: 437–54.

Holtz-Bacha, Christina and Norris, Pippa (2001) 'To entertain, inform and educate: still the role of public television in the 1990s?', *Political Communication* 18(2): 123–40.

Howard, John (2002) Keynote speech to the International Democratic Union luncheon, Ronald Reagan Building, Washington DC.

—— (2008) 'John Howard's Irving Kristol lecture', delivered to the American Enterprise Institute, Washington DC, 5 March, printed in the *Australian*, 6 March, http://www. theaustralian.news.com.au/story/0,25197,23328945–5014047,00.html.

Hudson, Phillip (2009) 'Internet will lure missing voters, says election chief', *Sydney Morning Herald*, 12 April.

Hudson, Repps (2008) 'The future of newspapers', *St Louis Journalism Review* 38, May: 17–19.

Hutcheon, Simon (2007) 'Kevin in '07 became a real click magnet', *Sydney Morning Herald*, 21 December.

Hyland, Tom (2009a) 'Fairfax, NEWS to charge for online', *Age*, 9 August.

—— (2009b) 'Calling the tune', *Age*, 13 December.

Iyengar, Shanto and Kinder, Donald R. (1987) *The News that Matters*, Chicago, University of Chicago Press.

—— and Simon, Adam F. (2000) 'New perspectives and evidence on political communication and campaign effects', *Annual Review of Psychology* 5: 149–69.

—— Norpoth, Helmut and Hahn, Kyu S. (2004) 'Consumer demand for election news: the horserace sells', *The Journal of Politics* 66(1): 157–75.

—— Peters, Mark D. and Kinder, Donald R (1982) 'Experimental demonstration of the not-so-minimal consequences of television news programs', *American Political Science Review* 76 (December): 848–58.

Jackson, Sally and Doman, Matthew (2003) 'Point scoring: pushing their opinions', *Australian*, 27 February: B01.

Jaensch, Dean (1995) *Election! How and Why Australia Votes*, St Leonards, NSW, Allen & Unwin.

—— (2001) '100 years later, our campaigns are driven by the jet set', *Advertiser*, 4 January: 18.

Jarvis, Jeff (2006) interview on *Frontline*, PBS, http://www.pbs.org/wgbh/pages/frontline/newswar/interviews/jarvis.html.

Javes, Sue (2007) 'Voters tune out election and Jones', *Sydney Morning Herald*, October 31: 5.

Jeffries, Stuart (2010) 'A rare interview with Jürgen Habermas', *Financial Times*, 30 April.

Jerit, Jennifer (2009) 'Understanding the knowledge gap: the role of experts and journalists', *The Journal of Politics* 71(2), April: 442–56.

Joint Standing Committee on Electoral Matters *see* JSCEM.

Jones, Paul and Pusey, Michael (2008) 'Mediated political communication in Australia: Leading issues, new evidence', *Australian Journal of Social Issues* 43(4), 583–600.

Jones, Roger, McAllister, Ian, Denemark, David and Gow, David (1993) *Australian Election Study 1993 [computer file]*, Canberra, Australian Social Science Data Archive, The Australian National University.

—— McAllister, Ian and Gow, David (1996) *Australian Election Study 1996 [computer file]*, Canberra, Australian Social Science Data Archive, Australian National University.

JSCEM [Joint Standing Committee on Electoral Matters] (2007) *Inquiry into Civics and Electoral Education*, Canberra, Parliament of Australia.

—— (2009) *Report on the Conduct of the 2007 Federal Election and Matters Related Thereto*, Canberra, Parliament of Australia.

Katz, Ian (2000) 'All aboard the sinking(?) ship', *British Journalism Review* 11(5): 5–11.

Katz, Richard, S. (2008) 'Political parties' in Daniele Caramani (ed), *Comparative Politics*, Oxford University Press, pp. 293–315.

Keane, John (1999) 'Some reflections on *The Good Citizen*', http://www.johnkeane.net/essays/essay_onthegoodcitizen.htm.

—— (2009) *The Life and Death of Democracy*, Simon & Schuster, London.

Keating, Paul (2000) 'Paul Keating on the Australian media', 14 June, http://www.australianpolitics.com/media/00–06-14keating.shtml.

Kellner, Douglas (1990) *Television and the Crisis of Democracy*, Boulder, Westview Press.

Kelly, Paul (2001) 'Keynote address to the ejournalism conference 2001', *ejournalism* 1(2), http://www.ejournalism.eu.com/ejournalist/kelly.pdf.

Kerbel, Matthew R. (1999) *Remote and Controlled* (2nd edn) Boulder CO, Westview.

Kermond, Clare (2004) 'Bagging the grab', *Age*, Green Guide, 9 September: 8.

Kerr, Christian (2007a) 'Bias-o-meter III: the federal Press Gallery', *Crikey*, 27 June.

—— (2007b) '1.368 million reasons Rudd chose Rove', *Crikey*, 19 November.

Kingdon, John W. (1970) 'Opinion leaders in the electorate', *The Public Opinion Quarterly* 34(2): 256–61.

Kingston, Margo (2001) *Off the Rails*, Crows Nest, NSW, Allen & Unwin.

Klapper, Joseph (1960) *The Effects of Mass Communication*, Gencoe, Illinois, Free Press.

Kohler, Alan (2009) 'Quality journalism will bloom online', *Crikey*, 9 April.

Kuttner, Robert (2007) 'The race', *Columbia Journalism Review* 45(6): 24–35.

Latham, Mark (2005) *The Latham Diaries*, Melbourne, Melbourne University Press.

Lazarsfeld, Paul F., Berelson, Bernard and Gaudet, Hazel (1944) *The People's Choice*, New York, Columbia University Press.

Leonard, Andrew (2008) 'Tribune bankruptcy', *salon,com*, 8 December, http://www.salon.com/tech/htww/2008/12/08/tribune_bankruptcy/.

Lewis, Justin, Cushion, Stephen and Thomas, James (2005) 'Immediacy, convenience or engagement? an analysis of 24-hour news channels in the UK', *Journalism Studies* 6(4): 461–77.

Lichter, S. Robert (2001) 'A plague on both parties: Substance and fairness in TV election news', *Press/Politics* 6(3): 8–30.

—— and Smith, Ted (1996) 'Why elections are bad news: media and candidate discourse in the 1996 presidential primaries', *Harvard International Journal of Press/Politics* 1(4): 15–35.

Lijphardt, Arend (1997) 'Unequal participation: democracy's unresolved dilemma', *American Political Science Review* 91: 1–14.

Lloyd, Clem J. (1988) *Parliament and the Press*, Melbourne, Melbourne University Press.

Lowrey, Wilson (2006) 'Mapping the journalism–blogging relationship', *Journalism* 7(4): 477–500.

Lucy, Niall and Mickler, Steve (2006) *The War on Democracy*, Crawley, WA, University of Western Australia Press.

Lumby, Catharine (1999) *Gotcha*, Sydney, Allen & Unwin.

McAllister, Ian (1992) *Political Behaviour*, Melbourne, Longman Cheshire.

—— (1998) 'Civic education and political knowledge in Australia', *Australian Journal of Political Science* 33(1): 7–23.

—— (2002) 'Calculating or capricious? The new politics of late deciding voters', in David Farrell and Rüdiger Schmitt-Beck (eds), *Do Political Campaigns Matter?*, London, Routledge, pp. 22–40.

—— and Clark, Juliet (2007) *Trends in Australian Political Opinion*, Canberra, Australian Social Science Data Archive, http://assda.anu.edu.au/aestrends.pdf.

—— and Mughan, Anthony (1987) *Australian Election Survey 1987 [computer file]*, Canberra, Australian Social Science Data Archive, Australian National University.

—— Jones, Roger, Papadakis, Elim and Gow, David (1990) *Australian Election Survey 1990 [computer file]*, Canberra, Australian Social Science Data Archive, Australian National University.

McCabe, Helen and Farr, Malcolm (2001) 'Round one leaves Beazley bruised', *Daily Telegraph*, 13 October: 33.

McCarthy, Patsy (1993) 'The men and their messages: Election 93', *Australian Journal of Communication* 20: 14–27.

McChesney, Robert W. (2003 [1999]) 'The new global media', pp. 260–96 in David Held and Anthony McGrew (eds), *The Global Transformations Reader: An Introduction to the Globalisation Debate*, Cambridge, Polity Press.

McCombs, Maxwell E. (2005) 'The agenda-setting function of the press' in Geneva Overholser and Kathleen Hall Jamieson (eds), *The Press*, Oxford, Oxford University Press, pp. 156–68.

—— and Shaw, Donald L. (1972) 'The agenda-setting function of mass media', *Public Opinion Quarterly* 36: 176–87.

MacCormack, David (2007) 'Turnbull should do whatever it takes', *Crikey*, 9 September: 8.

—— (2008) 'Private equity worse than the moguls? You're kidding', *Crikey*, 25 January.

McGuinness, Padraic P. (2002) 'Soiled ethics can no longer hide dirty secrets of the Canberra club', *Sydney Morning Herald*, 9 July.

Mackerras, Malcolm (2009) 'Describing the results', *Australian Cultural History* 27(2): 219–42.

McKnight, David (2005) 'Murdoch and the culture war' in Robert Manne (ed), *Do Not Disturb*, Melbourne, Black Inc, pp. 53–72.

McManus, Gerard (2004a) 'Greens back illegal drugs', *Herald Sun*, 31 August: 3.

—— (2004b) 'Polls show Greens are sprouting', *Herald Sun*, 30 August: 8.

McNair, Brian (2000) *Journalism and Democracy*, London, Routledge.

—— (2006) *Cultural Chaos*, London, Routledge.

Maddison, Sarah (2007) 'Lobbying government' in Sally Young (ed), *Government Communication in Australia*, Melbourne, Cambridge University Press, pp. 255–69.

Magazine Publishers of Australia *see* MPA.

Maiden, Malcolm (2007) 'Sir Rod gets Rudd and Labor off to a flying start', *Sydney Morning Herald*, 12 Feb 2007.

—— (2008) 'Crunch time for Fairfax as it faces its debt, cutting dividends', *Age*, 6 December.

Mair, Peter (2008) 'Democracies' in Daniele Caramani (ed), *Comparative Politics*, Oxford University Press, pp. 108–32.

Manin, Bernard (1997) *The Principles of Representative Government*, Melbourne, Cambridge University Press.

Manne, Robert (2007) 'The new bland and dull ABC', *Age*, 4 April.

Manning, Paul (2001) *News and News Sources: a Critical Introduction*, London, Sage.

—— (2007) 'The race to the bottom', *Age*, 26 April.

Marr, David and Wilkinson, Marian (2003) *Dark Victory*, Crows Nest, NSW, Allen & Unwin.

Marriner, Cosima (2004) 'Contender denies Murdoch and Packer are out to get him', *SMH*, 7 July: 8.

Marsh, David (ed) (2006) *Political Parties in Transition?* Sydney, Federation Press.

Masters, Chris (2006) *Jonestown*, Crows Nest, NSW, Allen & Unwin.

Mayer, Henry (1964) *The Press in Australia*, Melbourne, Lansdowne.

Mayne, Stephen (2008) 'Can the Murdoch and Fairfax families support their debt laden public empires?', *Crikey*, 16 October.

MEAA [Media Entertainment and Arts Alliance] (1996) *Women in the Media Survey*, Redfern, NSW, MEAA.

—— (2008) *Life in the Clickstream*, Redfern, NSW, MEAA.

Media Rules (1996) [videorecording], Sydney, Special Broadcasting Service.

Media Watch (2004) 'The ABC of elusive bias', *ABC Television*, 17 May, http://www.abc. net.au/mediawatch/transcripts/s1110154.htm.

—— (2007) 'How to vote', *ABC Television*, 12 November, http://www.abc.net.au/ mediawatch/transcripts/byyear/2007.htm#20071112.

Meyer, Phillip (1995) 'Learning to love lower profits', *American Journalism Review*, December http://www.ajr.org/article.asp?id=1461.

—— (2004) *The Vanishing Newspaper*, University of Missouri Press.

Miller, Joanne and Krosnick, Jon (1997) 'Anatomy of news media priming' in S. Iyengar and R. Reeves (eds), *Do the Media Govern?*, Thousand Oaks, Sage Publications.

Miller, Toby (2009) 'Approach with caution and proceed with care: campaigning for the US presidency "after" TV' in Graeme Turner and Jinna Tay (eds), *Television Studies After TV*, London, Routledge, pp. 75–82.

—— and Turner, Graeme (2002) 'Radio' in Stuart Cunningham and Graham Turner (eds) *The Media and Communications in Australia*, Crows Nest NSW, Allen & Unwin, pp. 133–151.

Mills, Stephen (1986) *The New Machine Men: Polls and Persuasion in Australian politics*, Ringwood, Vic., Penguin.

—— (1993) *The Hawke Years: The Story from the Inside*, Ringwood, Vic., Viking.

Morris, Grahame (2004) 'Dodgy journalists to blame for all the secrecy', *Australian*, 30 September: 18.

Moss, Stephen (2010) 'John Simpson', the *Guardian*, 15 March.

MPA [Magazine Publishers of Australia] (2008), 'Top 100 national magazine circulation (Australia only)', *MPA*, www.magazines.org.au.

Murphy, Damien and Debelle, Penelope (2007) 'Wentworth emails reveal two sides of reporter', *Age*, 14 November: 12.

Murray, Paul (2007) 'Follow the leader', *West Australian*, 22 December: 10.

NAA [National Archives of Australia] (2009) 'Robert Menzies – in office', *Australia's Prime Ministers*, Canberra, NAA: http://primeministers.naa.gov.au/prime-ministers/menzies/in-office.aspx.

New Matilda (2010) 'Advertise with us', http://newmatilda.com/advertise/.

Newsspace (2009a) 'The *Australian*', *Newspace Online*, http://www.newsspace.com.au/ theaustralian.com.au.

—— (2009b) 'The *Daily Telegraph*', *Newspace Online*, http://www.newsspace.com.au/ Daily_Telegraph.

—— (2009c) 'mX', *Newspace Online*, http://www.newsspace.com.au/mx_melbourne.

Newton, Kenneth (1999) 'Mass media effects: mobilization or media malaise?', *British Journal of Political Science* 29(4): 593–4.

—— (2007) 'The fourth estate: a weak force', *WZB-Mitteilungen*, http://www.wzb.eu/publikation/pdf/wm115/14–17.pdf.

NMRA [Nielsen Media Research Australia] (2007a) 'Population potentials by demographic', *2007 Radio Ratings Survival Kit*, www.nielsenmedia.com.au.

—— (2007b) 'Radio ratings survey no.8 2007' http://www.nielsenmedia.com.au/en/pdf/mri/13/TotalMetropolitanMarketsSurvey8–2007.pdf.

—— (2008) 'Survey No. 1 2008', www.nielsenmedia.com.au.

Norris, Pippa (1996) 'Does television erode social capital? a reply to Putnam', *PS: Political Science & Politics*, September: 474–80.

—— (1997a) *Electoral Change in Britain Since 1945*, Oxford, Blackwell.

—— (1997b) *Women, Media, and Politics*, Oxford University Press.

—— (1999) *Critical Citizens*, Oxford University Press.

—— (2000) *A Virtuous Circle*, Cambridge University Press.

—— (2001a) *Digital Divide*, Cambridge University Press.

—— (2001b) 'All spin and no substance: the 2001 British general election', *Harvard International Journal of Press/Politics* 6(4): 3–10.

—— Curtice, John, Sanders, David, Semetko, Holli and Scammell, Margaret (1999) *On Message*, Thousand Oaks, CA, Sage.

Oakes, Laurie (1972) 'An image-making, soft-sell campaign', the *Advertiser*, 5.

—— (2006) 'Centre of attention', the *Bulletin*, 4 January.

—— (2008) *Power Plays*, Sydney, Hachette Australia.

—— and Solomon, David (1973) *The Making of an Australian Prime Minister*, Melbourne, Cheshire.

Ofcom (2005) 'Viewers and voters: attitudes to television coverage of the 2005 general election', London, Ofcom.

OFW [Office for Women] (2007) *Women in Australia 07*, Canberra, Office for Women, Australian Government.

OzTAM (2007a) 'Universe Estimates Year 2007 – Individuals', Sydney, OzTAM.

—— (2007b) 'National subscription TV report: week 29, July 22', *OzTAM Online*, http://www.oztam.com.au/documents%5C2007%5CB1_20070715.pdf.

—— (2007c) 'National subscription TV report: week 47, 18 November–24 November 2007', *OzTAM Online*, http://www.oztam.com.au/documents/2007/B1_20071118.pdf.

—— (2008a) 'Metropolitan total TV share of all viewing – all homes: 5 City share report, week 30 2008 (20/07/08–26/07/08): Sun–Sat 06:00–23:59', Sydney, OzTAM.

—— (2008b) 'Metropolitan total TV share of all viewing – all homes: 5 City share report, Week 30 2008 (20/07/08–26/07/08): Sun–Sat 18:00–23:59', Sydney, OzTAM.

—— (2009) 'Top 20 Programs – 12–18 April', *OzTAM Online*, http://www.oztam.com.au/documents/2009/E_20090412.pdf.

Parker, Derek (1990) *The Courtesans*, North Sydney, Allen & Unwin.

Passey, Andrew and Lyons, Mark (2005) 'Voluntary associations and political participation' in Shaun Wilson, Gabrielle Meagher, Rachel Gibson, David Denemark, David and Mark Western (eds), *Australian Social Attitudes*, Sydney, UNSW Press, pp. 62–81.

Patterson, Thomas (1980) *The Mass Media Election*, New York, Praeger.

PEJ [Project for Excellence in Journalism] (2007) *The State of the News Media 2007*, http://www.stateofthenewsmedia.org/2007/narrative_newspapers_publicattitudes. asp?cat=7&media=3.

—— (2008) *The State of the News Media 2008*, www.stateofthenewsmedia.org/2008.

Penniman, Howard (ed) (1977) *Australia at the Polls*, ANU Press, Canberra.

Pew Project for Excellence in Journalism *see* PPEJ.

Pew Research Center for the People and the Press *see* PRC.

Phillips, Timothy, Tranter, Bruce, Mitchell, Deborah, Clark, Juliet and Reed, Ken (2008) *The Australian Survey of Social Attitudes, 2007* [computer file], Canberra: Australian Social Science Data Archive, Australian National University.

'Pieman' (2010) comments on *Andrew Bolt blog*, 'Media Watch impugns Oakes', 23 February   http://blogs.news.com.au/heraldsun/andrewbolt/index.php/heraldsun/ comments/media_watch_impugns_oakes/.

Posner, Richard A. (2005) 'Bad news', the *New York Times*, 31 July.

Post Click (2010) Report on Onlineopinion.com.au, provided 3 May 2010 by Graham Young, *Online Opinion*.

Postman, Neil (1985) *Amusing Ourselves to Death*, New York, Viking.

PPEJ [Pew Project for Excellence in Journalism] (2009) 'Daily Newspaper Readership by Race/Ethnicity', The State of the News Media, Pew Research Centre, http://www. stateofthenewsmedia.com/2009/index.htm.

PRC [Pew Research Centre for the People and the Press] (2004) 'News audiences increasingly politicized', *PRC Online*, 8 June, http://people-press.org/report/215/ news-audiences-increasingly-politicized.

—— (2005) 'Data memo: The state of blogging', January 2005.

—— (2006), 'Online papers modestly boost newspaper readership: Biennial News Consumption Survey', *PRC Online*, July 30, http://people-press.org/report/282/ online-papers-modestly-boost-newspaper-readership.

—— (2007) 'Public knowledge of current affairs little changed by news and information revolutions', *PRC Online*, 15 April, http://people-press.org/report/319/ public-knowledge-of-current-affairs-little-changed-by-news-and-information- revolutions.

—— (2008a), *Audience Segments in a Changing News Environment*, PRC, Washington DC.

—— (2008b) *The Web*, PRC, 17 March, http://people-press.org/reports/pdf/403.pdf.

—— (2008c), New numbers for blogging and blog readership', 22 July, http://www. pewinternet.org/Commentary/2008/July/New-numbers-for-blogging-and-blog- readership.aspx.

Price, Matt (1999) 'Solid as an Oakes', *Australian*, 13 May: M01.

—— (2004) 'Real tears in a political soap opera', *Australian*, 6 July: 4.

Prior, Markus (2003) 'Any good news in soft news?', *Political Communication* 20(2): 149–71.

—— (2007) *Post-Broadcast Democracy*, Melbourne, Cambridge University Press.

Project for Excellence in Journalism *see* PEJ.

Purcell, Charles (2010) 'Latham's passion is missing from the press corps', the *Age*, *National Times*, 9 August, http://www.theage.com.au/opinion/politics/ lathams-passion-is-missing-from-the-press-corps-20100809-11tmc.html.

Putnam, Robert D. (1995) 'Tuning in, tuning out: the strange disappearance of social capital in America', *PS: Political Science and Politics*, December: 664–83.

—— (2000) *Bowling Alone*, New York, Touchstone.

Rawson, D. W. (1961) *Australia Votes: The 1958 Federal Election*, Melbourne, Melbourne University Press.

Richardson, Graham (1994) *Whatever it Takes*, Sydney, Bantam Books.

Richardson, Nick (2002) 'Playing political games: ministers, minders and information' in Stephen Tanner (ed), *Journalism: Investigation and Research*, Pearson, Frenchs Forest NSW, pp. 170–83.

Ricketson, Matthew (2007) 'Big jump in online readership', *Age*, 16 February.

Riffe, Daniel, Aust, Charles F. and Lacy, Stephen R. (1993) 'The effectiveness of random, consecutive day and constructed week sampling in newspaper content analysis', *Journalism Quarterly* 70(1): 133–39.

RMR [Roy Morgan Research] (2004) 'Why Australians don't respect the media', March, *Roy Morgan Online*, http://www.roymorgan.com/resources/pdf/papers/20040903.pdf.

—— (2005) 'Labor supporters watch ABC, soap, Coalition supporters switch on to Nine, gardening, travel', 30 November, http://www.roymorgan.com/news/press-releases/2005/428/.

—— (2006) 'Journalists strongly oppose Government's media laws' http://www.roymorgan.com/news/press-releases/2006/541/.

—— (2007) 'Large majority of Australians think the media is "often biased"': Finding no. 4195', August 2007.

—— (2007–08) Data supplied to the author from Single Source Australia, July 2007–June 2008.

—— (2008) 'Image of professions survey', *Roy Morgan Online*, http://www.roymorgan.com/news/polls/2008/4283/.

—— (2009a) 'Press release: Australians still spend more time with TV than the internet', *Roy Morgan Online*, www.roymorgan.com/news/press-releases/2009/853/.

—— (2009b) 'Kid's: Less TV, more internet and more sport', July 2009, http://www.roymorgan.com/news/press-releases/2009/907/.

Robinson, John P. and Levy, Mark R. (1986) *The Main Source*, Thousand Oaks, CA, Sage.

Rosen, Jay (2006) 'The people formerly known as the audience', *PressThink*, 27 June http://journalism.nyu.edu/pubzone/weblogs/pressthink/2006/06/27/ppl_frmr.html.

Roy Morgan Research *see* RMR.

Saad, Lydia (2005) 'The group better known as "news junkies"', *Gallup Online*, 4 October, http://www.gallup.com/poll/18967/Group-Better-Known-News-Junkies.aspx.

Savva, Niki (2010) *So Greek: Confessions of a Conservative Leftie*, Melbourne, Scribe.

SBS (2007) *Codes of Practice*, http://www20.sbs.com.au/sbscorporate/

Scalmer, Sean and Goot, Murray (2004) 'Elites constructing elites: News Limited's newspapers, 1996–2002' in Marian Sawer and Barry Hindess (eds), *Us and Them: Anti-Elitism in Australia*, Perth, API Network, pp. 137–59.

Schudson, Michael (1994) 'Question authority: a history of the news interview in American journalism, 1860s–1930s', *Media, Culture & Society* 16(4): 565–87.

—— (1998) *The Good Citizen*, New York, Martin Kessler Books.

—— (2009) 'Ten years backwards and forwards', *Journalism* 10(3): 368–70.

Schultz, Julianne (1998) *Reviving the Fourth Estate: Democracy, Accountability and the Media*, Melbourne, Cambridge University Press.

Schulze, Jane (2009) 'Nine signs $500m Warner deal to launch youth digital channel', *Australian*, 22 June.

Schumpeter, Joseph (1943) *Capitalism, Socialism and Democracy*, London, Allen & Unwin.

SCIICMI [Senate Select Committee for an inquiry into a certain maritime incident] (2002) *A Certain Maritime Incident*, Parliament of Australia, Canberra.

Scott, Mark (2009) speech to *Australia's Right to Know* Conference, 24 March.

—— (2009b) *Annual Media Studies Lecture*, La Trobe University, 8 April.

Screen Australia (2008) 'Free-to-air TV viewing patterns', *Australian Film Commission*, http://www.afc.gov.au/gtp/wftvviewage.html.

—— (2009) 'Free-to-air TV viewing patterns', *Australian Film Commission*, http://www.afc.gov.au/gtp/wftvviewage.html.

SCRGSP [Steering Committee for the Review of Government Service Provision] 2007, *Overcoming Indigenous Disadvantage: Key Indicators 2007*, Productivity Commission, Canberra.

Seccombe, Mike (2001) 'The wages of spin', the *Sydney Morning Herald*, 5 November: 6.

Semetko, Holli A. (1996) 'Political balance on television: campaigns in the United States, Britain and Germany', *Press/Politics* 1(1): 51–71.

—— and Valkenburg, Peter M. (2000) 'Framing European politics: a content analysis of press and television news', *Journal of Communication* 50: 93–109.

—— Blumler, Jay G., Gurevitch, Michael, and Weaver, David H. (1991) *The Formation of Campaign Agendas*, Hillsdale, NJ, Erlbaum Associates.

Senate Select Committee for an inquiry into a certain maritime incident *see* SCIICMI.

Senior, Philip (2007) 'Reporting the Great Debate: press coverage of Australian televised leaders' debates', paper presented to the *Australasian Political Studies Association Conference*, Monash University, 24–26 September.

Shanahan, Dennis (2007a) 'Rudd faces late Howard surge', *Weekend Australian*, 24–25 November: 1.

—— (2007b) 'Kevin's sizzle not snag free', *Dennis Shanahan Blog*, the *Australian* online, 10 July, accessed 11 July 2007 and 10 May 2010 http://blogs.theaustralian.news.com.au/dennisshanahan/index.php/theaustralian/comments/kevins_sizzle_not_snag_free/.

Simons, Margaret (1999) *Fit to Print: Inside the Canberra Press Gallery*, Sydney, UNSW Press.

—— (2008a) 'Readership v circulation: curious newspaper mathematics', *Crikey*, 14 March.

—— (2008b) 'Catching up', *Australian Policy Online*, 12 March, http://www.apo.org.au/commentary/catching-0.

—— (2008c) 'The bad news about news – and why I disagree', *The Content Makers*, 22 December, http://blogs.crikey.com.au/contentmakers/2008/12/22/the-bad-news-about-news-and-why-i-disagree/.

—— (2009) 'A bumper boost: crunching the Fairfax circulation figures', *Crikey*, 16 February.

Simper, Errol (1998) 'Media spin a recognisable art form between the sheets', *Australian*, 21 October: 8.

Sky News (2007) 'About', *Sky News Online*, http://www.skynews.com.au/corporate/anc. aspx.

Smith, Aaron and Rainie, Lee (2009) 'The internet's role in campaign 2008', Washington DC, Pew Internet and American Life Project, Pew Research Center http://www. pewinternet.org/Reports/2009/6-The-Internets-Role-in-Campaign-2008.aspx.

Smith, Bridie (2004) 'Buzz wins election night tussle', *Age*, 12 October.

Solomon, David (ed) (2002) *Howard's Race*, Sydney, HarperCollins.

Sparks, Colin (2000) 'Introduction: The panic over tabloid news' in Colin Sparks and John Tulloch (eds), *Tabloid Tales*, Oxford, Rowman & Littlefield, pp. 1–40.

Speers, David (2008) Interview with the author, conducted 31 January.

Staff Writers (2007) 'News.com.au most clicked stories for 2007', 11 December, http:// www.news.com.au/story/0,23599,22905421-2,00.html.

Starick, Paul (2007) 'Political staff bullying doomed to fail', *Advertiser*, 18 April: 20.

Steering Committee for the Review of Government Service Provision *see* SCRGSP.

Steketee, Mike (2007) 'A candid candidate is a worry', *Australian*, 10 November: 22.

Sternberg, Jason (1998) 'Rating youth: A statistical review of young Australians' news media use', *Australian Studies in Journalism* 7: 84–135.

Stillwell, Frank and Jordan, Kirrily (2007) *Who Gets What?* Port Melbourne, Cambridge University Press.

Stoney, Tim (2001) 'Commuter papers suggest we're amusing ourselves to death', *Australian Journalism Review* 3 (1): 239–43.

Street, John (2001) *Mass Media, Politics and Democracy*, New York, Palgrave.

Strömbäck, Jesper and Kaid, Lynda Lee (eds) (2008) *The Handbook of Election News Coverage Around the World*, New York, Routledge.

Suich, Max (1988) 'Press Gallery in the dock', *Sydney Morning Herald*, 13 December: 17.

——— (2004a) 'The decline of the gallery', *Age*, 3 September: 13.

——— (2004b) 'Politics creates radio stars', *Age*, 1 October: 15.

——— (2004c) 'Media bias: read all about it', *Age*, 10 September.

Sussman, Gerald (2005) *Global Electioneering*, Lanham MD, Rowman & Littlefield.

Switzer, Tom (2007) 'Instinctive bias of its staff is not among ABC's virtues', *Australian*, 22 January.

Tabakoff, Nick (2009a) 'Fairfax dive undermines raising chances', *Australian*, 21 February.

——— (2009b) 'Readers not averse to paying for online content', *Australian*, 11 May.

Tadros, Edmund (2007) '2.4m viewers tuned in', *Sydney Morning Herald*, 22 October.

Tebbutt, John (2006) 'Imaginative demographics: the emergence of a radio talkback audience in Australia', *Media, Culture & Society* 28(6): 857–82.

Thompson, John B. (1993) 'The theory of the public sphere', *Theory, Culture and Society* 10: 173–89.

Thussu, Daya Kishan (2007) *News as Entertainment* [electronic source], London, Sage.

Tiffen, Rodney (1989) *News and Power*, St Leonards, NSW, Allen & Unwin.

——— (1999) *Scandals*, Sydney, UNSW Press.

——— (2007) 'Polls and elections: a primer for the perplexed', *Australian Policy Online*, available at http://www.sisr.net/apo/electionpolls.pdf.

—— (2008) 'Campaign tactics, media bias and the politics of explanations', *Communication, Politics & Culture* 41(2): 8–25.

—— (2009) 'The *Australian* at forty-five', *Inside Story*, 14 July, http://inside.org.au/the-australian-at-forty-five/.

—— and Gittins, Ross (2004) *How Australia Compares*, Melbourne, Cambridge University Press.

—— and Gittins, Ross (2009) *How Australia Compares* (2nd edn), Melbourne, Cambridge University Press.

Tranter, Bruce (2007) 'Political knowledge and its partisan consequences', *Australian Journal of Political Science* 42(1): 73–88.

Turner, Graeme (2005) *Ending the Affair*, Sydney, UNSW Press.

—— (2010) *Ordinary People and the Media*, London, Sage.

Varian, Hal (2010) 'Newspaper economics: online and offline', 9 March, http://googlepublicpolicy.blogspot.com/2010/03/newspaper-economics-online-and-offline.html.

Vromen, Ariadne (2008) 'Building virtual spaces: young people, participation and the internet', *Australian Journal of Political Science* 43(1): 79–97.

Walsh, Geoff (1982) 'NSW ALP branch candidates seminar', Canberra, Australian Labor Party. National Library of Australia, Manuscripts (MS4985, Box 523, folder 'Media courses 1984 election').

—— (2002) 'The Australian Labor Party', in John Warhurst and Marian Simms (eds), *2001: The Centenary Election*, St Lucia, Qld, University of Queensland Press, pp. 125–35.

Ward, Ian (1992) 'Rich, wrinkly, rowdy politicians: is this how teenagers "read" television news?', *Australian Journal of Political Science* 27: 213–29.

—— (1995) *Politics of the Media*, South Melbourne, Macmillan.

—— (2002a) 'Talkback radio, political communication, and Australian politics', *Australian Journal of Communication* 29(1): 21–38.

—— (2002b), 'The *Tampa*, wedge politics, and a lesson for political journalism', *Australian Journalism Review* 24(1): 21–39.

—— (2006) 'The media, power and politics' in Andrew Parkin, John Summers and Dennis Woodward (eds), *Government, Politics, Power and Policy* (8th edn), Pearson Education, Frenchs Forest NSW, pp. 363–79.

Ward, Stephen and Thierry Vedel (2006) 'Introduction: the potential of the internet revisited', *Parliamentary Affairs* 59(2): 210–25.

Warhurst, John (2002) 'International versus domestic issues' in John Warhurst and Marian Simms (eds), *2001: The Centenary Election*, St Lucia, Qld, University of Queensland Press, pp. 9–17.

—— (2007) 'Business can live with Rudd', *Canberra Times*, 10 May.

Watson, Don (2002) *Recollections of a Bleeding Heart*, Sydney, Random House.

Weaver, David H., and Drew, Dan (2006) 'Voter learning in the 2004 presidential election: did the media matter?' *Journalism and Mass Communication Quarterly* 83(1): 25–42.

Weller, Patrick (1983) 'Labor in 1980' in Howard R. Penniman (ed), *Australia at the Polls: The National Elections of 1980 and 1983*, Sydney, Allen & Unwin, pp. 55–78.

Western, John and Hughes, Colin (1983) *The Mass Media in Australia* (2nd edn), St Lucia, Qld, University of Queensland Press.

Williams, Pamela (1997) *The Victory*, St Leonards, NSW, Allen & Unwin.

Wilson, Rebecca (2000) 'Political interviewers – what makes them tick', *Australian*, 13 July.

Windschuttle, Keith (1988) *The Media*, Ringwood, Vic., Penguin Books.

Young, Graham (2010) personal correspondence with author, 7 May.

Young, Sally (2003) 'Selling Australian politicians', unpublished PhD, Political Science Department, University of Melbourne.

—— (2004) *The Persuaders*, North Melbourne, Vic., Pluto Press.

—— (2006) 'Biting the hand that feeds? Media reporting of government advertising in Australia', *Journalism Studies* 7(4): 554–74.

—— (2007) 'A history of government advertising in Australia' in Sally Young (ed), *Government Communication in Australia*, Melbourne: Cambridge University Press: 181–203.

—— (2008) 'The broadcast political interview and strategies used by politicians: how the Australian Prime Minister promoted the Iraq War', *Media, Culture & Society* 30(5): 623–40.

—— (2009a) 'Sky News Australia: the impact of local 24-hour news on political reporting in Australia', *Journalism Studies* 10(3): 401–16.

—— (2009b) 'The decline of traditional news and current affairs in Australia', *Media International Australia* 131: 147–59.

—— (2010) 'The journalism crisis: Is Australia immune or just ahead of its time?' *Journalism Studies* 11(4): 610–24.

—— and Hill, Lisa (2009) 'Uncounted votes: informal voting and political exclusion in Australia', *Australian Journal of Politics and History* 55(1): 64–79.

Zaller, John (1989) 'Bringing Converse back in: modelling information flow in political campaigns', *Political Analysis* 1: 181–234.

—— (1992) *The Nature and Origins of Mass Opinion*, New York, Cambridge University Press.

—— (2003) 'A new standard of news quality: burglar alarms for the monitorial citizen', *Political Communication* 20: 109–30.

Zapit.com (2009) 'Nielsen Television (TV) Ratings for Network Primetime Series Top 20 Network Primetime Series 04/13/09 – 04/19/09', http://tvlistings.zap2it.com/ratings/weekly.html.

Zappone, Chris (2009) 'Fairfax Media ready to discuss charging for online news: CEO McCarthy', *Business Day* (Fairfax Digital), 24 August, http://www.businessday.com.au/business/fairfax-ready-to-discuss-charging-for-online-news-ceo-mccarthy-20090824-evh4.html.

INDEX